An Annotated Critical Bibliography of Feminist Criticism

Harvester Annotated Critical Bibliographies

This major new series provides extensive guides to literary movements and to major figures in English literature. Each volume is edited by a scholar of international repute, and writings by authors and the location of manuscript collections are presented in detail together with information on the secondary writings of each author.

An Annotated Critical Bibliography of Modernism
Alistair Davies

An Annotated Critical Bibliography of Henry James
Nicola Bradbury

Forthcoming:

An Annotated Critical Bibliography of Milton
C. A. Patrides

An Annotated Critical Bibliography of Feminist Criticism
Maggie Humm

An Annotated Critical Bibliography of Browning
Philip Drew

An Annotated Critical Bibliography of Marlowe
John Russell-Brown

An Annotated Critical Bibliography of Wordsworth
Keith Harley

An Annotated Critical Bibliography of Augustan Literature
David Nokes

An Annotated Critical Bibliography of Langland
Derek Pearsall

An Annotated Critical Bibliography of James Joyce
Thomas Staley

An Annotated Critical Bibliography of Swift
Carole Fabricant

An Annotated Critical Bibliography of Jacobean Comedy
Peter Corbin and Douglas Sedge

An Annotated Critical Bibliography of Thomas Hardy
Ronald Draper and M. S. Ray

An Annotated Critical Bibliography of the Metaphysical Poets
William Zunder

An Annotated Critical Bibliography of the Brontës
Christine Alexander

An Annotated Critical Bibliography of William Morris
David Latham and Sheila Latham

An Annotated Critical Bibliography of George Eliot
George Levine

An Annotated Critical Bibliography of Feminist Criticism

Maggie Humm
Co-ordinator of Women's Studies
North East London Polytechnic

G.K. HALL &CO.
70 LINCOLN STREET, BOSTON, MASS.

Published in the United States of America and Canada by
G. K. Hall & Co., 70 Lincoln Street, Boston, Mass.

First published in Great Britain in 1987 by
THE HARVESTER PRESS LIMITED
Publisher: John Spiers
16 Ship Street, Brighton, Sussex

© Maggie Humm, 1987

Library of Congress Cataloging-in-Publication Data

Humm, Maggie
  An annotated critical bibliography of feminist
  criticism.

  Includes index.
  1. Feminist criticism—Bibliography. I. Title.
Z7963.F44H85 1987 [HQ1206] 016.3054′2 87–9078
ISBN 0–8161–8937–4

Phototypeset in Linotron Times, 10 on 11pt by
Input Typesetting Ltd, London SW19 8DR

Printed in Great Britain by
Biddles Ltd, Guildford and King's Lynn

All rights reserved

For Nancy Ann and Arthur Reed

The page was headed quite simply WOMEN AND POVERTY, in block letters; but what followed was something like this:

> Condition in Middle Ages of,
> Habits in the Fiji Islands of,
> Worshipped as Goddesses by,
> Weaker in Moral sense than.

What one wants, I thought . . . is a mass of information; at what age did she marry; how many children had she as a rule; what was her house like; had she a room to herself.

For you have a library, and a good one. A working library, a living library; a library where nothing is chained down and nothing is locked up; a library where the songs of the singers rise naturally from the lives of the livers. There are the poems, here the biographies. And what light do they throw upon the professions, those biographies? How far do they encourage us to think that if we help the daughters to become professional women we shall discourage war?

VIRGINIA WOOLF

Contents

Advice to the Reader	ix
Acknowledgements	xi
Theory and Sexual Politics	1
Literary Criticism	35
Sociology, Politics and Economics	71
Arts, Film, Theatre, Media, Music	105
Psychology	135
History	150
Anthropology and Myth	181
Education and Women's Studies	206
Index of Subjects	227
Index of Contributors	232

Advice to the Reader

Purpose and Scope

The subject of this bibliography is contemporary feminist criticism: its theories, techniques, debates and development in America and England. In annotating the major books and articles in most disciplines, my purpose is to provide a core collection of women-centred materials which can support feminist research, policy and studies.

Definition

The focus of this bibliography is on criticism which is exploring women's theory, ideology and culture through taking a women-centred perspective. The term 'criticism' is used in the sense of 'critique' not practical criticism. Texts were considered 'feminist' and were included if they give evidence of a re-evaluation or critique of existing disciplines, of traditional paradigms about women, nature or social roles or document such work by others or women's history.

Arrangement of Entries and Citations

This guide follows others in the series which arrange entries chronologically in sections so that readers can follow more easily the development of debates.

When citing a book I give the name of the author, full title, publisher and first date and place of publication.

When citing an article I give the name of the author, title of journal, volume and number, date and pagination.

The sections are in the broad categories most in use in Women's Studies today: Theory and Sexual Politics including the Women's Movement; Literary Criticism; Sociology with Politics and Economics; Arts including Film, Theatre, Music and Media; Psychology; History; Anthropology and Myth; Education and Women's Studies.

Each entry within these sections has been individually numbered with the following abbreviations: TSP, LIT, SOC, ART, PSY, HIST, ANTH, ED.

General Problematics

A few specifics should be given as to what this bibliography does and does not do. The main issue is how to select the most important and relevant material and write about it for the new generations of feminist readers who want a well-grounded idea of what are the 'classics' and also what to expect from very contemporary feminist writing.

Many texts and articles are not published by mainstream publishers but have had to be found through a variety of sources: reviews, citations, conferences, syllabuses as well as bibliographies. Some have been rewritten or retitled, are hard to cite in full, and of course have disappeared from library shelves if not from feminist memory.

The definition of mainstream is problematic since in many debates a short article, not a book, may have been of great significance as with Helen Hacker's 'Women As a Minority Group'.

Some areas have been considered in the past as less worthy of inclusion in disciplinary categories and a feminist bibliography has to redress the balance: for example, by including oral history collections in 'history', autobiography in 'psychology', and privileging a literary criticism of groups over that of the individual author.

Yet the bibliography should also be accurate and authoritative and some areas of feminist criticism, such as the Arts, have developed less quickly than others so that sections are necessarily unbalanced in length.

Finally the concept of 'discipline' is itself problematic. Assigning texts to separate sections at all in the multi-cultural, multi-disciplinary world of Women's Studies is bound to seem arbitrary and is often very difficult. For example the history of education is in history and not in education.

The problem of when to stop and omitting some crucial reference is every bibliographer's nightmare.

Acknowledgements

The research required for this bibliography would have been impossible without a semester study leave given by Professor Gerry Fowler, Rector of North East London Polytechnic. The Center for Research on Women (Crow), Stanford University, by inviting me to be a Visiting Scholar, provided an invaluable research base. As an Adjunct Faculty Member of San Diego State University I was able to use computer searches and Women's Studies materials. In Britain the Interlibrary Loans service of NELP and the excellent Women's Research and Resources Library, Hungerford House, London provided much source material. I would like to be able to thank, in the manner of most bibliographers, many research assistants but have to admit that since the book was prepared alone all errors are mine. I can however thank Peter and Daniel Humm, and my friends and students for their encouragement and advice; Sue Roe of Harvester Press for her continued interest and feminist support; Madeleine Scott of SDSU for her word-processing skill. Above all I wish to thank sister bibliographers without whose earlier work this bibliography could not have been completed.

Theory and Sexual Politics

This chapter is an eclectic collection of feminist polemics, major criticism by and about the women's movements in America and Britain and feminist theory.

TSP 1   de Beauvoir, Simone
THE SECOND SEX (New York: Alfred A. Knopf, 1953)

> This is a classic feminist text written as a huge historical, literary and mythical survey. de Beauvoir's main thesis is that women have been constructed as objects by men; 'woman' is 'Other' to man and denied the right to her own subjectivity. She shows how these assumptions dominate all social, political and cultural life and how women internalise this objectification. Most contemporary feminists acknowledge their debt to this text.

TSP 2   Friedan, Betty
THE FEMININE MYSTIQUE (New York: W. W. Norton, 1963; London: Victor Gollancz, 1963)

> An early critique of the unhappiness of middle-class American women in affluent post-war society. Friedan describes the psychology of suburban American women based on questionnaires and interviews with Smith College graduates. Friedan's idea is that consciousness-raising within an individual context would be sufficient to energise the reform of sexism. More influential for its ideas than its content, but it is cited by Ellen Moers as a reason for her decision to treat women as a separate group.

TSP 3   Daly, Mary
THE CHURCH AND THE SECOND SEX (New York: Harper and Row, 1958)

This is a radical attack on the anti-feminism of the Church from ancient time. Daly emphasises the insensitivity of various popes to the problems of women. It was reissued with a 'New Feminist Post-Christian Introduction' in 1975.

TSP 4   Long, Priscilla (ed.)
THE NEW LEFT: A COLLECTION OF ESSAYS (Boston, Mass.: Porter Sargent, 1969)

An anthology of radical writing on the women's movement.

TSP 5   Roszak, Betty and Roszak, T. (eds.)
MASCULINE/FEMININE: READINGS IN SEXUAL MYTHOLOGY AND THE LIBERATION OF WOMEN (New York: Harper and Row, 1969)

A brief history of modern anti-feminist thought, together with essays offering contemporary feminist responses from the 1950s and 1960s by de Beauvoir, Rossi, Dixon, and others. There are some more contemporary radical feminist pieces.

TSP 6   Wittig, Monique
LES GUERRILLIÈRES (Paris: Minuit, 1969; New York: Viking, 1971)

A woman-centred perspective creating a vision of women's sphere. Using utopian fragments depicting life in an Amazon society, Wittig creates a new form of feminist criticism in an imagery of the vulva and the safety of a women's world.

TSP 7   Cade, Toni (ed.)
THE BLACK WOMAN: AN ANTHOLOGY (New York: New American Library, 1970)

Cade presents the writings of black women, partly as a response to the mainstream feminist movement which she believes ignores the experience of black women.

TSP 8   Figes, Eva
        PATRIARCHAL ATTITUDES (London: Faber and
        Faber, 1970; New York: Stein and Day, 1970)

        A description of the bias and limitations of male patterns
        of thinking and forms of representation. The unifying
        theme is an exploration of the double standard as a manifestation of a fundamental patriarchal attitude. Figes
        concentrates on individual philosophers rather than
        presenting a systematic critique of the construction of
        knowledge.

TSP 9   Firestone, Shulamith
        THE DIALECTIC OF SEX: THE CASE FOR
        FEMINIST REVOLUTION (New York: William
        Morrow, 1970)

        Firestone asserts that the eradication of sexism in society
        is a political problem and that feminism is the ideological
        means of uniting society. She addresses herself to the
        relationship of the biological to the social and the importance of psychological power relations between men and
        women. Firestone argues for the transformation of sexual
        difference in advances in genetic technology.

TSP 10 Freeman, Jo
        THE BITCH MANIFESTO (Pittsburgh: Know, 1970)

        An early feminist pamphlet arguing that females need to
        be bitches—assertive, free and seeking our own identity.

TSP 11 Freeman, Jo
        THE BUILDING OF THE GILDED CAGE
        (Pittsburgh: Know, 1970)

        A similar short polemic describing the social controls over
        women.

TSP 12 Millett, Kate
        SEXUAL POLITICS (New York: Doubleday, 1970;
        London: Virago, 1977)

The first book to articulate a broad theoretical base for the ideas of the women's movement. Millett widened the concept of politics to refer to power structuring in general and shows that this concept is the essence of male/female arrangements. Using historical and literary models she argues that sexual politics, grounded in misogyny results in women's oppression both institutionally and at a personal level. Millett itemises realms and modes within which patriarchy operates—such as biology, ideology, class, sociology, education and rape, and shows that one of patriarchy's key features is its invisibility. A devastating analysis which transformed contemporary thinking about sex roles.

TSP 13 Morgan, Robin (ed.)
SISTERHOOD IS POWERFUL: AN ANTHOLOGY OF WRITINGS FROM THE WOMEN'S LIBERATION MOVEMENT (New York: Vintage, 1970)

A comprehensive collection of writings from 50 contributors covering the major social institutions, Black and Chicana liberation, psychology, autobiography and poetry. It is useful as an account of what women were doing at that time and by arguing for an autonomous women's movement it prepared the way for that development.

TSP 14 Reed, Evelyn
PROBLEMS OF WOMEN'S LIBERATION: A MARXIST APPROACH (New York: Pathfinder Press, 1970)

Reed writes of the economic and social oppression of women from a socialist viewpoint.

TSP 15 Reed, Evelyn
REVOLUTIONARY FEMINISM: WOMAN AS REASON (New York: Women's Liberation News and Letters, 1970)

Short essays on topics of the day including the origins of International Women's Day. Essays aim to present a total picture of women's revolutionary activity and potential.

TSP 16 Sherfey, Mary Jane
'A Theory on Female Sexuality', SISTERHOOD IS POWERFUL, ed. Robin Morgan (New York: Vintage, 1970) pp. 220–30

Sherfey's discussion of clitoral orgasm laid the groundwork of the second wave of American feminism. She argues that women's sexual capacity for multiple orgasms is radically different from and superior to that of men.

TSP 17 Solanas, Valerie
SCUM (New York: Olympia Press, 1970)

A cult book of feminism by the woman who shot Andy Warhol, which argues for the overthrow of capitalism and the male sex.

TSP 18 Staxbler, Sookie (ed.)
WOMEN'S LIBERATION: BLUEPRINT FOR THE FUTURE (New York: Ace, 1970)

A collection of writings by radical feminists such as Kate Millett and Susan Brownmiller.

TSP 19 Thompson, Mary Lou (ed.)
VOICES OF THE NEW FEMINISM (Boston, Mass.: Beacon Press, 1970)

An anthology of writings by feminists who touch on current problems, ideology and sex roles. Contributors include Mary Daly and A. Rossi. There is a good bibliography on women.

TSP 20 Ware, Cellestine
WOMAN POWER: THE MOVEMENT FOR WOMEN'S LIBERATION (New York: Tower Publications, 1970)

Ware portrays in general terms the state of women's liberation in the 1970s with interesting material on the contribution of black women.

TSP 21   Adams, Elsie and Briscoe, Mary Louise (eds.)
UP AGAINST THE WALL, MOTHER . . . ON
WOMEN'S LIBERATION (Beverley Hills, CA.:
Glencoe Press, 1971)

An anthology of essays, poems and articles organised as a source of introductory readings.

TSP 22   Altbach, Edith (ed.)
FROM FEMINISM TO LIBERATION (Cambridge, Mass.: Schenkman, 1971)

A collection of essays from the February 1970, 'Special Issue on Women's Liberation' journal *Radical America*. Most contributors are socialist feminist and the articles are classics of the women's liberation movement. Among these: 'Bread and Roses', by Kathy McAfee and Myrna Wood and 'Where Are We Going?' by Marlene Dixon.

TSP 23   Babcox, Deborah and Belkin, Madeleine (eds.)
LIBERATION NOW! WRITINGS FROM THE
WOMEN'S LIBERATION MOVEMENT (New York: Dell, 1971)

This is an excellent early anthology. It includes writings by Marlene Dixon, Margaret Benston, Marge Piercy, Juliet Mitchell, Vivian Cornick, Alice Rossi, Charlotte Bunch and others.

TSP 24   Davis, Angela
IF THEY COME IN THE MORNING: VOICES OF
RESISTANCE (New York: Third Press, 1971)

A collection of essays about black American women who have become the symbol of resistance to oppression all over the world.

TSP 25   Garskof, Michele Hoffnung (ed.)
ROLES WOMEN PLAY: READINGS TOWARD
WOMEN'S LIBERATION (Belmont, CA.: Brooks/Cole, 1971)

An anthology of women's liberation readings with essays by Weisstein, Freeman, Dixon, Cantarow among others.

TSP 26   Greer, Germaine
THE FEMALE EUNUCH (London: McGibbon and Kee, 1970; New York: McGraw-Hill, 1971)

The best-selling British competitor to Kate Millett's *Sexual Politics*. Greer's is a populist argument for female liberation in an all-inclusive study of women's cultural history, psychology and relationships with men.

TSP 27   Hanisch, Carol
'The Personal is Political', THE RADICAL THERAPIST, ed. J. Agel (New York: Ballantine Books, 1971) pp. 152–7

This is reprinted from *Notes from the Second Year: Women's Liberation: Major Writings of the Radical Feminists* ed. S. Firestone and A. Koedt (New York: Radical Feminists, 1970)
   Hanisch first coined the slogan 'the personal is political', the important slogan of the second wave of the women's liberation movement.

TSP 28   Janeway, Elizabeth
MAN'S WORLD, WOMAN'S PLACE: A STUDY IN SOCIAL MYTHOLOGY (New York: Delta Press, 1971; London: Michael Joseph, 1971). Elaborated as POWERS OF THE WEAK (New York: Alfred. A. Knopf, 1980)

An examination of myths about male and female behaviour. Janeway argues that 'social mythology' is a more useful term than patriarchy. Sex role differentiation, she claims to come from male propaganda, and she traces the historical development of the idea that women are domestic pointing out that 'home' is a relatively modern concept. Her account converges with that given by Kate Millett that the influence of sex roles is a key factor in the subordination of women. Unlike Ortner or Firestone, Janeway does not see the association of women with the domestic sphere as universal but as having developed in a historically-specific moment.

TSP 29   Koedt, Anne and Firestone, Shulamith (eds.)
NOTES FROM THE THIRD YEAR: WOMEN'S LIBERATION (New York: Notes, 1971)

An anthology of radical feminism including women's literature, nineteenth-century suffrage, black feminism, children's books, prostitution, lesbianism, media, religion and the problems of age and legal issues.

TSP 30   Mitchell, Juliet
WOMEN'S ESTATE (Harmondsworth: Penguin, 1971; New York: Pantheon, 1971)

Mitchell's book contributed to the continuity of feminist theory through its extensive coverage of Kate Millett and Shulamith Firestone. Her main focus is on women in the workplace and her concern is to link exploitation there with women's role in the family. Mitchell extended the framework of radical feminism into the methodology of historical materialism. The book was a blueprint for the new field of Women's Studies then being established in Britain.

TSP 31   Abbott, Sidney and Love, Barbara
SAPPHO WAS A RIGHT-ON WOMAN: A LIBERATED VIEW OF LESBIANISM (New York: Stein and Day, 1972)

This book is by two lesbian activists who discuss the historic oppression of gay women and the achievements of the Gay Movement.

TSP 32   Jay, Carla and Young, Allen (eds)
OUT OF THE CLOSETS: VOICES OF GAY LIBERATION (New York: Douglas Books, 1972)

A book of readings by both men and women homosexuals containing some of the early manifestos which made such a strong impression on the Gay Movement. Writings include 'The Woman-Identified Woman' by the Radicalesbians and Rita Mae Brown's 'Take A Lesbian to Lunch'.

TSP 33   Jenness, Linda (ed.)
FEMINISM AND SOCIALISM (New York: Pathfinder Press, 1972)

This addresses such questions as the possibility of women's liberation within capitalism? And, the connection between the oppression of women and racism? There are articles on Chicanas, Red-Baiting, Women's Liberation and Black Women.

TSP 34   Martin, Del and Lyon, Phyllis
LESBIAN/WOMAN (San Francisco: Glide Publications, 1972)

This is a book written by participants in the lesbian liberation movement. It deals with such topics as lesbian mothers, growing up gay, self-image and the liberation of gay women.

TSP 35   Rowbotham, Sheila
WOMEN, RESISTANCE AND REVOLUTION (Harmondsworth: Penguin, 1972; New York: Vintage, 1974)

Discusses language, meaning and symbolic order and their relationship to the future of women's liberation.

TSP 36   Wandor, M. (ed.)
THE BODY POLITIC: WOMEN'S LIBERATION IN BRITAIN (London: Stage I, 1972)

The first collection of specifically British women's liberation writings. It includes autobiographical aspects of women in contemporary society, family, the media, black women, prisons, trade unions together with a historical account of women's liberation and its famous campaigns.

TSP 37 Birkby, Phyllis et al. (eds.)
AMAZON EXPEDITION: A LESBIAN FEMINIST ANTHOLOGY (Washington, N.J.: Times Change Press, 1973)

An excellent collection of lesbian feminist articles with contributions from Ti-Grace Atkinson, Joanna Russ and Jill Johnston.

TSP 38 Cartledge, S. and Ryan J. (eds)
SEX AND LOVE (London: The Women's Press, 1973)

Illustrates the renewed feminist interest in sexuality and includes lesbian as well as heterosexual accounts in a range of approaches—journals, interviews and questionnaires. The book's central commitment is to the idea that sexuality is a social construct. It has a dominant model of love as nurturance based primarily on a mother and child relationship.

TSP 39 Cooke, Joanne et al. (eds.)
THE NEW WOMEN: A MOTIVE ANTHOLOGY ON WOMEN'S LIBERATION (Greenwich, CT.: Fawcett Publications, 1973)

Based on a special double issue of *Motive* magazine (March/April 1969). This collection of essays and poems is revealing for its introduction to the contemporary Women's Movement and as examples of the early writings of Marge Piercy, Charlotte Bunch among others.

TSP 40 Daly, Mary
BEYOND GOD THE FATHER: TOWARD A PHILOSOPHY OF WOMEN'S LIBERATION (Boston, Mass.: Beacon Press, 1973)

Daly exposes the limitations of male methods of knowledge construction. She raises the issue of the extent to which patriarchal reality would persist if women refused to acknowledge its existence.

TSP 41   Heilbrun, Carolyn
         TOWARD A RECOGNITION OF ANDROGYNY
         (New York: Alfred A. Knopf, 1973)

         Heilbrun argues that androgyny in western literature and mythology is a long-standing tradition. She proposes it as a solution to sex-role stereotyping and calls for the psychological homogenisation of the two sexes. Criticised, by Catherine Stimpson among others, as a static concept implying the integration of women into the political status quo.

TSP 42   Koedt, Anne (ed.)
         RADICAL FEMINISM (New York: Quadrangle/New York Times Books, 1973)

         Contains Koedt's classic essay 'The Myth of the Vaginal Orgasm', showing how men control women by means of their control over the sex act. Male power is based on the myth that, for women to achieve 'true' orgasm, they must experience penetration by a penis. The text is an anthology of key and now classic feminist writings with early essays by Mary Daly, Susan Brownmiller and Kate Millett.

TSP 43   Rowbotham, Sheila
         WOMAN'S CONSCIOUSNESS, MAN'S WORLD
         (Harmondsworth: Penguin, 1973)

         An account of the development of feminist consciousness and the social changes that inspired it, together with theories about the family in capitalism and the part it plays in maintaining commodity production. Rowbotham's is a systematic analysis of women's exclusion from the meanings and culture of a male dominated society and the implications for women's consciousness.

TSP 44   Atkinson, Ti-Grace
         AMAZON ODYSSEY (New York: Links Books, 1974)

         This is an argument for a lesbian perspective as an essential element in the development of a complete feminist theory. Using an axiom from the sociology of knowledge,

Atkinson turns an argument of women's liberation on itself, in her idea that if women are radically different from men then so are gay women different from straight women. Lesbians are the true radicals of feminism.

TSP 45   Bird, Caroline
BORN FEMALE: THE HIGH COST OF KEEPING WOMEN DOWN (New York: McKay, 1974)

Bird addresses major issues of women's liberation in America: women in the labour force; equal pay; educational discrimination and offers the moderate arguments that energised the women's movement in 1970.

TSP 46   Bunch, Charlotte and Myron, Nancy (eds.)
CLASS AND FEMINISM (Baltimore, MD.: Diana Press, 1974)

These are articles written by the Furies, a lesbian-feminist collective, on the efforts to deal with issues of class in their collective. The articles are a combination of the theoretical analysis of class and women's oppression and a reporting of the personal experiences of the writers.

TSP 47   Carden, Maren Lockwood
THE NEW FEMINIST MOVEMENT (New York: Russell Sage Foundation, 1974)

Carden discusses the ideas, issues and trends of the women's movement, focusing in particular on the National Organization of Women. As a sociologist she concentrates on questions about group behaviour.

TSP 48   Dworkin, Andrea
WOMAN HATING (New York: E. P. Dutton, 1974)

A significant contribution to feminist thought, partly through its linkage of fairy tale and pornography and because it deals with the diversity of women's experience. Dworkin tackles the exploitative and discriminatory nature of class and race structures.

TSP 49   Janeway, Elizabeth
BETWEEN MYTH AND MORNING: WOMEN AWAKENING (New York: William Morrow, 1974)

She describes some changes brought about by the women's movement and what new issues arise from the changes.

TSP 50   Johnston, Jill
LESBIAN NATION: THE FEMINIST SOLUTION (New York: Simon and Schuster, 1974)

The argument that lesbianism is more than a matter for sexual preference but is a political commitment. 'Lesbian' Johnston defines as a generic term signifying activism and resistance and what Johnston calls the 'envisioned goal of a woman-committed state'.

TSP 51   Klaich, Dolores
WOMAN PLUS WOMAN: ATTITUDES TOWARDS LESBIANISM (New York: Simon and Schuster, 1974)

Klaich calls her book a social history of lesbianism. She thinks that people erroneously think of women who are lesbians only in terms of their sexuality, never as whole people.

TSP 52   Peck, Ellen and Sanderowitz, Judith (eds.)
PRONATALISM: THE MYTH OF MOM AND APPLE PIE (New York: Thomas Y. Crowell, 1974)

A collection of essays on the social relations of reproduction and their control of women. The topics are pronatalism in the media; motherhood and political participation and child-free marriages with contributions from Hollingsworth and Lynn among others.

TSP 53   Brownmiller, Susan
AGAINST OUR WILL: MEN, WOMEN AND RAPE (New York: Simon and Schuster, 1975)

A classic polemic. Brownmiller's treatment of the concept of rape is historical, anthropological and political. Her thesis is that forcible rape is a conscious act of intimidation and the secret of patriarchy. Both the possibility and actuality of rape are the main agents of male domination over women. She views rape as coming from the biological origins of male enmity to women, and made the legal issue of rape a major focus in her political work. The text places radical feminism at odds with the socialist view of the centrality of class and with a black view of the centrality of racism.

TSP 54   Dalla Costa, Mariarosa and James, Selma
THE POWER OF WOMEN AND THE SUBVERSION OF THE COMMUNITY (Bristol: Falling Wall Press, 1975)

A classic of the women's movement which analyses the division of labour in marriage and thoughts on the significance and function of housework.

TSP 55   Deckard, B. S.
THE WOMEN'S MOVEMENT: POLITICAL, SOCIO-ECONOMIC AND PSYCHOLOGICAL ISSUES (New York: Harper and Row, 1975)

This attempts to synthesise in one account the social, economic and political status of women in past and present societies in a survey of women from primitive to nineteenth-century societies. Deckard covers the political functions of sexism and psychological and social theories about women.

TSP 56   Freeman, Jo
THE POLITICS OF WOMEN'S LIBERATION: A CASE STUDY OF AN EMERGING SOCIAL MOVEMENT AND ITS RELATION TO THE POLICY PROCESS (New York: David McKay, 1975)

An investigation of the development of public policy on women's rights using interviews with key women. Freeman examines the origins and organisational methods of the American women's movement in the first systematic study and evaluation of the processes of American feminism.

TSP 57   Freeman, Jo (ed.)
WOMAN: A FEMINIST PERSPECTIVE (Palo Alto, CA.: Mayfield Publishing, 1975)

Contributes to feminist theory the idea that a notion of communality underlies the diversity of women's experience and is the key substance of the politics of the women's movement.

TSP 58   Fritz, Leah
THINKING LIKE A WOMAN (New York: WIN Books, 1975)

A collection of essays published between 1967 and 1975. These document her developing feminist awareness of radical politics and the peace and civil rights movements.

TSP 59   Rubin, Gayle
' "Traffic in Women": Notes on the "Political Economy" of Sex', TOWARD AN ANTHROPOLOGY OF WOMEN, ed. R. Reiter (New York: Monthly Review Press, 1975)

The radical argument that heterosexuality is socially constructed in women, and entirely the product of enforcement by a kinship system. Rubin coined the term 'sex/gender system' to cope with the difficulty of defining women as a social group.

TSP 60   Ruether, Rosemary Radford
NEW WOMAN, NEW EARTH: SEXIST IDEOLOGIES AND HUMAN LIBERATION (New York: Seabury Press, 1975)

Liberation seen from the perspective of socialist-feminism. It is interesting to compare this work with Mary Daly's *Beyond God the Father* since both address issues of religion and sexism but Ruether includes forms of oppression experienced by blacks and Jews.

TSP 61   West, Uta (ed.)
WOMEN IN A CHANGING WORLD (New York: McGraw-Hill, 1975)

A collection of writings which examine the impact of shifting sex roles on women's experience. They look at how women have changed and how they feel about themselves and new definitions of their roles. The contributors are M. Daly, E. Janeway with fiction by G. Paley and D. Lessing, among others.

TSP 62 Yates, Gayle
WHAT WOMEN WANT: THE IDEAS OF THE MOVEMENT (Cambridge, Mass.: Harvard University Press, 1975)

Yates characterises the women's movement as having three ideological divisions; feminist, women's liberationist and androgynous.

TSP 63 Bardwick, Judith
IN TRANSITION: HOW FEMINISM, SEXUAL LIBERATION AND THE SEARCH FOR SELF-FULFILMENT HAVE ALTERED OUR LIVES (New York: Holt, Rinehart and Winston, 1976)

A psychologist who examines how women's identities have been changed by the women's movement.

TSP 64 Brown, Rita Mae
A PLAIN BROWN RAPPER (Oakland, CA.: Diana Press, 1976)

A collection of essays written between 1969 and 1975 and originally published in *The Furies*, *Quest* and *Rat*. The essays trace her growth through issues of race, class, the Left, lesbianism and there is an introduction describing her political career to date.

TSP 65 Dworkin, Andrea
OUR BLOOD: PROPHECIES AND DISCOURSES ON SEXUAL POLITICS (New York: Harper and Row, 1976)

Dworkin writes a series of essays on issues facing women utilising a radical-feminist perspective. She addresses such topics as rape, non-violence, lesbianism, as well as the causes of oppression.

TSP 66   Gould, Carol C. and Wartofsky, Marx W. (eds.)
WOMAN AND PHILOSOPHY: TOWARD A THEORY OF LIBERATION (New York: G. P. Putnam, 1976)

This collection of essays attempts to outline the fundamental philosophic assumptions of the women's liberation movement and how they apply to specific issues.

TSP 67   Millett, Kate
PROSTITUTION PAPERS: A QUARTET FOR FEMALE VOICE (New York: Ballantine Books, 1976)

A radical feminist view of prostitution based on essays from four prostitutes written in an original form.

TSP 68   Redstockings
FEMINIST REVOLUTION (New York: Random House, 1976)

An important document of the contemporary women's movement in the United States. Redstockings was one of the earliest feminist organisations and the authors include Judy Grahn, Carol Hanisch, Pat Mainardi and others.

TSP 69   Rich, Adrienne
OF WOMAN BORN: MOTHERHOOD AS EXPERIENCE AND INSTITUTION (New York: W. W. Norton, 1976; London: Virago, 1977)

The classic text of feminism recuperating the concept of motherhood for women. Rich distinguishes between motherhood as 'experience' and as 'institution'. She claims that the institution is controlled by men but that the experience of motherhood can transform women. She gives the concept a symbolic architecture of history and myth, autobiography and poetry in a new form of feminist scholarship.

TSP 70　Coward, Rosalind and Ellis, John
LANGUAGE AND MATERIALISM: DEVELOPMENTS IN SEMIOLOGY AND THE THEORY OF THE SUBJECT (London: Routledge & Kegan Paul, 1977)

This was the first introduction into Britain of an unfamiliar body of French theory. The authors describe theories of the subject as constituted in and by language and the relationship of ideological and signifying practices. They throw out fertile ideas for feminism on the importance of signification and the centrality of the 'subject-in-process'.

TSP 71　Morgan, Robin
GOING TOO FAR: THE PERSONAL CHRONICLE OF A FEMINIST (New York: Random House, 1977)

This includes her angry manifesto of her departure from the New Left and is a collection of her articles from 1967–1977. In them she argues for radical feminism as a new source of change since it goes well beyond any previously known form of political or cultural transformation.

TSP 72　Vetterling-Braggin, M. et al. (eds.)
FEMINISM AND PHILOSOPHY (Totowa, N.J.: Littlefield, Adams, 1977)

An account of the phenomenology of feminist consciousness, together with a description of current ideologies in feminism from liberalism, Marxism and lesbian separatism.

TSP 73　Foss, Paul and Morris, Meaghan (eds.)
LANGUAGE, SEXUALITY AND SUBVERSION (Darlington, Australia: Feral Press, 1978)

This discusses contemporary radical European thought by Umberto Eco, Jean Baudrillard and Luce Irigaray in relation to feminism and sexuality.

TSP 74   Gornick, Vivian
ESSAYS IN FEMINISM (New York: Harper and Row, 1978)

A collection of Gornick's essays written for the *Village Voice* which reveals her developing feminism. There are accounts of Alice Paul, Agnes Smedley and discussions about Radcliffe women and feminist experience.

TSP 75   Griffin, Susan
WOMAN AND NATURE: THE ROARING INSIDE HER (New York: Harper and Row, 1978)

An encyclopedic form of essay, collage and polemic which traces the history of the pervasive metaphors of western science which Griffin sees as the means of men's control of, and domination over nature, perceived as female. Griffin shows women inhabiting a world outside of culture as nurturers and thinks that women's love making evokes a natural inheritance of beauty and harmony in a wilderness away from the destructive violence of man-made culture.

TSP 76   Jagger, Alison and Struhl, P. R.
FEMINIST FRAMEWORKS: ALTERNATIVE THEORETICAL ACCOUNTS OF THE RELATIONS BETWEEN WOMEN AND MEN (New York: McGraw-Hill, 1978)

An examination of contemporary social arrangements and problems for women in the areas of work, the family and sexuality. The theoretical frameworks are: conservatism, liberalism, Marxism, radical feminism and socialist feminism.

TSP 77   Lipshitz, Susan (ed.)
TEARING THE VEIL: ESSAYS ON FEMININITY (Boston, Mass.: Routledge & Kegan Paul, 1978)

Essays written from the perspectives of psychoanalysis, anthropology, history and literature by Mandy Merck, Barbara Taylor and Mary Jacobus among others. The topics are prostitution, maternity, Hardy's *Tess* and feminism in early British socialism.

TSP 78 Lorde, Audrey
USES OF THE EROTIC: THE EROTIC AS POWER (Trumansburg, N.Y.: Out and Out Books, The Crossing Press, 1978)

Lorde believes that the erotic (seen from a lesbian perspective) is our most creative source and can be female and self-affirming in a racist patriarchy.

TSP 79 Weinbaum, Batya
THE CURIOUS COURTSHIP OF WOMEN'S LIBERATION AND SOCIALISM (Boston, Mass.: South End Press, 1978)

Weinbaum describes the treatment of women by socialist regimes in the twentieth century and discusses the relationship of feminism and Marxism. She proposes a strategy which encompasses Marx, Freud and radical feminism.

TSP 80 Bishop, S. and Weinzsweig, M. (eds.)
PHILOSOPHY AND WOMEN (Belmont, CA: Wadsworth, 1979)

This contains a range of essays including one by Bartsky on female narcissism arguing that the social identification of a woman with her body affects her self image.

TSP 81 Daly, Mary
GYN/ECOLOGY (Boston: Beacon Press, 1978: London: Women's Press, 1979)

An influential feminist text. Daly lists male atrocities both on women's bodies and on language. Central to Daly's arguments is the idea that women are constrained by systems of meaning and we need to link our symbols and myths to formulate linguistic strategies, which will reclaim for women the right to name.

TSP 82   Eisenstein, Zillah (ed.)
CAPITALIST PATRIARCHY AND THE CASE FOR SOCIALIST FEMINISM (New York: Monthly Review Press, 1979)

A collection of essays on socialist-feminist theory and its applications to specific historical contexts, for example antebellum America, the nineteenth-century suffrage movement, and others. It includes statements of principles by several contemporary socialist-feminist collectives.

TSP 83   Fritz, Leah
DREAMERS AND DEALERS: AN INTIMATE APPRAISAL OF THE WOMEN'S MOVEMENT (Boston, Mass.: Beacon Press, 1979)

Fritz dismisses the possibility of any further connection between feminism and the political Left, since the 'male' style of SDS politics eventually doomed the Left revolutionary project to failure.

TSP 84   Griffin, Susan
RAPE: THE POWER OF CONSCIOUSNESS (New York: Harper and Row, 1979)

Griffin characterises rape as the all-American crime. She connects the crime of rape at home and American crimes abroad, particularly in Vietnam, in her theory that rape and imperialism have common elements.

TSP 85   Heilbrun, Carolyn
RE-INVENTING WOMANHOOD (New York. W. W. Norton, 1979)

Heilbrun writes a book essay on how woman's identity has been lost in history. She suggests some ways to understand 'womanhood' independently of pervasive male definitions.

TSP 86   Hope, Carol and Young, Nancy
          OUT OF THE FRYING PAN: A DECADE OF
          CHANGE IN WOMEN'S LIVES (Garden City, N.Y.:
          Anchor Press, 1979)

          The authors interviewed many women who felt affected
          by the contemporary feminist movement. They describe
          using real-life experiences how these women have
          changed.

TSP 87   Raymond, Janice
          THE TRANSSEXUAL EMPIRE: THE MAKING OF
          THE SHE-MALE (Boston, Mass.: Beacon Press, 1979)

          Argues that the androgynous ideal ignores issues of
          power, since it combined the language of dominance and
          servitude and cannot define a free person.

TSP 88   Rich, Adrienne
          ON LIES, SECRETS, AND SILENCE: SELECTED
          PROSE 1966–1978 (New York: W. W. Norton, 1979;
          London: Virago, 1980)

          Essays revealing Rich's ability to name and found a
          women's culture. There are accounts of feminist litera-
          ture, education, lesbian writing, motherhood, racism and
          feminist theory in a subtle interweaving of autobiography
          with theory.

TSP 89   Rowbotham, Sheila et al. (eds.)
          BEYOND THE FRAGMENTS: FEMINISM AND
          THE MAKING OF SOCIALISM (London: Merlin
          Press, 1979)

          A reappraisal of the relationship of the women's move-
          ment to the Left in Britain. It argues for new approaches
          to theory and political organisation both at community
          and national level.

TSP 90   Sabrosky, Judith
          FROM RATIONALITY TO LIBERATION: THE
          EVOLUTION OF FEMINIST IDEOLOGY
          (Westport, CT.: Greenwood Press, 1979)

Sabrosky looks at the origins of feminist thought in the Enlightenment of the eighteenth century. She goes on to describe contemporary feminist ideology as a coherent set of beliefs and proposes some guidelines for strengthening feminism as an ideology.

TSP 91　Stamboulian, G. and Marks, Elaine (eds.)
HOMOSEXUALITIES AND FRENCH LITERATURE: CULTURAL CONTEXTS/CRITICAL TEXTS (Ithaca, N.Y.: Cornell University Press, 1979)

Fifteen essays rethink the relationship between sexuality and literature addressing the question: What effect has the women's and gay liberation movements had on the context of literary discussion? The essays are by leading psychoanalysts, feminists and writers in France and the United States raising questions about desire and textuality from the eighteenth century to the present.

TSP 92　Dixon, Marlene
WOMEN IN CLASS STRUGGLE (San Francisco: Synthesis Publications, 1980)

This was expanded into *The Future of Women* (San Francisco: Synthesis, 1983). It is a study of the exploitation of women in capitalism by the founder of the Democratic Workers Party. Written from the perspective of American Marxism, it deals with the issue of sexism to women in socialist movements.

TSP 93　Gay Left Collective (eds.)
HOMOSEXUALITY: POWER AND POLITICS (London: Allison and Busby, 1980; New York: Schocken Books, 1980)

Written by contributors to the journal *Gay Left*, this sums up the progress of the gay and women's movements in Britain in the 1970s. The essays examine and integrate ideas from the women's movement, Gramsci, Freud and Foucault. They include personal accounts of lesbian experiences; lesbians in literature; the media representation of lesbianism; the morality of lesbianism and the relationship of lesbianism and socialism.

TSP 94 Lederer, Laura (ed.)
TAKE BACK THE NIGHT: WOMEN ON PORNOGRAPHY (New York: William Morrow, 1980)

Essays argue that an analysis of pornography requires a different set of axes than those defining the traditional political grid since pornography is the ideology of a culture of violence towards women.

TSP 95 Marks, Elaine and de Courtivron, Isabelle (eds.)
NEW FRENCH FEMINISMS: AN ANTHOLOGY (Amherst: The University of Massachusetts Press, 1980; Brighton: Harvester Press, 1980)

An anthology of 50 pieces of French theory emphasising dialectical thought, psychoanalysis and linguistic theory. Included are de Beauvoir, Cixous, Kristeva and Irigaray with an introductory essay discussing the history of French feminism and French discourses.

TSP 96 O'Reilly, Jane
THE GIRL I LEFT BEHIND (New York: Macmillan, 1980)

A collection of magazine articles on many feminist issues including housework, sexuality, pornography, the New Right, ERA and Third World women. A kaleidoscope of contemporary feminism.

TSP 97 Rich, Adrienne
'Compulsory Heterosexuality and Lesbian Existence', *Signs* 5: 4 (1980) 631–61

Written as a critical response to Miller, Chodorow and Dinnerstein. Rich argues for the dissection of compulsory heterosexuality as an oppressive social institution. Rich's is an expanded and exciting definition of lesbianism including lesbian 'experience'—the historical and contemporary existence of lesbians, and lesbian 'continuum'—woman-identified experience.

TSP 98   Shulman, Alix Kate
'Sex and Power: The Sexual Bases of Radical Feminism',
Signs 5: 4 (Summer 1980) 590–604

A description by one of the first users of how consciousness-raising is a means of sharing reliable information about female experience. Discusses the fundamental critique of sex relations undertaken in CR groups and uses of CR as data collection.

TSP 99   Stimpson, Catherine and Person, E. S. (eds.)
WOMEN AND SEXUALITY (Chicago and London: University of Chicago Press, 1980)

A range of essays, reprinted from *Signs*, on topics such as desire, eroticism, reproduction and metaphors of sexuality. The volume demonstrates 'the folly of obsessive insistence on one normative pattern of female sexuality'.

TSP 100   Bunch, Charlotte
FEMINISM IN THE '80s: FACING DOWN THE RIGHT (New York: Inkling Press, 1981)

The keynote address at the Second National Lesbians Conference. In her discussion of the threat of the right wing to feminism, Bunch argues for the necessity of a radical vision of fundamental change.

TSP 101   Bunch, Charlotte et al. (eds.)
BUILDING FEMINIST THEORY: ESSAYS FROM *QUEST*, A FEMINIST QUARTERLY (New York: Longman, 1981)

The essays argue that lesbianism is a major element in women's culture since lesbians are more able to perceive the ways in which heterosexuality has supported male domination.

TSP 102   Califia, Pat et al. (eds.)
COMING TO POWER: WRITINGS AND GRAPHICS ON LESBIAN S/M (San Francisco: Samois, 1981)

This makes a case for consensual lesbian S/M (sadomasochistic practices followed by lesbian partners as expression of dominance/submission fantasies). It attacks the moralism of some feminists, particularly the campaign against pornography.

TSP 103   Davis, Angela
WOMEN, RACE AND CLASS (New York: Random House, 1981)

Davis argues that the white feminist analysis of rape omitted historical background to create a 'myth' of the black rapist.

TSP 104   Dworkin, Andrea
PORNOGRAPHY: MEN POSSESSING WOMEN (New York: G. P. Putnam's, 1981; London: Women's Press, 1981)

Dworkin argues that the chief engine of male history is male sexual violence, possibly rooted in biology. She extends the critique of masculinity begun by Chodorow to define for women how pornography is at the heart of male supremacy. Women can be free only when pornography ceases to exist.

TSP 105   Eisenstein, Zillah (ed.)
THE RADICAL FUTURE OF LIBERAL FEMINISM (New York: Longman, 1981)

This looks at the implications of legal reform for radicalising liberal feminists. Eisenstein shows how feminism grew out of liberal theory and seeks to transcend it and explode it. It is a rehabilitation of the theories of liberal feminism.

TSP 106   Friedan, Betty
THE SECOND STAGE (New York: Summit Books, 1981)

Friedan argues that radical feminists are destroying the gains of NOW (The National Organization of Women) and reformist feminism.

TSP 107 Griffin, Susan
PORNOGRAPHY AND SILENCE: CULTURE'S REVENGE AGAINST NATURE (New York: Harper and Row, 1981)

Griffin argues that pornography expresses a fundamental theme of the western Christian tradition: a hatred of the flesh since women are associated with the body. Pornography is a form of ritualised desecration of women and the sadism of pornography lies in its objectification of women. She argues that pornography has spilled over into everyday life since it has taught women silence and self-annihilation as a cultural form. Griffin is more sensitive to history than Andrea Dworkin and acknowledges the pervasive influence of pornography on men as well as women.

TSP 108 Hooks, Bell
AIN'T I A WOMAN: BLACK WOMEN AND FEMINISM (Boston: South End Press, 1981)

Correctly castigates white feminists for impressing on the American public their sense that 'woman' meant white woman by drawing endless analogies between 'women' and 'blacks'.

TSP 109 Joseph, Gloria and Lewis, Jill
COMMON DIFFERENCES: CONFLICTS IN BLACK AND FEMINIST PERSPECTIVES (Garden City, N.Y.: Anchor Press, 1981)

A black and a white feminist examine key features of mother–daughter relationships; media representation; sexuality and sexual socialisation and the political nature of women's liberation each from their own perspective. They argue for black and white women connecting their specific understandings of oppression.

TSP 110 Sargent, Lydia (ed.)
WOMEN AND REVOLUTION: A DISCUSSION OF THE UNHAPPY MARRIAGE OF MARXISM AND FEMINISM (Boston, Mass.: South End Press, 1981; London: Pluto Press, 1981)

Analysing patriarchy, these feminists claim, has brought about a questioning both of Marxist materialism and economistic Marxism. Essays by Hartmann, Ehrlich, Vogal and others put forward ideology, psychology and culture as either equal with the 'base' or part of it.

TSP 111 Willis, Ellen
BEGINNING TO SEE THE LIGHT: PIECES OF A DECADE (New York: Wideview Books, 1981)

Magazine articles on aspects of feminism first published in *Village Voice* and *The New York Times*. Willis focuses on abortion rights but argues that the feminist preoccupation with pornography converges too much with the family fundamentalism of the New Right.

TSP 112 Brunt, Rosalind and Rowan, Caroline (eds.)
FEMINISM, CULTURE AND POLITICS (London: Lawrence and Wishart, 1982)

The collection shows how feminism has broadened our definitions of politics since culture here includes everyday experience, cultural products, media and visual representations. There are essays on the politics of ageing, Radclyffe Hall, psychoanalysis and history.

TSP 113 Coote, Anna and Campbell, Beatrix
SWEET FREEDOM: THE STRUGGLE FOR WOMEN'S LIBERATION (London: Picador, 1982)

This explores the main areas where the women's liberation movement in Britain has been politically engaged. The authors see women's liberation as both reformist and revolutionary and that the key to women's liberation is the transformation of the social construction of feminine psychology.

TSP 114 Evans, Mary (ed.)
THE WOMAN QUESTION: READINGS ON THE SUBORDINATION OF WOMEN (London: Fontana, 1982)

A collection of extracted readings in feminist theory from historical, cross-cultural and literary perspectives on themes of sexuality, work, domesticity and culture. Each section has a useful editorial comment and there is a good bibliography.

TSP 115 Keohane, N. O., Rosaldo, M. Z. and Gelpi, B. C.
FEMINIST THEORY: A CRITIQUE OF IDEOLOGY (Chicago: University of Chicago Press, 1982; Brighton: Harvester Press, 1982)

This contains key essays by Kristeva, Griffin, Jehlen and Keller, among others, covering psychology, political theory and literary criticism from the different political perspectives of liberal, Marxist, socialist and radical feminism. The editors aim to prevent ideology becoming 'frozen theory'.

TSP 116 Rosenberg, Rosalind
BEYOND SEPARATE SPHERES: INTELLECTUAL ROOTS OF MODERN FEMINISM (New Haven, CT: Yale University Press, 1982)

Rosenberg shows how Millett and others, by insisting on the cultural origins of sex differences, were building on the work of Margaret Mead and an earlier generation of feminist researchers.

TSP 117 Coward, Rosalind
PATRIARCHAL PRECEDENTS (London: Routledge & Kegan Paul, 1983)

Coward shows how many of our contemporary approaches to feminist questions originate in nineteenth-century discourses, for example the evolutionist theory of the family.

TSP 118   Eisenstein, Hester
CONTEMPORARY FEMINIST THOUGHT (Boston, Mass: G. K. Hall, 1983; London: Allen and Unwin, 1984)

A history and critique of feminist theory, principally in the United States, from 1970. She focuses on the ideas of radical feminism, as given by Kate Millett and Shulamith Firestone, and elaborated by Nancy Chodorow, Mary Daly and Adrienne Rich. Eisenstein shows the shifts in feminist theory from the idea that socially constructed differences was the chief source of female oppression; through the second phase of theory which was the rejection of androgyny and the adoption of a woman-centred perspective to the idea that difference from men is liberating rather than oppressive.

TSP 119   Jagger, Alison
FEMINIST POLITICS AND HUMAN NATURE (Brighton: Harvester Press, 1983)

A summary of the kinds of feminism in political philosophy. In a brief history of feminism, Jagger decides in favour of socialist-feminism because it combines class and gender in its explanation of patriarchy.

TSP 120   McGavran, Murray Meg
FACE TO FACE: FATHERS, MOTHERS, MASTERS, MONSTERS: ESSAYS FOR A NONSEXIST FUTURE
(Westport, CT.: Greenwood Press, 1983)

Theoretical perspectives from a number of disciplines on the nature of gender relationships in western (mainly American) culture. Contributors include Bernard, Dinnerstein, on the topics of parenting, myth, work, politics, psycho-analysis and the future.

TSP 121   Rowbotham, Sheila
DREAMS AND DILEMMAS: COLLECTED WRITINGS (London: Virago, 1983)

A collection of her early women's liberation movement

pieces from the 1960s in Britain on issues of sexuality, race, motherhood, the Welfare State and trade unions.

TSP 122   Snitow, Ann Barr (ed.)
POWERS OF DESIRE: THE POLITICS OF SEXUALITY (New York: Monthly Review Press, 1983) published as DESIRE: THE POLITICS OF SEXUALITY (London: Virago, 1984)

An anthology of feminist essays on pornography, violence, rape, gay rights and race and class in sexual relationships. Contributors include Walkowitz, Schulman, Rich, Ann E. Kaplan and others.

TSP 123   Spender, Dale (ed.)
FEMINIST THEORISTS (London: Women's Press, 1983)

Spender brings together contemporary feminists writing on original feminist thinkers from Aphra Behn to Simone de Beauvoir. The essays describe artificial classifications imposed on women and annotate their intellectual traditions. Each is a good account of the life and career of these feminist thinkers.

TSP 124   Steinem, Gloria
OUTRAGEOUS ACTS AND EVERYDAY REBELLIONS (New York: Holt, Rinehart and Winston, 1983)

A compendium of her articles arranged into chronological order of her awakening feminism and political involvement.

TSP 125   Daly, Mary
PURE LUST (Boston: Beacon Press, 1984: London: Women's Press, 1984)

Daly extends the argument of *Gyn/Ecology* and creates an alternative naming process, for women, of eroticism and bodies. As in her other work, Daly elaborates fresh symbolic codes.

TSP 126   Darty, T. and Potter, S. (eds.)
WOMEN-IDENTIFIED WOMEN (Palo Alto, CA.: Mayfield Publishing, 1984)

An anthology of essays on lesbian identity, theory, ethnicity, oppression, culture and community, Black lesbians, music and health care. The majority are published here for the first time and the book contains a bibliography and list of feminist periodicals.

TSP 127   Greer, Germaine
SEX AND DESTINY: THE POLITICS OF HUMAN FERTILITY (London: Secker & Warburg, 1984)

Greer covers western and non-western ideas of fertility, motherhood and population control. She argues for a return to large and extended families in her view of the superiority of the non-western family unit.

TSP 128   Harford, B. and Hopkins, S. (eds.)
GREENHAM COMMON: WOMEN AT THE WIRE (London: The Women's Press, 1984)

The first serious attempt to examine the peace camp and what it has taught women about patriarchy. Founded after a protest march in 1981 from South Wales to Greenham, the camp has created a growing politicisation of women about the nature of imperialism, racism and militarism. The book is a collection of oral and written accounts by the many women visitors to the camp.

TSP 129   Lorde, Audrey
SISTER OUTSIDER: ESSAYS AND SPEECHES (Trumansberg, N.Y.: Crossing Press, 1984)

Contains Lorde's key essays including 'Uses of the Erotic: The Erotic as Power' and 'An Open Letter to Mary Daly'.
  Lorde shows the importance of creating theory from a concept of the different realities of black and lesbian. She attacks the false universalism of white feminist theory as a form of neo-colonialism and shows that autobiographical experiences are central to the development of feminist theory.

TSP 130　　Mitchell, Juliet
　　　　　　WOMEN: THE LONGEST REVOLUTION (London: Virago, 1984; New York: Pantheon, 1984)

This includes Mitchell's seminal essay of that title first published in *New Left Review* 40 (1966) where Mitchell argued that four structures of society needed to be transformed before women could be liberated: production, reproduction, sexuality and the socialisation of children. The anthology also includes her other essays on psychoanalysis and literary criticism.

TSP 131　　Vance, Carole S. (ed.)
　　　　　　PLEASURE AND DANGER: EXPLORING FEMALE SEXUALITY (Boston, Mass.: Routledge & Kegan Paul, 1984)

Papers from the 1982 Barnard Conference on Politics of Sexuality. Contributors discuss the sexuality of children, nineteenth-century feminism, sex manuals, sexuality and ethnic women and pornography. There are contributions from Kate Millett, Cherrie Moraga, Gayle Rubin and others.

TSP 132　　Vogel, Lisa
　　　　　　MARXISM AND THE OPPRESSION OF WOMEN: TOWARDS A UNITARY THEORY (New Brunswick, N.J.: Rutgers University Press, 1984)

She discusses the debate about Firestone's biological materialism among socialist-feminists, and gives a direction to the development of socialist-feminist theory on the 'mode of reproduction'.

TSP 133　　Freedman, E. B. and Gelpi, B. C. (eds.)
　　　　　　THE LESBIAN ISSUE (Chicago: University of Chicago Press, 1985)

This is a collection from *Signs* 9: 4 (Summer 1984) with a focus on lesbian identity, lesbian literature and a history of discrimination against lesbians. The collection reveals the breadth of lesbian studies and scholarship in coverage of history, anthropology, literature and political science.

There are essays by Bonnie Zimmerman, Martha Vicinus, Ruby Rich and Adrienne Rich.

TSP 134 Russ, Joanna
MAGIC MOMMAS, TREMBLING SISTERS, PURITANS AND PERVERTS: FEMINIST ESSAYS (Trumansburg, N.Y.: Crossing Press, 1985)

Russ deals with the issues of sex and pornography combined with her own autobiography. She attempts to demystify pornography and offers some alternative conceptions of eroticism drawing on science fiction.

TSP 135 Spender, Dale
FOR THE RECORDS: THE MAKING AND MEANING OF FEMINIST KNOWLEDGE (London: Women's Press, 1985)

An account of the writings of feminist theorists from the 1970s including Kate Millett, Greer, Friedan, Morgan and others. Spender collected some letters written by critics in response to her essays about them.

Literary Criticism

This is defined as feminist criticism about *literature* rather than feminist criticism about specific writers except where an account of an individual writer suggests an interesting new critical approach or paradigm. Feminist literary criticism is not new but what is distinctive about contemporary criticism is its use of theory and politics.

LIT 1   Rogers, Katherine, M.
THE TROUBLESOME HELPMATE: A HISTORY OF MISOGYNY IN LITERATURE (Seattle: University of Washington Press, 1966)

A thesis about the cultural causes of male misogyny which had a strong influence on Kate Millett's *Sexual Politics*. Rogers lists the rejection of, or guilt about, sex by men; idealisations with which men have glorified women and a patriarchal wish to keep women subject to men. The last is the most important Rogers claims because it is most entrenched.

LIT 2   Ellman, Mary
THINKING ABOUT WOMEN (New York: Harcourt Brace, 1968; London: Macmillan, 1969)

A basic text for subsequent 'images of women' criticism, Ellman searches for female stereotypes in male writing. Her main purpose is to expose the illogical nature of males' analogies and to show how men's assertive mode has confined women to a language of sensibility.

LIT 3   Cornillon, Susan K. (ed.)
IMAGES OF WOMEN IN FICTION: FEMINIST PERSPECTIVES (Ohio: Bowling Green University Press, 1972)

Organised in four categories of women as heroine, invisible women, woman as hero and feminist aesthetics. Essays by Donovan, Howe, Robinson, among others take a basically reflectionist stance that literature encapsulates life—that of the reader and the writer's autobiography.

LIT 4   Hoffman, Nancy, Secor, Cynthia and Tinsley, Adrien (eds.)
FEMALE STUDIES VI: CLOSER TO THE GROUND (Old Westbury, N.Y.: Feminist Press, 1972)

A collection of writings on feminist pedagogy which influenced literature classes in America.

LIT 5   Appignanesi, Lisa
FEMININITY AND THE CREATIVE IMAGINATION: A STUDY OF HENRY JAMES, ROBERT MUSIL AND MARCEL PROUST (London: Vision Press, 1973; New York: Barnes and Noble, 1973)

She examined definitions and concepts of femininity in these writers using a mode of cultural criticism.

LIT 6   Brée, Germaine
WOMEN WRITERS IN FRANCE: VARIATIONS ON A THEME (New Brunswick, N.J.: Rutgers University Press, 1973)

Describes the concept of *l'écriture feminine* and applies it to French writing.

LIT 7   Ferguson, Mary Anne
IMAGES OF WOMEN IN LITERATURE (Boston., Mass: Houghton Mifflin, 1973)

An anthology of literature arranged in groups to reflect the social stereotyping of women (as in 'old maid'). Ferguson shows the tension between these and women's aspirations and social expectations.

LIT 8   Showalter, Elaine
'Women writers and the female experience', RADICAL FEMINISM, ed. Anne Koedt (New York: Quadrangle, 1973)

This early essay of feminist criticism appeared first in *Notes from the Third Year* (1971) and focuses on four books: *Jane Eyre, Adam Bede, The Awakening* and *The Group* to demonstrate how criticism applies double standards to women's books.

LIT 9   Basch, Françoise
RELATIVE CREATURES: VICTORIAN WOMEN IN SOCIETY AND THE NOVEL (New York: Schocken Books, 1974)

Basch looks at caricatures of Victorian women in the work of Dickens, the Brontës, Gaskill, Eliot and Thackeray from three points of view—imagery of wives and mothers, single women and impure women. She shows how women are deprived of an integral dialectic of the social with the psychological.

LIT 10   Berkinow, Louise
'Introduction', THE WORLD SPLIT OPEN: FOUR CENTURIES OF WOMEN POETS IN ENGLAND AND AMERICA 1552–1950 (New York: Random House, 1974)

An influential account of hitherto unregarded women poets.

LIT 11   Cixous, Hélène
'The character of character', *New Literary History* 5: 2 (Winter 1974)

Argues that characters in fiction are too static for feminist critics to be examining since they are to do with authorial ownership—a patriarchal concept.

LIT 12   Donovan, Josephine (ed.)
FEMINIST LITERARY CRITICISM: EXPLORATIONS IN THEORY (Lexington, Kentucky.: University Press of Kentucky, 1975)

An important early collection which aims at a reader unfamiliar with feminist criticism. Essays by Register, Currier Bell among others on aesthetics end with a dialogue between Carolyn Heilbrun and Catherine Stimpson on the aims, function and future of feminist criticism.

LIT 13   Gelpi, Barbara and Gelpi, A. (eds.)
ADRIENNE RICH'S POETRY (New York: W. W. Norton, 1975)

Although on a single author this collection represents a very useful form of feminist criticism. It includes a representative selection of Rich's work, critical essays about that writing and a series of fascinating conversations between Rich and the editors on the intersection of poetry, politics and psychology in her writing career. There is a chronology and bibliography.

LIT 14   Kaplan, Sydney
FEMINIST CONSCIOUSNESS IN THE MODERN BRITISH NOVEL (Urbana, Illinois: University of Illinois Press, 1975)

An interesting linguistic analysis of the writings of Lehmann, Sinclair, Woolf, Richardson and Lessing. By examining the relation between sentence structure and character's consciousness, Kaplan is able to deal more adequately with metaphors of femininity than do more traditional 'images of women' feminist critics.

LIT 15   Key, Mary
MALE/FEMALE LANGUAGE (Metuchen, N.J.: Scarecrow Press, 1975)

Shows, cross-culturally, that languages need not have masculine and feminine gender. There is a comprehensive bibliography.

LIT 16   Kolodny, Annette
THE LAY OF THE LAND: METAPHOR AS EXPERIENCE IN AMERICAN LIFE AND LETTERS (Chapel Hill, N.C.: University of North Carolina Press, 1975)

Kolodny focuses on the works of male writers she feels can alter our ways of understanding the male literary tradition and how it has dealt with us.

LIT 17   Kolodny, Annette
'Some Notes on Defining a "Feminist Literary Criticism" ', *Critical Inquiry* 2: 1 (1975) 75–92

This is reprinted in Brown, Cheryl and Olson, Karen (eds.) *Feminist Criticism: Essays on Theory, Poetry and Prose* and was the source of much subsequent feminist debate. Kolodny argues that because feminist criticism is not established an appropriate feminist stance is pluralism.

LIT 18   Rule, Jane
LESBIAN IMAGES (Trumansburg, N.Y.: The Crossing Press, 1975)

An important account by another lesbian writer of the main examples of lesbian writing. Rule includes writers as diverse as Maureen Duffy and Willa Cather as well as Gertrude Stein and Vita Sackville-West. It is the first good introduction to the main themes, characters and plots in a significant area of women's writing.

LIT 19   Spacks, P. M.
THE FEMALE IMAGINATION (New York: Knopf, 1975)

Spacks gives a helpful historical account of the nineteenth-century novels written by women. She has a very broad definition of feminist criticism which she takes to be any mode that approaches a text with a primary concern for the nature of female experience.

LIT 20   *Women and Literature* 3: 1 (Spring 1975); 4: 1 (Spring 1976); 4: 2 (Fall 1976)

Three collections of articles on women writers.

LIT 21   Allen, Mary
THE NECESSARY BLANKNESS: WOMEN IN
MAJOR AMERICAN FICTION OF THE SIXTIES
(Urbana, Illinois: University of Illinois Press, 1976)

A feminist critique of gender, genre and representation in the work of Roth, Updike, Plath and Oates. She examines mysogynist imagery taking the 'images of women' approach of early feminist criticism.

LIT 22   Cixous, Hélène
'The Laugh of the Medusa', *Signs* 1 (Summer 1976), 875–93

Argues that patriarchy is binary versus the multiple difference of women's writing. A forceful feminist appropriation of Derridean theory.

LIT 23   Juhasz, S.
NAKED AND FIERY FORMS: MODERN
AMERICAN POETRY BY WOMEN: A NEW
TRADITION (New York: Harper and Row, 1976)

Examining a range of poets including Dickinson, Moore, Levertov, Plath, Sexton, Rich, Brooks and Giovanni, Juhasz tackles the issue of women's 'different' voices claiming they represent a need to integrate public with private worlds.

LIT 24   Kaplan, Cora
'Language and Gender', PAPERS ON PATRIARCHY
(Lewes, Sussex: Women's Publishing Collective, 1976)

An early attempt to grapple with the issue of difference and its syntactical representation in women's writing.

LIT 25   Miller, Casey and Swift, Kate
WORDS AND WOMEN (Garden City, New York: Anchor Books, 1976)

The book examines sexism in language and takes the

position that language, reflecting consciousness, is a serious issue.

LIT 26 Moers, Ellen
LITERARY WOMEN: THE GREAT WRITERS (New York: Doubleday, 1976; London: Women's Press, 1976)

A pioneering work mapping an uncharted territory of women's writing. Moers provides a history of women's styles and themes in an overview of English, American and French writing from the eighteenth to twentieth centuries with plot summaries and an emphasis on biography. Moers adopts a traditional canonic approach using traditional aesthetic criteria.

LIT 27 Myers, Carol Fairbanks (ed.)
WOMEN IN LITERATURE: CRITICISM OF THE SEVENTIES (Metuchen, N.J.: Scarecrow Press, 1976)

This text is representative of early feminist criticism focusing on women characters in myth and literature. They examine women characters and social relations, women characters as myth and symbol, biographical studies and interviews. It is weighted more towards American writing.

LIT 28 Diamond, Arlene and Edwards, Lee (eds.)
THE AUTHORITY OF EXPERIENCE: ESSAYS IN FEMINIST CRITICISM (Amherst, Mass.: University of Massachusetts Press, 1977)

The essays focus on the impact of culture, history and politics on critical analysis. Critics include Fetterley, Rogers and Kahn among others who examine Virginia Woolf, Doris Lessing, Kate Chopin and male authors.

LIT 29 Douglas, Ann Wood
THE FEMINIZATION OF AMERICAN CULTURE (New York: Alfred A. Knopf, 1977)

Looking in particular at the period 1820–1875 Douglas

examines the intimate connection between women's domestic and religious concerns and American literature of which they were the prime consumers.

LIT 30 Ferrier, Carole
'The Inadequacy of the Imagination: Towards a Feminist Literary Criticism,' THE RADICAL READER, eds. Stephen Knight and Michael Wilding (Sydney: Wild and Woolley Press, 1977)

A functionalist discussion of the role of literature and criticism as a political tool. Contains a bibliography.

LIT 31 Showalter, Elaine
A LITERATURE OF THEIR OWN: BRITISH WOMEN NOVELISTS FROM BRONTË TO LESSING (Princeton, N.J.: Princeton University Press, 1977)

A guided tour of female literary landscape in Britain since the 1840s. A major contribution to literary history is the emphasis she places on the rediscovery of forgotten or neglected women writers. Showalter describes three major phases of development: the 'feminine' period of male pseudonyms which ended with the death of George Eliot in 1880; the 'feminist' phase from 1880 to 1920 and a 'female' phase from the 1920s.

LIT 32 Smith, Barbara
TOWARDS A BLACK FEMINIST CRITICISM (Trumansburg, N.Y.: Out and Out Books and Crossing Press, 1977)

The pioneering account of black lesbian writing. Smith attacks the misrepresentation and construction of black women in texts by black or white men and makes valid connections between the politics of black women and what they write.

LIT 33 Spacks, P. M. (ed.)
CONTEMPORARY WOMEN NOVELISTS (Englewood Cliffs, N.J.: Prentice-Hall, 1977)

Eleven essays by men and women critics from Mailer to Oates probe the styles of Welty, Murdoch, Rhys, McCarthy, Lessing and Sparks. The collection does ask questions about the representation of sexuality but only marginally can it be called feminist.

LIT 34   Springer, Marlene (ed.)
WHAT MANNER OF WOMAN: ESSAYS ON ENGLISH AND AMERICAN LIFE AND LITERATURE (New York: New York University Press, 1977; Oxford: Basil Blackwell, 1977)

A chronological survey of major literary periods. Essays by Heilbrun, Banta, Baym and others describe literary portraits of women within a historical-cultural framework. A well-documented account of genre, imagery and black writing in poetry, drama and the novel.

LIT 35   Auerbach, Nina
COMMUNITIES OF WOMAN: AN IDEA IN FICTION (Cambridge, Mass.: Harvard University Press, 1978)

Auerbach gives narrative descriptions of the kinds of women's communities in *Pride and Prejudice*, *Little Women*, *Cranford*, *Villette*, *The Bostonians*, *The Odd Women* and *The Prime of Miss Jean Brodie*.

LIT 36   Baym, Nina
WOMEN'S FICTION: A GUIDE TO NOVELS BY AND ABOUT WOMEN IN AMERICA, 1820–1870 (Ithaca, New York: Cornell University Press, 1978)

A feminist critique of popular fiction which illustrates a crucial question in feminist literary criticism: How to defend the quality of popular fiction while trying to redefine 'literary quality' as represented by the canon.

LIT 37   Brown, Carol and Olson, K. (eds.)
FEMINIST CRITICISM: ESSAYS ON THEORY, POETRY AND PROSE (Metuchen, N.J. and London: The Scarecrow Press, 1978)

A woman-centred approach with no male contributors which is an excellent text for women's studies courses. It combines theoretical with practical criticism in assessment of novels, poetry, autobiography. Includes Pratt, Kolodny, Robinson and Nin among others.

LIT 38   Cunningham, Gail
THE NEW WOMAN AND THE VICTORIAN
NOVEL (London: Macmillan, 1978)

Brief surveys of conventions and stereotypes in the depiction of women in the Victorian novel. Includes such popular novelists as Grant Allan and Sarah Grand and examines their historical significance.

LIT 39   Fetterley, Judith
THE RESISTING READER: A FEMINIST
APPROACH TO AMERICAN FICTION
(Bloomington, Indiana: Indiana University Press, 1978)

A critique of male authors including D. H. Lawrence and Hemingway which aims to make feminist criticism be an 'act of resistance' to existing judgements and canons.

LIT 40   Garvin, Harry (ed.)
WOMEN, LITERATURE, CRITICISM (Lewisburg: Bucknell University Press, 1978)

The essays range from the historical to the biographical with two essays by M. Farwell and Jane Marcus on the aims, function and range of feminist criticism. The focus is on a disjunction between inherited ideas of women's roles and the critical perceptions of many women.

LIT 41   Kennard, Jean
VICTIMS OF CONVENTION (Hamden, CT: Archon Books, 1978)

Deals with the broader question of feminism as applied to the work of Austen, Brontë and Eliot.

Literary Criticism

LIT 42 Marxist-Feminist Literature Collective
'Women's Writing: *Jane Eyre, Shirley, Villette, Aurora Leigh,*' *Ideology and Consciousness* 1: 3 (Spring 1978) 27–48

A pioneering article which draws on the theories of French Marxists such as Louis Althusser and Pierre Macherey to analyse the marginalisation of the woman writer and her work in terms of both class and gender.

LIT 43 Olsen, Tillie
SILENCES (New York: Dela Corte Press, 1978)

By describing her own autobiographical experiences of writing Olsen pioneered a form, now more common in feminist criticism, of encyclopedic essay combined with private thoughts and polemic. Olsen demonstrates that silence is central in women's culture and that women's voices have gone unheard under male power realities incorporated into language. A stimulating challenge to male aesthetics.

LIT 44 Rigney, Barbara Hill
MADNESS AND SEXUAL POLITICS IN THE FEMINIST NOVEL: STUDIES IN BRONTË, WOOLF, LESSING AND ATWOOD (Madison: University of Wisconsin Press, 1978)

Rigney uses the theories of R. D. Laing, the British psychoanalyst to make a feminist study of women writers uses of the doppelganger.

LIT 45 Robinson, Lillian
SEX, CLASS, AND CULTURE (Bloomington, Indiana: Indiana University Press, 1978)

The essays range from Virginia Woolf and Austen to autobiography, employment, TV commercials, popular reading, soap operas and women's reading. Robinson provides a cohesive collection of feminist theory and applied criticism very adequately grounded in social history.

LIT 46   Bell, P. Roseann, Parker, J. Bettye and Guy-Sheftall, Beverley (eds.)
STURDY BLACK BRIDGES: VISIONS OF BLACK WOMEN IN LITERATURE (Garden City, N.Y.: Anchor Books, 1979)

An exciting new criticism which draws on biogenetics, the performing arts, economics as well as history, politics and sociology. It counterposes the historical reality of black women from many countries with fiction, prophecies and dreams. Including art and photographic essays and extensive bibliographies in African-American, African and Caribbean Studies.

LIT 47   Gilbert, Sandra and Gubar, Susan
THE MADWOMAN IN THE ATTIC: THE WOMAN WRITER AND THE NINETEENTH-CENTURY LITERARY IMAGINATION (New Haven, CT.: Yale University Press, 1979)

This is a major and influential study of women writers: Austen, the Brontës, Shelley, Eliot, Browning, Rossetti, Dickinson. The text demonstrates a new critical understanding of women's creativity in revealing how a feminist poetics can enable women to overcome their 'anxiety of authorship' (from Harold Bloom) and recover their lost foremothers. Feminist critical strategies, claim Gilbert and Gubar, are those which deconstruct and reconstruct images of women inherited from the male tradition. The madwoman they take to be a literary emblem of an imagery of disease and escape.

LIT 48   Gilbert, Sandra and Gubar, Susan (eds.)
SHAKESPEARE'S SISTERS: FEMINIST ESSAYS ON WOMEN POETS (Bloomington, Indiana: Indiana University Press, 1979)

The authors consider women poets who were pulled between careers and domesticity or religious constraints. Nineteen essays examine the poetry of Anne Bradstreet, H.D., Muriel Rukeyser, Denise Levertov, Edna St Vincent Millay, Christina Rossetti, Emily Dickinson, Gwendolyn Brooks and Afro-American poetry.

Literary Criticism

LIT 49   Jacobus, Mary (ed.)
WOMEN WRITING AND WRITING ABOUT WOMEN (London: Croom Helm, 1979; New York: Barnes and Noble, 1979)

Examples of 'female' modes of expression and experience in the writers Rossetti, Woolf, Dickinson, Ibsen, Hardy and the Brontës. Includes a wide variety of genres and disciplines with an essay by Laura Mulvey on feminist cinema and one on feminist poetics by Elaine Showalter.

LIT 50   Mason, M. A. and Green, C. H. (eds.)
JOURNEYS: AUTOBIOGRAPHICAL WRITINGS BY WOMEN (Boston, Mass.: G. K. Hall, 1979)

A collection of writers as varied as Levertov, Sontag and Beatrice Webb made to exemplify the editors' claim that the journey is a metaphor in women's writing for freedom, goals and action.

LIT 51   Mickelson, Anne
REACHING OUT: SENSITIVITY AND ORDER IN RECENT AMERICAN FICTION BY WOMEN (Metuchen, N.J.: Scarecrow Press, 1979)

Examining the work of Jong, Gould, Godwin, Didion, black writing and writing of the future, Mickelson assesses each writer's regard for women's liberation and how they have criticised or rejected the American social system.

LIT 52   Showalter, Elaine
'Towards a Feminist Poetics', WOMEN WRITING AND WRITING ABOUT WOMEN, ed. Mary Jacobus (London: Croom Helm, 1979), pp. 22–41

Showalter distinguishes two forms of feminist criticism: woman as reader and woman as writer which she calls gynocritics. Showalter argues for the second form of female culture.

LIT 53 Stewart, Grace
A NEW MYTHOS: THE NOVEL OF THE ARTIST AS HEROINE 1877–1977 (Vermont: Eden Press, 1979)

In reading Plath, Sinclair, Atwood, Richardson, Lessing and Woolf, Stewart focuses on rape myths, menstruation, mother/daughter relations, the mythic power of motherhood and the demonic powers of fathers.

LIT 54 Stubbs, Patricia
WOMEN AND FICTION: FEMINISM AND THE NOVEL 1880–1920 (Brighton: Harvester Press, 1979; New York: Barnes and Noble, 1979)

Stubbs examines how women writers' often radical techniques, such as Dorothy Richardson's stream of consciousness, are rejected by the male literary establishment. Stubbs still accepts, however, the concept of a literary tradition as objective.

LIT 55 Coward, Rosalind
' "This novel changes lives": Are women's novels feminist novels?', *Feminist Review* 5 (1980)

Influential essay showing how women's writing is a term which conceals contradictory ideologies. Argues that women's writing is a very dispersed field.

LIT 56 Davidson, C. N. and Broner, E. H.
THE LOST TRADITION: MOTHER AND DAUGHTERS IN LITERATURE (New York: Frederick Ungar, 1980)

A comprehensive chronological survey from ancient to modern literature of links between mothers and daughters in myths, poems, autobiographies, songs, novels and the oral tradition. With twenty-four essays the text contains a long bibliography of the field.

LIT 57 Eisenstein, Hester and Jardine, Alice (eds.)
THE FUTURE OF DIFFERENCE (Boston, Mass.: G. K. Hall, 1980)

Edited from a collection of conference papers given at Barnard College Women's Center. The issue of difference is considered from the perspectives of psychoanalysis, French feminism and black and lesbian positions. Essays by Lorde, Heilbrun, Chodorow among others represent a shift in feminist criticism to a woman-centred perspective.

LIT 58 Feminist Criticism Special Issue
Enclitic 4: 2 (Fall 1980)

Applying psychoanalytic and deconstructive techniques to feminism, essays by Jardine, Cixous and Gallop among others examine narrative strategies in de Sade, Kristeva, *Wuthering Heights*. There is a crucial essay by Sarah Kofman on Freud's fear of women.

LIT 59 Fox-Genovese, E.
'A New Female Literary Culture', *Antioch Review* 38 (Spring 1980), 193–217.

A Marxist-Feminist analysis of literary history.

LIT 60 Jelinek, Estelle (ed.)
WOMEN'S AUTOBIOGRAPHY: ESSAYS IN CRITICISM (Bloomington, Indiana: Indiana University Press, 1980)

A collection which includes early black feminist criticism and essays on Hong Kingston. A wide range of autobiographies, from Golda Meir to Doris Lessing are examined and Jelinek and others argue that women's autobiography is markedly different from those by men. Women write about their children not their careers in an oblique or humorous way to camouflage their feelings.

LIT 61 Johnson, Barbara
THE CRITICAL DIFFERENCE (Baltimore, MD.: Johns Hopkins Press, 1980)

Not explicitly feminist, yet Johnson provides a good introduction of concepts and techniques from psychoanalysis pertinent to feminism. She discusses the concept of difference as valorised both by Saussurean linguistics and by the Nietzschean tradition in philosophy arguing that to make a critical difference is the object of all criticism as such.

LIT 62   Kramarae, Chris (ed.)
THE VOICES AND WORDS OF WOMEN AND MEN
(Oxford: Pergamon Press, 1980)

An extensive collection of criticism about all aspects of sex/gender construction in language and speech. Essays by Henley, Martyna and others cover language uses in disciplines, in textbooks, in syntactics, in oral culture, in schools and in Indo-European culture. They answer questions about language and social change and the learning of gender.

LIT 63   McConnell-Ginet, S., Borker, R. and Furman, N.
WOMEN AND LANGUAGE IN LITERATURE AND SOCIETY (New York: Praeger, 1980)

An interdisciplinary investigation into language and its uses. Essays by Gallop, Spivak, Kramarae and others offer ethnographic studies of Spanish communities, Derridean deconstructions of Woolf, language uses in Chopin. The text connects very well the social study of language with the study of women in literature.

LIT 64   Miller, Nancy
THE HEROINE'S TEXT: READINGS IN THE FRENCH AND ENGLISH NOVEL (New York: Columbia University Press, 1980)

A semiological inquiry into 'euphoric' and 'dysphoric' novels and the semiotics of female vulnerability.

LIT 65   Perry, Ruth
WOMEN, LETTERS AND THE NOVEL (New York: AMS Press, 1980)

Focuses on the epistolary strain in fiction since Perry considers that letters are a significant part of written culture and have a special importance for women. She looks at the ways in which novels provided eighteenth-century women with a coherent world.

LIT 66 Spender, Dale
MANMADE LANGUAGE (London: Routledge & Kegan Paul, 1980)

An important account of sexism and language. Spender argues that patriarchal uses of written and spoken language structure much of women's subordination in society. She proposes that women must encode their own language to move towards self-determination. Some of Spender's ideas were accurately described as confused and incorrect by later feminists (in particular D. Cameron LIT 131 and T. Moi LIT 139), but her book is a comprehensive survey of gender difference studies in the field of linguistics.

LIT 67 Sternburg, Janet (ed.)
THE WRITER ON HER WORK: CONTEMPORARY WOMEN WRITERS REFLECT ON THEIR ART AND SITUATION (New York: W. W. Norton, 1980)

A collection of personal, literary and female landscapes by Kingston, Jong, Rukeyser, Godwin, Burroway, Didion, Milford, Alice and Margaret Walker, Bambara and Griffin. Each describes having to write against social construction creating, as Kingston suggests 'a trail of words' to escape patriarchy.

LIT 68 Todd, Janet
WOMEN'S FRIENDSHIP IN LITERATURE (New York: Columbia University Press, 1980)

Part of the new wave of feminist critics interested in studying relationships between women either as mothers and daughters, or in female communities.

LIT 69   Todd, Janet
GENDER AND LITERARY VOICE (New York: Holmes and Meier, 1980)

The book debates the presence of a distinctive female style, voice or content in literature written by women from the Middle Ages to the twentieth century. Wollstonecraft and Burney wrote about the linguistic difficulties of writing prose; Virginia Woolf looks at an androgynous literature. The authors consider the role of female experience; the passive mode; the female appropriation of traditional male genres such as bildungsroman. Contributors include Wilt and Butler with a review of feminist criticism by Nina Auerbach.

LIT 70   Bulkin, Elly
'A Look at Lesbian Short Fiction', LESBIAN FICTION (Watertown, Mass.: Persephone Press, 1981)

An illuminating account of lesbian criticism and teaching which Bulkin repeats in her account of lesbian poetry in the same series.

LIT 71   Cixous, Hélène
'Castration or Decapitation', *Signs* (Autumn 1981)

Elaborates her idea that theoretical discourse is oppressive and that women are outside the symbolic. Argues that women's language is closer to the voice and the future of criticism must be to change the metalanguage.

LIT 72   Faderman, Lillian
SURPASSING THE LOVE OF MEN: ROMANTIC FRIENDSHIP AND LOVE BETWEEN WOMEN FROM THE RENAISSANCE TO THE PRESENT (New York: William Morrow, 1981; London: Junction Books, 1981)

An important cultural history of women-identified women and their representation, in literature. Faderman defines what 'writing lesbian' might entail and describes fictional strategies such as non-linear writing and fantasy.

Although Faderman was later attacked by some feminists for not centralising sexuality, the book remains a very comprehensive account of romantic friendship in literature.

LIT 73 Grier, B.
THE LESBIAN IN LITERATURE (Tallahassee, FLA: Naiad Press, 1981)

An extensive bibliography of novels, short stories, drama and fictionalised biography concerned with lesbianism. A crucial introduction to a rapidly growing field, the text also includes autobiography and magazine material.

LIT 74 Jehlen, Myra
'Archimedes and the Paradox of Feminist Criticism', *Signs* 6: 4 (1981) 575–601

Jehlen argues for radical comparativism by not simply restricting feminist criticism to woman-centred works.

LIT 75 Mitchell, Sally
THE FALLEN ANGEL: CHASTITY, CLASS AND WOMEN'S READING 1835–1880 (Bowling Green, Ohio: Bowling Green University Popular Press, 1981)

Mitchell looks at fictional variations of theme, moral intent and literary style in terms of sexual and moral attitudes towards and by women in early and mid-Victorian fiction. She chooses the period as the one in which organised feminism had its birth and initial successes.

LIT 76 Moragu, C. and Anzaldua, G. (eds.)
THIS BRIDGE CALLED MY BACK: WRITINGS BY RADICAL WOMEN OF COLOR (New York: Kitchen Table Press, 1981)

A superb collection of prose, poetry, personal narrative and analysis by Afro-American, Asian American, Latina, and native American women. The themes are racism, culture, Third World writing and the future.

LIT 77   Newton, Judith Lowder
WOMEN, POWER AND SUBVERSION: SOCIAL
STRATEGIES IN BRITISH FICTION 1778–1860
(Athens, Georgia: University of Georgia Press, 1981)

Newton takes a basically thematic and imagistic approach to focus on the conjuncture of class and gender in British nineteenth-century literature.

LIT 78   Pearson, Carol and Pope, Catherine
THE FEMALE HERO IN AMERICAN AND
BRITISH LITERATURE (New York: R. R. Bowker, 1981)

An example of myth criticism which challenges a number of assumptions about women characters and provides evidence from Chaucer to Doris Lessing to substantiate a rewriting of mythical themes from a feminist perspective.

LIT 79   Pratt, Annis
ARCHETYPAL PATTERNS IN WOMEN'S FICTION
(Bloomington, Indiana: Indiana University Press, 1981; Brighton: Harvester Press, 1982)

Pratt describes archetypes (mainly from Jung) and applies them to a variety of women's literature including both major and minor writers. It is a synchronic study de-emphasising history which uses women's fiction in order to explore questions of women's identity.

LIT 80   Roberts, J. R.
BLACK LESBIANS: AN ANNOTATED
BIBLIOGRAPHY (Tallahassee, Florida: Naiad Press, 1981)

Roberts argues that the bibliographic situation mirrors the denial and invalidation of black lesbian experience in society. This is an exemplary collection of essays, autobiography, bibliographies, and poetry arranged in helpful categories of literature, lives, oppression, periodicals, music and research.

Literary Criticism

LIT 81 Stetson, Erlene
BLACK SISTER: POETRY BY BLACK AMERICAN WOMEN 1764–1980 (Bloomington, Indiana: Indiana University Press, 1981)

Black feminist criticism which introduces many obscure black voices.

LIT 82 Abel, Elisabeth (ed.)
WRITING AND SEXUAL DIFFERENCE (Chicago: University of Chicago Press, 1982; Brighton: Harvester Press, 1982)

Demonstrates a shift in feminist criticism towards the reading of women's texts by women and the displacement of male bias as a centre of critical attention. The text is based on a special issue of *Critical Inquiry* 8: 2 (Winter 1981) and includes contributions by Jacobus, Gilbert and Gubar, Spivak, Showalter and Stimpson. They elucidate the subversive acts that constitute a female text and celebrate pluralism by including psychoanalytic, deconstructive, and generic criticism with historical studies.

LIT 83 Auerbach, Nina
WOMAN AND THE DEMON (Cambridge, Mass.: Harvard University Press, 1982)

She examines Victorian constructions of the heroine, spinster and the outcast in fiction, criticism and painting.

LIT 84 Boumelha, Penny
THOMAS HARDY AND WOMEN: SEXUAL IDEOLOGY AND NARRATIVE FORM (Brighton: Harvester Press, 1982)

An ideological critique using Althusserian, and Marxist-feminist models.

LIT 85   Brickman, Richard, McDonald, Susan and Stark, Myra (eds.)
CORRUPT RELATIONS: DICKENS, THACKERAY, TROLLOPE, COLLINS AND THE VICTORIAN SEXUAL SYSTEM (New York: Columbia University Press, 1982)

Feminist criticism in the 'resisting reader' tradition.

LIT 86   Brownstein, Rachel Mayer
BECOMING A HEROINE: READING ABOUT WOMEN IN NOVELS (New York: Viking Press, 1982)

Brownstein's central thesis is that novels help determine the lives of readers. She examines heroine-centred novels by Richardson, Brontës, Meredith, Austen, Eliot and James.

LIT 87   Carter, Angela
NOTHING SACRED (London: Virago, 1982)

Accounts of images of women in the media and Colette and Mansfield.

LIT 88   Clausen, Jan
A MOVEMENT OF POETS: THOUGHTS ON POETRY FROM FEMINISM (Brooklyn, New York: Long Haul Press, 1982)

A short monograph on the relation of women's poetry to the American feminist movement. Clausen outlines the problems involved in using a 'correct' feminist line in poetry.

LIT 89   Figes, Eva
SEX AND SUBTERFUGE: WOMEN WRITERS TO 1850 (London: Macmillan, 1982)

Shows how women writers have reshaped the novel away from the male picaresque tradition to uses of first-hand experience and the descriptions of women's roles.

LIT 90   Gardiner, Judith Kegan et al.
'An Interchange on Feminist Criticism on "Dancing Through the Minefield" ', *Feminist Studies* 8: 3 (Fall 1982) 629–75

A collection of important responses to the criticism of Annette Kolodny. Each, although from the very different perspectives of lesbian, Marxist-feminist or black, proves that white feminist criticism is often racist and homophobic.

LIT 91   Hanscombe, Gillian
THE ART OF LIFE: DOROTHY RICHARDSON AND THE DEVELOPMENT OF FEMINIST CONSCIOUSNESS (London: Peter Owen, 1982)

Although on a single author, the text uses an interesting mode of feminist criticism in which Hanscombe mixes autobiography with fiction to demonstrate how the experimental form of *Pilgrimage* sprang directly from Richardson's feminist convictions.

LIT 92   Heilbrun, Carolyn and Higonnet, M. (eds.)
THE REPRESENTATION OF WOMEN IN FICTION (Baltimore, MD: Johns Hopkins University Press, 1982)

Essays by Marcus, Miller, Gubar, Poovey and other feminists consider both individual writers (as George Sand or Katherine Mansfield) and the pastoral or *Kunstlerroman* traditions in which they were writing.

LIT 93   Kristeva, Julia
DESIRE IN LANGUAGE: A SEMIOTIC APPROACH TO LITERATURE AND ART, trans. L. S. Roudiez with A. Jardine and T. Gora (New York: Columbia University Press, 1982; Oxford: Basil Blackwell, 1982)

A leading exponent of French feminist psychoanalytic criticism, Kristeva defines the semiotic as pre-verbal displaced by the symbolic order of men but represented in it through rupture and contradictions.

Not explicitly feminist the text is supportive in Kristeva's portrait of motherhood as a conceptual challenge to phallocentrism.

LIT 94   Modleski, Tania
LOVING WITH A VENGEANCE (Hamden, CT.: Shoe String Press, 1982; London: Methuen, 1984)

A serious study of Harlequin romances, female Gothics and soap operas. Modelski argues that mass-produced feminine narratives are popular because they speak to real desires in women which capitalism cannot cope with in other ways. She demonstrates that each type of narrative contains elements of resistance which attract women readers.

LIT 95   Mulford, Wendy
'Socialist-feminist Criticism: A Case Study, Women's Suffrage and Literature 1906–1914', RE-READING ENGLISH, ed. Peter Widdowson (London: Methuen, 1982)

An authoritative article which argues a convincing case for feminist criticism to be both socio-historical *and* centred on women's writing and autobiography.

LIT 96   Piercy, Marge
PARTI-COLORED BLOCKS FOR A QUILT (Ann Arbor: University of Michigan Press, 1982)

A collection of essays and interviews and Piercy's reviews of other writers such as Robin Morgan and Joanna Russ. The themes are autobiography and feminist criticism.

LIT 97   Rogers, Katherine M.
FEMINISM IN EIGHTEENTH-CENTURY ENGLAND (Urbana, Ill.: University of Illinois Press 1982; Brighton: Harvester Press, 1982)

Narrative and plot summaries of literary approaches to feminism in male and female writers of the period.

LIT 98   Staley, Thomas (ed.)
TWENTIETH-CENTURY WOMEN NOVELISTS
(London: Macmillan, 1982)

In ten essays on Lessing, Murdoch, Manning, Pym, Hill, P. D. James, Drabble, Spark, O'Brien and Johnston each critic considers each writer's use of social experience. Contributors include Sydney Kaplan and Benstock together with male critics.

LIT 99   Walker, Cheryl
THE NIGHTINGALE'S BURDEN: WOMEN POETS AND AMERICAN CULTURE BEFORE 1900
(Bloomington, Indiana: Indiana University Press, 1982)

Walker describes poetry as part of women's culture in essays on Dickinson, Bradstreet and Wilcox. Studying poetic autobiography and popular and serious poets side by side Walker makes a feminist semiotics of American women's poetry.

LIT 100   Abel, Elizabeth, Hirsch, Marianne and Landland, Elizabeth (eds.)
THE VOYAGE IN: FICTIONS OF FEMALE DEVELOPMENT (Hanover, New Hampshire: University Press of New England, 1983)

Sixteen essays examine the female *Bildungsroman* from a comparative perspective. The authors expand the standard male genre to embrace the special social and cultural ideologies of women. They combine feminist literary analysis with Freudian revision to approach *Jane Eyre*, *Mrs. Dalloway*, fairy tales, lesbian coming-out stories and black writing.

LIT 101   Beaumann, Nicola
A VERY GREAT PROFESSION: THE WOMAN'S NOVEL 1914–1939 (London: Virago, 1983)

She looks at the relationship of class and gender in categories of domesticity, sex, surplus women and love. This includes an account of best-sellers like Glyn and Delafield.

LIT 102   Clements, Patricia and Grundy, Isobel (eds.)
VIRGINIA WOOLF: NEW CRITICAL ESSAYS
(London: Vision Press, 1983)

These essays trace the linking elements among Woolf's novels, critical and other essays, journals, letters, autobiographical and biographical material, and observe some of the correspondences between her work and that of some of her predecessors and contemporaries.

LIT 103   Delany, Sheila
WRITING WOMEN: WOMEN WRITERS AND WOMEN IN LITERATURE, MEDIEVAL TO MODERN (New York: Schocken Books, 1983)

A Marxist-feminist examination of the connections in literature between sexual and political behaviour. Delany cross-compares writers from different centuries and countries such as Margery Kempe, and Marge Piercy.

LIT 104   Fleenor, Julianne
THE FEMALE GOTHIC (Montreal: Eden Press, 1983)

A survey of writers which includes Victoria Holt, the Brontës, Stead, Dinesan, Atwood, Shelley, Perkins Gilman and O'Connor. Fleenor aims to show how women have used the gothic to protest against patriarchal paradigms of the female body. Claims that French feminism and feminist history reveals the possibility of female subcultures and the polarity of language.

LIT 105   Flynn, Elizabeth
'Gender and Reading', *College English* 45: 3 (March 1983), 236–54

Describes freshmen's responses to writing by men and women. Flynn found that men were 'detached' readers in Iser's sense and overly judgemental while women were interested in resolving tensions in stories.

Literary Criticism

LIT 106   Huf, Linda
A PORTRAIT OF THE ARTIST AS A YOUNG WOMAN: THE WRITER AS HEROINE IN AMERICAN LITERATURE (New York: Frederick Ungar, 1983)

Huf criticises autobiographical novels by Chopin, Cather, Hall and Plath depicting their struggles to become creative artists and their subsequent problems with self-portrayals of sexuality, professionalism and womanhood.

LIT 107   Light, Alison
'Feminism and the Literary Critic', *LTP* 2 (1983) 61–81

Along with a critique of Millett and Showalter, Light includes her autobiography as a feminist critic. She steps 'outside' feminism to critical theory in Marxism, history and psychoanalysis to avoid the privileging of the literary and calls for collective work outside of the academy.

LIT 108   Little, Judith
COMEDY AND THE WOMAN WRITER: WOOLF, SPARK AND FEMINISM (Lincoln, Nebraska: University of Nebraska Press, 1983)

Little distinguishes between traditional comedy or satire and the festive or 'liminal' comedy to which she claims feminism belongs.

LIT 109   Ostriker, Alicia
WRITING LIKE A WOMAN (Ann Arbor: University of Michigan Press, 1983)

In essays about American women poets, Ostriker addresses the question: Do women write differently from men? She agrees that the marginal position of the woman poet generates a different way of thinking about politics and language but not that there is an *essentialist* mode of female writing.

LIT 110   Owen, Ursula
FATHERS (London: Virago, 1983)

The book examines father/daughter relationships with autobiographical contributions from Doris Lessing, Angela Carter, Sheila Rowbotham among others. The collection brings together memoirs, poems and photographs which cover the topics of childhood, religion, literature, psychology, anthropology and family life.

LIT 111   Ozick, Cynthia
ART AND ARDOR (New York: Alfred A. Knopf, 1983)

Although about the representation of the Judaic in contemporary writing, the text includes essays on Woolf and Wharton together with essays on feminism and Ozick's autobiography of her childhood.

LIT 112   Perry, Ruth and Brownley, Martine Watson (eds.)
MOTHERING THE MIND: TWELVE STUDIES OF WRITERS AND THEIR SILENT PARTNERS (New York and London: Holmes and Meier, 1983)

Maternity as metaphor and experience in writing.

LIT 113   Russ, Joanna
HOW TO SUPPRESS WOMEN'S WRITING (Austin: University of Texas Press, 1983)

A stimulating and funny monograph by a novelist about other women's writing. Russ describes the range of prohibitions on women's writing from denial of authorship, fallacies about femininity, inaccessibility of training, to the suppression of names and exclusion of women from the literary tradition. An exciting conversational mode of feminist criticism.

LIT 114   Smith, Barbara
HOME GIRLS: A BLACK FEMINIST ANTHOLOGY (New York: Kitchen Table Press, 1983)

A crucial collection which addresses issues of black sexual politics from a solidly pro-woman and feminist perspective. The book focuses on the meanings that home and family have for black women. It describes the challenge for women of combining an identity as black women with that of the artist. There are extensive sections on black lesbianism and black feminist issues.

LIT 115　Spivak, Gayatri
'Displacement and the Discourse of Women', DISPLACEMENT; DERRIDA AND AFTER, ed. M. Krupnick (Bloomington, Indiana: Indiana University Press, 1983)

Following on from her other essays in *Yale French Studies* and elsewhere, this account of Kristeva again demonstrates Spivak's sophisticated amalgam of feminism with deconstruction. Unlike some other feminists, Spivak provides a more pointed critique of Kristeva's writings and her concept of the semiotic. Spivak proves conclusively that Kristeva is removed from feminism.

LIT 116　Tate, Claudia (ed.)
BLACK WOMEN WRITERS AT WORK (New York: Continuum Publishing, 1983)

Fourteen writers answer questions about the impact of the Women's Movement on Afro-American women and their feelings about Michelle Wallace's *Black Macho and Myth of the Superwoman* (New York: Dial Press, 1979).
　A good introduction to the interview as a literary genre appropriate to feminism.

LIT 117　Walker, Alice
IN SEARCH OF OUR MOTHERS' GARDENS: WOMANIST PROSE (New York: Harcourt Brace Jovanovich, 1983; London: Women's Press, 1984)

A stimulating collection of the important essays—such as her essays on Zora Neale Hurston, on a retrospective view of the Civil Rights Movement, on her mother and the 'nature' of women's art.

LIT 118   Wandor, M.
ON GENDER AND WRITING (London: Pandora Press, 1983; Boston and London: Routledge & Kegan Paul, 1983)

Twenty-two writers look at their own writing and assess how their families, childhood and changes wrought by feminism have influenced their lives. Contributions from many British contemporary writers, including playwrights and journalists.

LIT 119   Bemstock, Shari (ed.)
FEMINIST ISSUES IN LITERARY SCHOLARSHIP: Special Issue of *The Tulsa Studies in Women's Literature* 3: 1/2 (Spring/Fall 1984)

Essays on feminist criticism by Auerbach, Robinson, Baym, Showalter, Marcus, Donovan among others.

LIT 120   Edwards, Lee, R.
PSYCHE AS HERO: FEMALE HEROISM AND FICTIONAL FORM (Middletown, CT.: Wesleyan University Press, 1984)

Finds an imagery of metaphysical femininity in a diverse collection of writing. There are essays on Woolf, Lessing, Morrison, Hurston, Sayers and the Brontës, Hardy and James.

LIT 121   Evans, Marcia
BLACK WOMEN WRITERS: ARGUMENTS AND INTERVIEWS (Garden City, New York: Anchor Press, 1984; London: Pluto Press, 1985)

First definitive collection of criticism and bibliographies on black women combined with autobiographical accounts of their writing experience. Writers include Margaret and Alice Walker and Morrison.

Literary Criticism

LIT 122 Felman, Shoshana
THE LITERARY SPEECH ACT: DON JUAN WITH J. L. AUSTIN OR SEDUCTION IN TWO LANGUAGES (Ithaca, New York: Cornell University Press, 1984)

Imagining an encounter between Don Juan and J. L. Austin, Felman explores the relation between speech and the erotic. Felman's exciting use of psychoanalytic theory continues from her other essays in *Yale French Studies* and *Diacritics* on hysteria, deconstruction and literature.

LIT 123 Foster, Shirley
MARRIAGE AND FREEDOM IN VICTORIAN WOMEN'S FICTION (London: Croom Helm, 1984)

Foster exposes the contradiction in Victorian writing between the challenges extended by heroines and their eventual marriages to controlling husbands. She looks at writing strategies in popular as well as high culture including Yonge and Brontë.

LIT 124 Jensen, Margaret Ann
LOVE'S SWEET RETURN: THE HARLEQUIN STORY (Toronto, Canada: The Women's Educational Press, 1984)

An institutional analysis of the company combined with a stereotypic analysis of the novels which it publishes.

LIT 125 Martin, Wendy
AN AMERICAN TRIPTYCH: ANNE BRADSTREET, EMILY DICKINSON, ADRIENNE RICH (Chapel Hill, N.C. and London: University of North Carolina Press, 1984)

Good narrative and analytic account of each poet's work. Martin looks at the relation between literary phrasing and external pressures on women poets.

LIT 126   Poovey, Mary
THE PROPER LADY AND THE WOMAN
WRITER: IDEOLOGY AS STYLE IN THE WORKS
OF MARY WOLLSTONECRAFT, MARY SHELLEY
AND JANE AUSTEN (Chicago: University of
Chicago Press, 1984)

A skilful integration of feminism and Marxist literary criticism. Poovey examines how writing techniques—of effaced narrative centres or irony—can serve both conservative values and female self expression. Poovey describes important continuities between writing style and larger social questions.

LIT 127   Radway, Janice
READING THE ROMANCE: WOMEN,
PATRIARCHY AND POPULAR LITERATURE
(Chapel Hill, N.C.: University of North Carolina Press, 1984)

Radway convincingly questions the notion that romance fiction simply accepts a repressive ideology. By extensive interviews of women readers Radway argues that women use fiction to escape patriarchal culture. The text is a useful combination of feminist psycho-analysis, ethnography and feminist criticism.

LIT 128   Ruthven K. K.
FEMINIST LITERARY STUDIES: AN
INTRODUCTION (Cambridge: Cambridge University Press, 1984)

Ruthven shows how feminist criticism is an important contribution to literary studies. As a male critic, he 'appropriates' feminist criticism adding it as simply another 'area' to deconstruction, Marxism et al. since he claims that feminist criticism can be equally well taught by both sexes.

LIT 129   Squier, Susan Merrill (ed.)
WOMEN WRITERS AND THE CITY (Knoxville: University of Tennessee Press, 1984)

Covering the continental British and American writings of Tristan, Eliot, Sackville-West, Rich, Shange among others. Each essay positions its topic in an appropriate literary tradition as with Jane Marcus's account of Rebecca West and Sylvia Townsend Warner set in the context of feminine fantasy novels. Squier provides a checklist of relevant secondary works.

LIT 130 Williams, Merryn
WOMEN IN THE ENGLISH NOVEL 1800–1900 (London: Macmillan, 1984)

Examines the ways in which nineteenth-century novelists wrote about women—as sex symbols, old maids or evil women—and their responses to social change.

LIT 131 Cameron, Deborah
FEMINISM AND LINGUISTIC THEORY (London: Macmillan, 1985)

An examination of recent theories about the relation of women's oppression and language. A clear account of recent work in sociolinguistics, Lacanian theory and radical feminism. She attempts to demystify feminist ideas about language.

LIT 132 Christian, Barbara
PERSPECTIVES ON BLACK WOMEN WRITERS (London and Oxford: Pergamon Press, 1985)

Documents an extensive range of contemporary black writing including studies of Marshall, Lorde, Emecheta, Shange, and Morrison. She encapsulates a sense of the contemporary history of each black writer she considers.

LIT 133 Díaz-Diocaretz, Myriam and Zavala, I. M. (eds.)
WOMEN, FEMINIST IDENTITY AND SOCIETY IN THE 1980s (Amsterdam and Philadelphia: John Benjamins, 1985)

Essays on sexuality, literature and racism by Cliff, Coward and Rich among others.

LIT 134   DuPlessis, Rachel Blau
WRITING BEYOND THE ENDING (Bloomington, Indiana: Indiana University Press, 1985)

An ideological and syntactical reading of writers such as Woolf, Schreiner and H. D. to show how they were able to rupture conventional literary practice with bisexual and lesbian strategies, sentence and sequence disruption and make alternative statements about gender and literature.

LIT 135   Irigaray, Luce
THIS SEX WHICH IS NOT ONE, trans. Catherine Porter with Carolyn Burke (Ithaca, New York: Cornell University Press, 1985)

With *Speculum* this is a key example of the French mode of psychoanalytic feminist criticism. It is a translation of 'Ce sexe qui n'en est pas un', which is an analysis of the suppression of the feminine from Plato through Hegel to Lévi-Strauss. Phallocentric concepts can only be transformed, Irigaray argues when women find ways to assert their specificity as women.

LIT 136   Irigaray, Luce
SPECULUM OF THE OTHER WOMAN, trans. Gillian Gill (Ithaca, New York: Cornell University Press, 1985)

A major text of the French psychoanalytic feminist school. It is a translation of 'Speculum de l'autre femme'. Argues that representation in literature is a product of *hom(m)osexualité* and that women mime or are silent in patriarchy. Irigaray proposes a theory of writing making an analogy between women's 'morphology' and literary jouissance which is 'multiple' and non-unified.

LIT 137   James, Selma
THE LADIES AND THE MAMMIES: JANE AUSTEN AND JEAN RHYS (Bristol: Falling Wall Press, 1985)

Written by the campaigner for Wages for Housework and

the Prostitutes Collective. This is a political account of these women writers which 'retrieves' Austen.

LIT 138 McNaron, T. (ed.)
THE SISTER BOND: A FEMINIST VIEW OF A TIMELESS CONNECTION (Oxford: Pergamon Press, 1985)

Sisters and comrades as represented in the work of writers as varied as Rossetti, Nightingale, Woolf and Levertov.

LIT 139 Moi, Toril
SEXUAL/TEXTUAL POLITICS: FEMINIST LITERARY THEORY (London: Methuen, 1985)

Moi examines American and French modes of feminist criticism from the 1970s. She pays particular attention to the work of Kristeva, Cixous and Irigaray who she privileges over what she sees as the false 'realism' of many American critics.

LIT 140 Sage, Lorna
CONTEMPORARY WOMEN NOVELISTS (London: Macmillan, 1985)

Sage explores how women challenge the conventions of the novel in their uses of fantasy, melodrama and emotionalism.

LIT 141 Showalter, Elaine (ed.)
THE NEW FEMINIST CRITICISM: ESSAYS ON WOMEN, LITERATURE AND THEORY (New York: Pantheon Books, 1985)

Eighteen essays by pioneers of feminist criticism including Gilbert and Gubar, Coward, Zimmerman, Smith, Kolodny, Heilbrun and Robinson which challenge literary patriarchy. It is a very useful overview of feminist critical theory and practice since Showalter has collected the major and controversial essays.

LIT 142 Humm, Maggie
FEMINIST CRITICISM: WOMEN AS CONTEMPORARY CRITICS (Brighton: Harvester Press, 1986)

A survey of the forms of feminist literary criticism being written since 1970. It includes myth, black, lesbian, Marxist, feminist criticism together with substantial chapters on pioneers, Virginia Woolf, Rebecca West and Adrienne Rich.

Sociology, Politics and Economics

The aim of this chapter is to survey the current major sociological critiques of women-related topics. These include marriage, the family, work, trade unions, ethnic studies, the division of labour, crime, leisure and urban and political policy.

SOC 1   Komarovsky, Mirra
'Cultural Contradictions and Sex Roles', *American Journal of Sociology* 52 (1946) pp. 182–9

The first study of the way college girls 'play dumb' to men students. In 1970s a repeated study showed men were still frightened of women.

SOC 2   Hacker, Helen Mayer
'Women As a Minority Group', *Social Forces* 30 (October 1951) pp. 60–9

An early feminist essay applying the methodology used by sociologists when describing minority groups (blacks, Jews, etc.) to women. Hacker treats notions of separate sub-cultures, class/caste conflicts, and gender role differentiation.

SOC 3   Komarovsky, Mirra
WOMEN IN THE MODERN WORLD: THEIR EDUCATION AND THEIR DILEMMAS (Boston, Mass.: Little Brown, 1953)

The first dissenting voice from the conventional sociology of sex roles which had defined feminine behaviour as a cluster of psychological traits (of homemaker and passivity) and women's 'effective' roles versus the male 'instrumental'.

SOC 4   Moberley, Bell E.
STORMING THE CITADEL (London: Constable, 1953)

One of the first accounts of women's entry into medicine—a hitherto under-critiqued part of sociology.

SOC 5   Rosser, C. and Harris, C.
THE FAMILY AND SOCIAL CHANGE (London: Routledge & Kegan Paul, 1965)

An early investigation of adolescence in Swansea. The work reveals the solidarity women give other female members of their families in female kinship and group solidarity. The text traces a series of complex kinship networks across three and four generations.

SOC 6   Gavron, Hannah
THE CAPTIVE WIFE: CONFLICTS OF HOUSEBOUND MOTHERS (London: Routledge & Kegan Paul, 1966)

An investigation of housework which sparked off a debate in the quality press between women at home and those with independent careers. Gavron describes the experience of East London women trying to raise children rather than giving a political analysis. The text has a polemically useful concentration on the depressive effects for women of being shut up with young children.

SOC 7   Jones, Beverley and Brown, Judith
TOWARD A FEMALE LIBERATION MOVEMENT (Cambridge, Mass.: New England Free Press, 1968)

This puts forward sensible and realisable social programmes for women's liberation and women's studies.

SOC 8   Morgan, Robin (ed.)
WOMEN IN REVOLT (New York: Random House, 1969)

An extensive compendium of writings on psychology, education, birth control and sexuality.

SOC 9 Epstein, Cynthia
WOMAN'S PLACE (Berkeley, CA.: University of California Press, 1970)

A key text on women in professional occupations. Using Merton and Goffman's frameworks Epstein shows how women are treated as deviants in professions and kept marginal and subordinate through the internal dynamics of professions. Epstein shows that women lack sponsorship and are unsuccessful because aspects of men's everyday routines are denied to them. A good mixture of data from law, medicine, science, engineering and academia.

SOC 10 Herzog, Elizabeth
'Social Stereotypes and Social Research', *Journal of Social Issues* 26: 3 (1970) pp. 109–25

Questions existing social methods for measuring masculinity and femininity in relation to male/female dominance in the Negro family. Claims research on the effects of fatherlessness comes from social scientists' need to prove deprivation.

SOC 11 Rossi, Alice (ed.)
ESSAYS ON SEX EQUALITY (Chicago: University of Chicago Press, 1970)

Case study of men claiming to be feminist, such as J. S. Mill, revaluating the role of their supportive women. An anthology of articles on women's changing status which was an important contribution to revisionist sociology and helped to provide some of the historical background for the contemporary women's movement.

SOC 12 Amir, M.
PATTERNS IN FORCIBLE RAPE (Chicago: Chicago University Press, 1971)

The only sociologist to have studied rape scientifically is American, who found that none of the popular stereotypes of victim or rapist was valid in the majority of cases.

SOC 13   Andreas, Carol
SEX AND CASTE IN AMERICA (Englewood Cliffs, N.J.: Prentice-Hall, 1971)

Andreas analyses sexism and its roots in the economic system.

SOC 14   Ballan, Dorothy
FEMINISM AND MARXISM (New York: World View Publishers, 1971)

A publication of the Youth Against War and Fascism. It supplies a feminist-materialist analysis of current world conditions. It also traces the development of theories of the oppression of women in Marxist history and postulates the existence of a matriarchal society in early history.

SOC 15   Bart, Pauline
'Sexism and Social Science: From the Gilded Cage to the Iron Cage, or, The Perils of Pauline', *Journal of Marriage and the Family* 33 (November 1971) pp. 734–45.

About discrimination against professional women in social sciences. Bart reviews other feminist critiques to this date in sociology and includes a bibliography.

SOC 16   Bernard, Jessie
WOMEN AND THE PUBLIC INTEREST: AN ESSAY ON POLICY AND PROTEST (New York: Atherton, 1971)

An excellent study analysing the public interest in terms of women's rights and women in the labour market. Bernard examines the sexual division of labour and the functions of women.

SOC 17   Glazer, Nona and Waehrer, Helen Youngelson (eds.)
WOMEN IN A MAN-MADE WORLD (Chicago: Rand-McNally, 1971)

A vast collection of seminal essays covering the topics of feminist scholarship (Dorothy Smith); history (Hartmann); gender roles (Hacker); economics (Benston); marriage and black matriarchy (Berger); job market (Almquist); myths about women (Ostriker); and toward equality (Heller). Each topic area contains readings by several other feminists and all major economic, sociological, theoretical and empirical approaches are addressed. A classic handbook.

SOC 18   Gornick, V. and Moran, B. K. (eds.)
WOMAN IN SEXIST SOCIETY: STUDIES IN POWER AND POWERLESSNESS (New York: Basic Books, 1971)

Articles by 38 authors illuminate the political nature of women's condition with a natural emphasis on family relations. There are sections on psychology, marriage, images of women, women at work, social issues and feminism with many authors being represented for the first time such as Nancy Chodorow. Essays by most important feminists are included such as Phyllis Chesler, Showalter, Stimpson and Kate Millett.

SOC 19   Klein, Viola
THE FEMININE CHARACTER (Chicago: University of Illinois Press, 1971)

Originally published in 1946, Klein's book received little attention at the time but is considered now to be the first contemporary work to have a woman's perspective in sociology.

SOC 20   Kreps, Juanita
SEX IN THE MARKET PLACE: AMERICAN WOMEN AT WORK (Baltimore, MD.: Johns Hopkins Press, 1971)

This book discusses the prejudices women confront in pursuing careers in the semi professions. A bibliography is included.

SOC 21   Ladner, Joyce A.
TOMORROW'S TOMORROW: THE BLACK
WOMAN (Garden City, N.Y.: Doubleday, 1971)

A culmination of a four-year study of black adolescent girls in St Louis, Missouri. In her honest introduction Ladner writes of her conflicts as a black woman and doctoral candidate in a racist society. She decided to break from academic traditions and write from a fresh perspective.

SOC 22   Lopata, Helena Z.
OCCUPATION: HOUSEWIFE (New York: Oxford
University Press, 1971)

A study of housewives in Chicago. Lopata's sociological perspective is that of 'role theory' and she conceptualises the housewife role as one moving through a specifiable series of stages and constituting a life cycle. Lopata's study of role shifts in widowhood is separately published as *Widowhood in An American City* (New York: Schenkman, 1973).

SOC 23   *Valparaiso University Law Review*
'Symposium', *Valparaiso University Law Review* 5: 2 (1971)

An issue devoted to women and law with articles by Jo Freeman, Mary Eastwood, Sonia Fuentos and others.

SOC 24   Frankfurt, Ellen
VAGINAL POLITICS (New York: Quadrangle Books, 1972)

Frankfurt has written one of the early works of the contemporary women's movement about the politics of women's health care. She covers a range of issues including the drug industry, the media and advertising imagery.

SOC 25   Oakley, Ann
SEX, GENDER AND SOCIETY (London: Maurice
Temple-Smith, 1972)

Oakley sets out to clarify meanings of 'nature', 'sex difference' and 'gender' in biology, psychology, culture and convention. There is detailed and fascinating evidence from biology, anthropology, sociology, and animal behaviour. Oakley aims to separate value judgements from statements of fact and questions the 'inevitability' of women's oppression.

SOC 26   Safilios-Rothschild, Constantina (ed.) TOWARD A SOCIOLOGY OF WOMEN (New York: John Wiley, 1972)

A collection of seminal essays: Pamela Roby 'Institutional and Internalized Barriers to Women in Higher Education'; Diana Warshay 'Sex Differences in Language Style'; and policy proposals to change both society and the discipline itself.

SOC 27   Wortis, Helen and Rubinowitz, Clara (eds.) THE WOMEN'S MOVEMENT: SOCIAL AND PSYCHOLOGICAL PERSPECTIVES (New York: AMS Press, 1972)

A collection of essays examining the entire social structure and goals pertaining to the changing roles of women.

SOC 28   Bernard, Jessie
THE FUTURE OF MARRIAGE (New York: Bantam Books, 1973)

Bernard makes distinctions between men's and women's experience of marriage, and gives a study of its nature and possible future with a good bibliography.

SOC 29   Bernard, Jessie
'My Four Revolutions: An Autobiographical History of the ASA', *American Journal of Sociology* 78 (1973) 773–91.

Discusses shifts in sociology method from empiricism to commitment with an account of her shift to feminism. She describes women's critiques of women on functionalism and advocates 'communal' content and method.

SOC 30   Boslooper, Thomas and Hayes, Marcia
THE FEMININITY GAME (New York: Stein and Day, 1973)

A challenge to the American message that women are not supposed to take strenuous activity. They provide detailed statistics to show how women's sports are underfinanced.

SOC 31   Boston Women's Health Book Collective
OUR BODIES, OUR SELVES: A BOOK BY AND FOR WOMEN (New York: Simon and Schuster, 1973)

Written by women for women to prove that women are the best experts on their bodies. A polemic on the struggle for adequate health care. Chapters of superb information about female physiology, health and child care.

SOC 32   Huber, Joan (ed.)
'Changing Women in a Changing Society: A Special Issue', *American Journal of Sociology* 78: 4 (January 1973)

Also reprinted in 1973 by the University Press of Chicago. This is an entire issue of the journal consisting of articles by Bernard, Freeman, Komarovsky, Lapata et al., about women in work; the origins of women's liberation; and women in the book industry.

SOC 33   Lakoff, Robin
LANGUAGE AND WOMEN'S PLACE (New York: Harper Colophon, 1973)

Lakoff argues that gender stratification in society has resulted in different male and female language styles. There are gender differences in intonation and syntax, and she plots many differences in women's use of vocabulary and linguistic space.

SOC 34   Rossi, Alice (ed.)
THE FEMINIST PAPERS: FROM ADAMS TO de BEAUVOIR (New York: Columbia Press, 1973)

A collection of articles which helped to replace women in social science history.

SOC 35   Scully, Diane and Bart, Pauline
'A Funny Thing Happened on the Way to the Orifice: Women in Gynaecological Textbooks', *American Journal of Sociology* 78: 4 (January 1973) 1045–50

An analysis of 27 gynaecological texts which revealed a persistent bias towards maintaining traditional sex-role stereotypes.

SOC 36   Comer, Lee
WEDLOCKED WOMEN (London: Feminist Books, 1974)

Combines personal anecdotes, and readings from academic studies in a lucid and crisp attack on monogamous marriage. Comer argues that home and world are the locus of male power and that an ideology of romantic love supports this. Describes similarities across class and racial boundaries.

SOC 37   Critcher, C.
'Women in Sport', *Contemporary Cultural Studies* 5 (Spring 1974) pp. 3–13

Examines the contradictions between the role of sport in Britain and the role of women. Discusses press coverage of women in sport and describes media misrepresentation.

SOC 38   Currell, Melville
POLITICAL WOMEN (London: Croom Helm, 1974)

Focuses on the House of Commons. A survey of all women MPs still alive who sat in the Commons from 1923 to 1974 including two studies of women candidates. The socialisation of future women politicians is discussed.

SOC 39   Hoffman, Lois W. and Nye, F. J. (eds.)
          WORKING MOTHERS (San Francisco, CA.: Jossey-Bass, 1974)

          This pulls together research findings about the effect of maternal employment on the family from the fields of psychology and sociology. The focus of the book is on maternal employment in America since 1940, looking at studies of women's commitment to work in relation to fertility patterns. A good overview of knowledge to date with suggestions for further research.

SOC 40   Hubert, Jane
          'Belief and Reality', THE INTEGRATION OF A CHILD INTO A SOCIAL WORLD, ed. Richards, M. (Cambridge: Cambridge University Press, 1974)

          Hubert interviewed 54 women at an antenatal clinic and describes their erroneous beliefs about contraception. She reveals conflicting attitudes to pregnancy between the women and health services.

SOC 41   Jaquette, Jane (ed.)
          WOMEN IN POLITICS (New York: John Wiley, 1974)

          An anthology of essays and studies of women around the world. Contributors include Jo Freeman, Elsa Chaney, Susan Kaufman among others.

SOC 42   Oakley, Ann
          THE SOCIOLOGY OF HOUSEWORK (London: Martin Robertson, 1974; New York: Pantheon, 1974)

          This is a key feminist text. Oakley examines the conventional treatment of women in sociology and through interviews with 40 young London housewives covers such areas as: women's perceptions of housework and themselves as housewives; length of working weeks; housework routines as reward. The influence of upbringing on women's domesticity and the division of labour in the home is charted. The importance of the book lies in the correction of the traditional view that women 'work' outside the home but not in it.

SOC 43 Oakley, Ann
HOUSEWIFE (London: Allen Lane, 1974; New York: Pantheon Books, 1974 as *Women's Work: The Housewife Past and Present*)

This is the second half of *The Sociology of Housework*. There are chapters on the organisation of work and family life in non-industrialised cultures; the role of women historically and in modern industrial society; and the ideology of domesticity. The book provides a background and context for *The Sociology of Housework*.

SOC 44 'Masculine Blinders in the Social Sciences', *Social Science Quarterly* LV: 3 (December 1974)

A special issue and symposium.

SOC 45 Arms, Suzanne
IMMACULATE DECEPTION: A NEW LOOK AT WOMEN AND CHILDBIRTH IN AMERICA (Boston, Mass.: Houghton, Mifflin, 1975)

This demystifies pregnancy and pleads for a rehumanisation, a rewomanisation of the entire pregnancy, birth and post-partum process. She describes the technology of American obstetrics with its psychic and physical stress and concludes that 'childbirth' is part of the socialisation of women.

SOC 46 Bernard, Jessie
WOMEN, WIVES, MOTHERS: VALUES AND OPTIONS (Chicago: Aldine, 1975)

A portion of this collection of essays is taken from Bernard's earlier book, *The Future of Motherhood*. The other articles are not available elsewhere and include accounts of research on sex differences; adolescence and socialisation for motherhood; and the impact of sexism and racism on employment status.

SOC 47 Chamberlain, Mary
FENWOMEN (London: Virago, 1975)

About courtship and premarital relationships. The first study of women's lives in rural areas. She claims that men's lives changed with modernisation but that women's are still traditional. She claims too that the male study *Coal is our Life* is a very out-of-date, male perspective on women. Chamberlain shows women use leisure in socially responsible ways.

SOC 48   Collins, Randall
CONFLICT SOCIOLOGY: TOWARD AN EXPLANATORY SCIENCE (New York: Academic Press, 1975)

Uses cross-cultural methods to pursue the question of the specific conditions under which females have more or less power than males.

SOC 49   Davies, Ross
WOMEN AT WORK (London: Arrow, 1975)

Revelation/examination of the concentration of women in low-paying occupations. Discusses the power and influence of trade unions on male high-paying occupations, and the exclusion of women.

SOC 50   Duberman, Lucile (ed.)
GENDER AND SEX IN SOCIETY (New York: Praeger, 1975)

An effort to bring together current theory and research about the sociology of sex, status and gender roles. Chapters on class and race differences; cross-cultural perspectives and work differences.

SOC 51   Goot, Murray and Reid, Elizabeth
WOMEN AND VOTING STUDIES (London: Sage, 1975)

Devastating critique of studies of voting behaviour, casting serious doubt on so-called established findings about women. This text is mainly an academic study of politics in Britain, but the authors do raise serious doubts about the design of research instruments and the conclusions of researchers about women's political behaviour. They attempt to provide a detailed critique of the received idea that women are less interested in politics and redefine politics accordingly in a feminist direction.

SOC 52   Millman, Marcia and Kanter, Rosabeth Moss (eds.)
ANOTHER VOICE: FEMINIST PERSPECTIVES ON SOCIAL LIFE AND SOCIAL SCIENCE (Garden City, N.J.: Anchor, 1975)

A classic critique of empirical sociology. It proposes an alternative model of women negotiating their own political reality. The collection includes an excellent overview of research on deviance, criminology and accounts of women in working-class jobs.

SOC 53   Roby, Pamela (ed.)
CHILD CARE—WHO CARES? FOREIGN AND DOMESTIC INFANT AND EARLY CHILDHOOD DEVELOPMENT POLICIES (New York: Basic Books, 1975)

An excellent primer about the history and theory of child care in America and Europe, Soviet Union, Japan, Israel, Sweden, Finland, Norway.

SOC 54   Rosenberg, Marie Barovic and Bergstrom, Len V.
WOMEN AND SOCIETY: A CRITICAL REVIEW OF THE LITERATURE WITH A SELECTED ANNOTATED BIBLIOGRAPHY (Beverly Hills, CA.: Sage, 1975)

Contains an annotated bibliography which includes a listing of other bibliographies in addition to citations under such categories as sex roles, socialisation, lifestyles, customs, women in ethnic minorities.

SOC 55   Ross, Heather L. and Sawhill, Isabel
TIME OF TRANSITION: THE GROWTH OF FAMILIES HEADED BY WOMEN (Washington: The Urban Institute, 1975)

Transition is used in two contexts. The first context describes divorced women in marital transition. The second describes how economic factors governing the traditional roles of women and marriage are changing. Ross and Sawhill use 'the new home economics' to apply economic models to quantifiable data on the family in order to suggest that social policy should meet the needs of the transitional family.

SOC 56 Thorne, Barrie and Henley, Nancy (eds.)
LANGUAGE AND SEX: DIFFERENCE AND DOMINANCE (Rowley, Mass.: Newbury House, 1975)

An important collection of essays about gender difference in language use. The authors argue that males and females have two overlapping language styles and demolish popular myths about speech which put women in a 'double bind'.

SOC 57 Walton, R. G.
WOMEN IN SOCIAL WORK (London: Routledge & Kegan Paul, 1975)

One of the few studies of women in social work and social work training.

SOC 58 Westergaard, John and Resler, Henrietta
CLASS IN A CAPITALIST SOCIETY (London: Heinemann, 1975)

The authors offer startling figures of sharp inequality in earnings which reinforce sex and class inequalities.

SOC 59 Barker, Diana L. and Allen, Sheila (eds.)
SEXUAL DIVISIONS AND SOCIETY: PROCESS AND CHANGE (London: Longman, 1976)

Contains essays about the implications of sex-segregated education, and work on the relationship between school and gender dichotomies.

Sociology, Politics and Economics

SOC 60   Barker, Diana L. and Allen, Sheila (eds.)
DEPENDENCE AND EXPLOITATION IN WORK AND MARRIAGE (London: Longman, 1976)

Papers from a British Sociological Association Conference. Fourteen contributors look at ways in which marriage relationships are shaped by male dominance and the labour market. Domestic violence and equal pay are also items included.

SOC 61   Boserup, Ester
WOMEN'S ROLE IN ECONOMIC DEVELOPMENT (London: G. Allen and Unwin, 1970)

Documents case studies of how women's status declines sharply under colonial regimes. A comprehensive discussion supported by data from different geographical regions.

SOC 62   Chiplin, B. and Sloane, P. J.
SEX DISCRIMINATION IN THE LABOUR MOVEMENT (London: Macmillan, 1976)

The text aims to move consideration of unequal pay and unequal opportunity away from social issues to an examination of economic cause and effect. This is a good introduction to the microeconomics of discrimination and it compares American and British Equal Pay Acts.

SOC 63   Hart, Nicky
WHEN MARRIAGE ENDS (London: Tavistock, 1976)

A study of divorced women which destroys the stereotype of the divorced women as grasping but rather describes them as objects of discrimination and derision.

SOC 64   Hartmann, Heidi
'Capitalism, Patriarchy and Job Segregation by Sex', WOMEN AND THE WORKPLACE, eds. Blaxall, M. and Reagan, B. (Chicago: University of Chicago, 1976)

An important essay describing the role of men in creating

and reproducing job segregation. Men maintain power by controlling hierarchical organisations, through the exclusionary powers of male unions, and by denying women training. Criticises dual labour market theory and Marxist theory for paying insufficient attention to gender divisions.

SOC 65 Iglitzein, L. and Ross, R. (eds.)
WOMEN IN THE WORLD (Santa Barbara, CA.: Clio Press, 1976)

A cross-cultural account of the social and political roles of women in countries around the world. The collection looks particularly at the interaction of categories of patriarchy and liberation.

SOC 66 Rapoport, R. and Rapoport, R.
DUAL-CAREER FAMILIES RE-EXAMINED (London: Martin Robertson, 1976)

Shows that even couples who wish to break down the traditional division of labour give responsibility for housework to the woman.

SOC 67 Roberts, Joan (ed.)
BEYOND INTELLECTUAL SEXISM: A NEW WOMAN, A NEW REALITY (New York: David McKay, 1976)

This collection draws important parallels between bias in the social realm and bias in the intellectual realm. Contributors such as Julia Sherman and Annis Pratt look at biological interventions; social work, psychology, women in literature, legal and social institutions; women and education and sex-role innovations in Sweden, China and Israel.

SOC 68 Rubin, Lillian B.
WORLDS OF PAIN: LIFE IN THE WORKING-CLASS FAMILY (New York: Basic Books, 1976)

A superb evocation of the texture of working-class life in

America. Rubin conducted extensive interviews to assess the effect of class on family life and the contradictory nature of the family as both a constricting institution and a source of security. The perspective is clearly feminist.

SOC 69　Chetwynd, J. and Hartnett, O. (eds.)
THE SEX ROLE SYSTEM: PSYCHOLOGICAL AND SOCIOLOGICAL PERSPECTIVES (London: Routledge & Kegan Paul, 1977)

Essays by Lipshitz, Land, Weinreich and others trace sex-role stereotyping at work; in psychiatry; in the social security and income tax systems; in biology and sociology; and describe the influence of schools on the formation of gender roles.

SOC 70　Foreman, Ann
FEMININITY AS ALIENATION (London: Pluto Press, 1977)

Attempts to fuse the Marxist and Freudian approaches have failed, Ann Foreman claims. She argues that the decisive task is to establish that women's oppression is central to the organisation of the work process in capitalism.

SOC 71　Henley, Nancy M.
BODY POLITICS: POWER SEX AND NON-VERBAL COMMUNICATION (Englewood Cliffs, N.J.: Prentice-Hall, 1977)

An important study of body language from a feminist perspective. Henley shows how body language is used by men to maintain a social hierarchy and gives an outline of useful further research and priorities for non-verbal research that does *not* blame the victim.

SOC 72　Howe, Louise Kapp
PINK-COLLAR WORKERS (New York: Avon, 1977)

A new research area which describes settings and issues of female-dominated occupations and of patterns of behaviour generally thought to be more characteristic of women at work than of men.

SOC 73   Kanter, R. M.
MEN AND WOMEN OF THE CORPORATION (New York: Basic Books, 1977)

An exhaustive feminist critique of American business organisation. Kanter establishes that differences in behaviour in corporations depended on the powerlessness of or control over an individual's situation which affects women more than men. She includes proposals for altering the hierarchical nature of organisations.

SOC 74   King, J. and Stott, Mary (eds.)
IS THIS YOUR LIFE? (London: Virago, 1977)

An important collection of feminist criticisms of the mass media and advertising's image of women.

SOC 75   Macintyre, Sally
SINGLE AND PREGNANT (London: Croom Helm, 1977)

This demonstrates how beliefs of the general public, medical professions and sociologists about women and maternity in Britain are based on an unexamined assumption that women only want to be mothers within marriage. Sociologists have unconsciously adopted a perspective that marriage and babies 'belong' together and that unmarried mothers are deviant. She shows clearly that the medical profession's treatment of biological facts is normally determined by social facts. The book is based on an account of the pregnancy careers of 28 women in Aberdeen in the early 1970s. She examined their trajectories with particular emphasis on what she calls their 'moral careers' and how those related to their interactions with medical personnel.

SOC 76   Mackie, L. and Pattullo, P.
WOMEN AT WORK (London: Tavistock, 1977)

The authors reveal the lack of opportunity for day release and further education for women. They include an examination of inequalities at work and also a study by the Low Pay Unit. They conclude that recruitment figures are most important for the future.

SOC 77   Mayo, M. (ed.)
WOMEN IN THE COMMUNITY (London: Routledge & Kegan Paul, 1977)

The text contains an important account of women's aid centres—the only British groups to consistently argue that women are genuine victims and men the criminals.

SOC 78   Rossi, Alice
'A Biosocial Perspective on Parenting', *Daedalus* 106: 2 (Spring 1977) 1–31

Rossi suggests that feminists may have gone too far in rejecting women's nurturing role. Her analysis of the 'biosocial' aspects of parenting created a debate in the feminist academic community. Nancy Chodorow in particular challenged Rossi's view that there is some 'biosocial' basis for female mothering.

SOC 79   Safilios-Rothschild, Constantina
LOVE, SEX AND SEX ROLES (Englewood Cliffs, N.J.: Prentice-Hall, 1977)

The author examines issues of sexuality and love and the way in which the social conventions of both have served to oppress women.

SOC 80   Smart, Carol
WOMEN, CRIME AND CRIMINOLOGY (London: Routledge & Kegan Paul, 1977)

This points out the absurdity of a psychiatric treatment based on a rigid adherence to conventional sex roles. It analyses in some detail the argument that female deviance in Britain and America manifests itself as mental illness whereas males deviate by committing crime.

SOC 81   Walum, Laurel Richardson
THE DYNAMICS OF SEX AND GENDER: A SOCIOLOGICAL PERSPECTIVE (Chicago: Rand-McNally, 1977)

This describes the different norms governing women's and men's behaviour in the same social settings.

SOC 82   Watson, James (ed.)
BETWEEN TWO CULTURES (Oxford: Basil Blackwell, 1977)

Good data on women in ethnic groups as diverse as Cypriots, Chinese and Poles.

SOC 83   Dreifus, Claudia (ed.)
SEIZING OUR BODIES: THE POLITICS OF WOMEN'S HEALTH (New York: Random House, 1978)

This is a group of essays by feminists about the oppression of women by the health care system. The contributors include Adrienne Rich and Ellen Frankfurt.

SOC 84   Hamilton, Roberta
THE LIBERATION OF WOMEN: A STUDY OF PATRIARCHY AND CAPITALISM (London: George Allen and Unwin, 1978)

A historical inquiry into the relation of feminism and marxism. Hamilton argues a need for both perspectives but that marriage between the two is not yet feasible.

SOC 85   Kessler, Suzanne J. and McKenna, Wendy
GENDER: AN ETHNOMETHODOLOGICAL ACCOUNT (New York: John Wiley, 1978)

An academic account of male and female transsexuals.

SOC 86   Kuhn, A. and Wolpe A. M. (eds.)
FEMINISM AND MATERIALISM: WOMEN AND MODES OF PRODUCTION (London: Routledge & Kegan Paul, 1978)

A systematic analysis of women's relationship to modes of production and reproduction within a materialist framework. Essays cover patriarchy; paid and unpaid labour; and the role of the state. The centrality of the book's two themes: family and the labour process, suggests that an understanding of women's situation is necessarily based on an analysis of structures of production and reproduction.

SOC 87   Smart, Carol and Smart, Barry (eds.)
WOMEN, SEXUALITY AND SOCIAL CONTROL (London: Routledge & Kegan Paul, 1978)

This collection shows how much sociological research has been biased by current preconceptions about sexuality rather than being based on empirical evidence.

SOC 88   Stromberg, A. H. (ed.)
WOMEN WORKING: THEORIES AND FACTS IN PERSPECTIVE (Palo Alto, CA.: Mayfield Publishing, 1978)

A collection of essays giving special attention to women workers frequently overlooked in empirical and theoretical accounts: minority women, women in blue-collar jobs, and private household workers. Writers such as Acker, Almquist and Blau examine how women's socialisation and education prepare them for different work roles from those of men and how their life-cycle and careers interact in distinct ways.

SOC 89   Wilson, Amrit
FINDING A VOICE: ASIAN WOMEN IN BRITAIN (London: Virago, 1978)

She discusses the situation of Asian women workers in terms of a concept of the sub-proletariat. She argues that it is a combination of the dynamic of capitalist production—the imperative for profit, and racism which results in the specific situation of Asian women within the occupational structure of Britain today.

SOC 90 Amsden, A. H.
THE ECONOMICS OF WOMEN AND WORK
(Harmondsworth: Penguin, 1979)

Shows how the relative wages of men and women are less the outcomes of supply and demand—they are more a mirror of the relative positions of men and women in society.

SOC 91 Barrett, M. et al. (eds.)
IDEOLOGY AND CULTURAL PRODUCTION
(London: Croom Helm, 1979)

Contains essays about the representation of women, sexuality and reproduction and stereotyping and the media.

SOC 92 Beck, Evelyn Torton and Sherman, Julie (eds.)
THE PRISM OF SEX: ESSAYS IN THE SOCIOLOGY OF KNOWLEDGE (Madison: University of Wisconsin Press, 1979)

Ten essays about the effects of male domination in the disciplines of literature, history, sociology, philosophy, political science, psychology. They conclude that the omission of women's experience creates a faulty framework of knowledge and argue for a woman-centred epistemology.

SOC 93 Breugal, Irene
'Women as a Reserve Army of Labour', *Feminist Review* 3 (1979) 12–23

A seminal essay which sparked much feminist debate. Breugal examines patterns of women's and men's employment between 1974 and 1978 and shows reasons why women are disposed of more easily than men in manufacturing industry if not in the service sector. This is due, she claims, to a prevailing familial ideology of the male breadwinner.

SOC 94　Hakim, C.
OCCUPATIONAL SEGREGATION: A COMPARATIVE STUDY OF THE DEGREE AND PATTERN OF THE DIFFERENTIATION BETWEEN MEN AND WOMEN'S WORK IN BRITAIN, THE UNITED STATES AND OTHER COUNTRIES (London: Dept of Employment, 1978)

Hakim makes a useful distinction between two kinds of occupational segregation—horizontal and vertical. She provides a more sophisticated analysis of women at work than previous theories showing that although women worked in more occupations, between 1901 and 1971, the pattern of horizontal segregation remains strong.

SOC 95　Hochschild, A.
'Emotion, Work, Feeling Rules, and the Social Structure', *American Journal of Sociology* 85: 3 (November 1979) 551–46

Building on her work published in Millman and Kanter (eds.) *Another Voice*, Hochschild considers why sociologists have not developed a sociology of feeling and emotion. This opens up, she feels, an entire new sub-field in sociology and psychology.

SOC 96　Lloyd, C. and Niemi, B.
THE ECONOMICS OF SEX DIFFERENTIALS (New York: Columbia University Press, 1979)

This pieces together data to describe women's commitment to the work place.

SOC 97　Mandle, Joan D.
WOMEN AND SOCIAL CHANGE IN AMERICA (Princeton, N.J.: Princeton Book Company, 1979)

This examines various aspects of American society using a theoretical framework drawn from Marx, Freud and the women's movement. It proposes a new ideology for social change.

SOC 98   Newland, Kathleen
THE SISTERHOOD OF MAN (New York: W. W. Norton, 1979)

Newland analyses women's roles in several spheres—law, education, politics, work and others—and the way economic issues are intertwined.

SOC 99   Oakley, Ann
BECOMING A MOTHER (London: Martin Robertson, 1979)

A phenomenological study of female experience based on verbatim quotes transcribed from interviews with urban, middle-class and working women in England, structured around sub-themes such as childbirth, baby care and domestic politics.

SOC 100 Okin, S. M.
WOMEN IN WESTERN POLITICAL THOUGHT (Princeton, N.J.: Princeton University Press, 1979)

A feminist study of the nature and roles of women in classical political philosophy. She argues that contemporary modes of thought parallel classical philosophy; for example, that the functionalist treatment of women is still alive today. She concludes that philosophy is determined by its conception of women's role in the family.

SOC 101 Reinharz, Shulamit
ON BECOMING A SOCIAL SCIENTIST: FROM SURVEY RESEARCH AND PARTICIPANT OBSERVATION TO EXPERIENTIAL ANALYSIS (San Francisco: Jossey-Bass, 1979)

She synthesises some key approaches in contemporary sociology in an extensive discussion of the strengths and weaknesses of methods such as survey research or participant observation from a feminist perspective. With detailed autobiographical accounts of her own case studies she discusses ideas about uses of personal experience and scientific integrity.

SOC 102 Rubin, Lillian B.
WOMEN OF A CERTAIN AGE: THE MIDLIFE SEARCH FOR SELF (New York: Harper and Row, 1979)

A sociological study of contemporary women between the ages of 35 and 54 who earlier gave up careers to become wives and mothers. Rubin examines their plans for the future.

SOC 103 Segal, Marcia Texler and Berheide, Catherine White
'Towards a Women's Perspective in Sociology: Directions and Prospects', THEORETICAL PERSPECTIVES IN SOCIOLOGY, ed. Scott McNall (New York: St Martin's Press, 1979)

A good survey of current directions.

SOC 104 Snyder, Eloise (ed.)
THE STUDY OF WOMEN: ENLARGING PERSPECTIVES OF SOCIAL REALITY (New York: Harper and Row, 1979)

With a foreword and afterword by Jessie Bernard, this collection provides an excellent overview of the new feminist scholarship making this knowledge accessible to Women's Studies courses. There are essays about women and religion, history, black women, Chicanas, Native Americans, psychology, constitutional rights, literature and women in the workforce.

SOC 105 Barrett, M.
WOMEN'S OPPRESSION TODAY: PROBLEMS IN MARXIST-FEMINIST ANALYSIS (London: Verso, 1980; New York: Schocken Books, 1981)

From the perspective of Marxist-feminism, this analyses the construction of femininity and cultural practice in the formation of gender, concepts of the family and the role of the state in sexual relations. It also examines the relationship of feminism and socialism.

SOC 106　Eichler, M.
THE DOUBLE STANDARD: A FEMINIST CRITIQUE OF FEMINIST SOCIAL SCIENCE (London: Croom Helm, 1980; New York: St Martin's Press, 1980)

Argues for the promotion of anti-sexist research, concepts, language and methods in social science. A more sophisticated response to early feminist theories, for example that the inside/outside dichotomy of women's and men's lives may not be a totally adequate description of reality.

SOC 107　Ettore, E. M.
LESBIANS, WOMEN AND SOCIETY (London: Routledge & Kegan Paul, 1980)

A major contention of this book is that theories of lesbianism, along with society's ideas about sexuality and women, have subverted lesbian consciousness. Social lesbianism, an important concept introduced in the text, refers to the emergence of a public expression of lesbianism. Based on a study of 500 lesbians in London.

SOC 108　Gittell, M. and Shtob, T.
'Changing Women's Roles in Political Volunteerism and Reform of the City', *Signs* 5: 3 (Spring 1980) 564–78

By conceptualising electoral politics as the sole arena of political behaviour political scientists, the authors feel, offer incomplete and inaccurate analysis of political processes. They exclude the vast political work of voluntary women's organisations.

SOC 109　Lewenhak, Sheila
WOMEN AND WORK (London: Fontana, 1980)

A history of working women from matriarchy to post-war labour and new technologies. Lewenhak uses anthropological and historical evidence to look at key moments in the changing patterns of women's work.

Sociology, Politics and Economics

SOC 110   Oakley, Ann
WOMEN CONFINED: TOWARDS A SOCIOLOGY OF CHILDBIRTH (New York: Schocken Boom, 1980)

Oakley describes her own and other women's feelings about their experience of pregnancy. She looks at the societal-medical context of childbirth and how this influences women becoming mothers.

SOC 111   Rogers, R. L. (ed.)
THE BLACK WOMAN (Beverly Hills, CA.: Sage Publications, 1980)

Contains Beale Frances on 'Double Jeopardy: To be Black and Female'.

SOC 112   Sokoloff, Natalie J.
BETWEEN MONEY AND LOVE: THE DIALECTICS OF WOMEN'S HOME AND MARKET WORK (New York: Praeger, 1980)

A radical feminist analysis of sex roles in relation to employment. It argues that social conditioning still prevents women from contesting their assignment to low-paid work.

SOC 113   Cambridge Women's Studies Group
WOMEN IN SOCIETY (London: Virago, 1981)

This mixes the disciplines of history, economics, sociology and psychology, to provide provocative perspectives on the family, work, the state, the economy, sexuality, the nature/culture debate. A good bibliography. There are key essays on history and concepts of family and mental health. The essays tend to concentrate on the position of women under capitalism, but give past and present feminist theoretical frameworks.

SOC 114   Elshtain, J. B.
PUBLIC MAN, PRIVATE WOMAN: WOMEN IN SOCIAL AND POLITICAL THOUGHT (Oxford: Martin Robertson, 1981; Princeton, N.J.: Princeton University Press, 1981)

Claims that the dichotomy of public and private is an abstraction which ignores the complexities of human life. She examines these areas as they appear in western philosophy. She ends with a consideration of feminist thinking.

SOC 115 Epstein, C. and Coser, Lamb, R. (eds.)
ACCESS TO POWER (London: George Allen and Unwin, 1981)

A synthesis of research about political behaviour. It challenges theories of political socialisation which indicate that women are only influenced by men and children by parents.

SOC 116 Leghorn, L. and Parker, K.
WOMAN'S WORTH: SEXUAL ECONOMICS AND THE WORLD OF WOMEN (London: Routledge & Kegan Paul, 1981)

The authors question production statistics which do not include the production of leisure by women for men. The text helped raise the whole issue of what leisure is for women; what places are allocated for it and what form it takes.

SOC 117 McRobbie, A. and McCabe, T. (eds.)
FEMINISM FOR GIRLS: AN ADVENTURE STORY (London: Routledge & Kegan Paul, 1981)

An important introduction to feminist cultural studies, with perspectives on aspects of girls' adolescence. Themes and topics include girls' magazines, romance and sexuality, careers and ethnicity in Britain. The collection includes interviews and ethnographic accounts.

SOC 118 Oakley, Ann
SUBJECT WOMEN (New York: Pantheon Books, 1981)

This shows how social differentiation begins at birth since adults vary their behaviour depending on whether they are told children are male or female.

SOC 119   Roberts, Helen (ed.)
           DOING FEMINIST RESEARCH (London:
           Routledge & Kegan Paul, 1981)

           Fascinating and very useful accounts of research undertaken by feminist sociologists. The problems raised in personal accounts of research are themselves of sociological importance. For example Ann Oakley's critique of 'objective' interviewing techniques shows how research can be improved by a feminist perspective.

SOC 120   Stacey, M. and Price, M.
           WOMEN, POWER AND POLITICS (London:
           Tavistock, 1981)

           This builds on Stacey's previous work in *Tradition and Change* (London: Oxford University Press, 1960) and *Power, Persistence and Change* (London: Routledge & Kegan Paul, 1975) to develop a distinctive feminist theory. They argue that the ideology of the family has many forms and widen definitions of power and politics by including ideas from sociology and Marxism. They conclude that the idea of matriarchy has provided an important alternative political vision as well as acting as a stimulus for feminist research.

SOC 121   Stimpson, Catherine et al.
           WOMEN AND THE AMERICAN CITY (Chicago:
           University of Chicago Press, 1981)

           This is a collection of *Signs* essays which focus on problems unique to women in the urban environment. It contains, in essays by Dolores Hayden and others, non-sexist arguments for new city maps, urban policy and accounts of crime, city life and ethnic women. There is an extensive review essay by Gerda Wekerle.

SOC 122   Thorne, Barrie and Yalom, Marilyn (eds.)
           RETHINKING THE FAMILY: SOME FEMINIST
           VIEWS (New York: Longmans, 1981)

           Essays cover history, anthropology, law, economics, psychiatry to focus on the debate between challengers to and defenders of the family. There is an essay by Nancy Chodorow 'Fantasy of the Perfect Mother'.

SOC 123 Andersen, Margaret
THINKING ABOUT WOMEN: SOCIOLOGICAL AND FEMINIST PERSPECTIVES (London: Macmillan, 1983)

About contemporary research and theoretical perspectives on the sociological character of women's lives in American society. Review of feminist scholarship about biology and culture, crime, work and economy, the family, health and reproduction, early feminists and the social construction of knowledge.

SOC 124 Barrett, M. and McIntosh, M. (eds.)
THE ANTI-SOCIAL FAMILY (London: Verso, 1982)

Family–state relations are centrally considered and issues of moralism and censure within and between feminists on the theme of the family.

SOC 125 Elshtain, J. B. (ed.)
THE FAMILY IN POLITICAL THOUGHT (Brighton: Harvester Press, 1982)

This includes work on Aristotle, family metaphors in Nietzsche as well as accounts of contemporary feminist theory by Dinnerstein and Chodorow.

SOC 126 Greenglass, E. R.
A WORLD OF DIFFERENCES: GENDER ROLES IN PERSPECTIVE (Toronto: John Wiley, 1982)

Research on the career decisions of professional women and men.

SOC 127 Leonard, Eileen B.
WOMEN, CRIME AND SOCIETY: A CRITIQUE OF CRIMINOLOGY THEORY (New York: Longmans, 1982)

The author critically explores five influential theories of criminology to demonstrate their inadequacy in explaining female patterns of crime. She shows that they are not general theories but particular understandings of male behaviour. She also suggests a non-sexist theory of crime.

SOC 128 Barrett, N. S.
'How the Study of Women has Restructured the Discipline of Economics', A FEMINIST PERSPECTIVE IN THE ACADEMY, ed. Langland, E. and Gore, W. (Chicago: University of Chicago Press, 1983)

A review of economic theories and their relation to the history of women. Some mention of recent feminist approaches.

SOC 129 Boneparth, Ellen (ed.)
WOMEN, POWER AND POLICY (Oxford: Pergamon Press, 1983)

About how public policies affect women. Essays are on the record of the 1960s and 1970s; pay equity; alternative work patterns; motherhood; and policy failures.

SOC 130 Harding, S. and Hintikka, M. B. (eds.)
DISCOVERING REALITY (Boston, Mass.: D. Reidel, 1982)

An attempt to provide feminist theories and definitions throughout epistemology, the philosophy of science and metaphysics. There are essays about concepts of equality, individualism and feminist historical materialism by Fox Keller, Flax, Hartsock among others.

SOC 131   Hartsock, Nancy
           MONEY, SEX AND POWER: TOWARD A
           FEMINIST HISTORICAL MATERIALISM (New
           York: Longmans, 1983)

           Hartsock demonstrates that women writing about power, even those women who are not explicitly feminist such as Hannah Arendt, do offer descriptions of power different from those of male political theorists.

SOC 132   Lowe, M. and Hubbard, R. (eds.)
           WOMAN'S NATURE: RATIONALIZATIONS OF
           INEQUALITY (Oxford: Pergamon Press, 1983)

           Natural and social scientists address the claims of sociobiologists from a feminist perspective. They reveal that claims about 'woman's nature' are political and have no scientific meaning. There are accounts of scientific myths; black and Indian women; and the social effects of contemporary myths.

SOC 133   Phillips, Anne
           HIDDEN HANDS: WOMEN AND ECONOMIC
           POLICIES (London: Pluto Press, 1983)

           Mixing feminism and socialism, she looks at ways of changing waged employment and discusses an economic policy for a feminist future.

SOC 134   Rothschild, J. (ed.)
           MACHINA EX DEA: FEMINIST PERSPECTIVES
           ON TECHNOLOGY (Lowell, Mass.: University of
           Lowell, 1983; Oxford: Pergamon Press, 1983)

           A reassessment of the relationship of technology to women's work and lives that offers some new approaches to evaluating the social impact of new technologies. Essays on engineering, office technology and mathematics.

SOC 135 Stanley, L. and Wise, S.
BREAKING OUT (London: Routledge & Kegan Paul, 1983)

The authors argue that feminist social science must break out of the confines of existing research models. They discuss differing conceptions of the experiential and suggest that a key theme in a feminist critique is its relationship to the women's movement.

SOC 136 Hussein, Freda (ed.)
MUSLIM WOMEN (London: Croom Helm, 1984)

These papers refuse prevailing sociological misconceptions of Muslim women: that they are a social problem or should be judged by western standards. Instead, authors use a general theory of role behaviour to examine the contradictions between Islamic ideals and social context; the history of Islam and the problems of feminism and employment. Countries included are Turkey, Egypt, North Africa and Pakistan.

SOC 137 McRobbie, A. and Nava, M. (eds.)
GENDER AND GENERATION (London: Macmillan, 1984)

Essays about recent work in the youth service and adolescence discourse; psychoanalytic theory; the social significance of dance; youth photography projects; and the development of adolescent consumerism since the Second World War.

SOC 138 Siltanen, Janet and Stanworth, Michelle
WOMEN AND THE PUBLIC SPHERE (London: Hutchinson, 1984)

An examination of the traditions and methods of political analysis which finds that methods of statistical analysis are often inaccurate. Dealing with a spread of contemporary evidence in politics and sociology they pinpoint conceptual problems and argue for a more problematic conception of women's roles.

SOC 139 Edwards, Susan (ed.)
GENDER, SEX AND THE LAW (London: Croom Helm, 1985)

Explores some of the problems involved in the law's complicity with women's inequality. Essays discuss immigration laws, women and employment; and the failure of the Sex Discrimination and Equal Pay Acts in Britain to adequately protect women.

SOC 140 O'Donovan, K.
SEXUAL DIVISION IN LAW (London: Weidenfeld and Nicolson, 1985)

An original study about the unequal legal status of women and men. The author argues that this is due to the dichotomy between private and public with men's lives being seen as public (and legal) and women's as private (and unregulated). Examining the history of marriage, divorce, property and the regulation of sexuality O'Donovan looks at how the law constructs categories of 'man' and 'woman'. A major contribution to feminist legal theory.

Arts, Film, Theatre, Media, Music

The arts represent an underdeveloped area of feminist criticism. Materials have been included to suggest the future breadth of the area as well as its current priorities. Film, theory, media studies, fine art, music, fashion and textiles, photography, autobiography by creative women, and theatre studies are here as well as art history.

ART 1   Lippard, Lucy
        SURREALISTS ON ART (Englewood Cliffs, N.J.: Prentice-Hall, 1970)

        Lippard examines women's involvement in surrealism looking at the surrealist intention to initiate a new humanism, its opposition to prevailing notions and its interest in psychoanalysis. Lippard sees those positions as ideologically important to feminism.

ART 2   Chicago, Judy (ed.)
        'Miss Chicago and the California Girls', *Everywoman* 18 (May 1971)

        A special issue with interviews, articles on female imagery, and studio work written by Chicago and her students in the feminist programme at Fresno.

ART 3   *Film Library Quarterly* (Winter 1971–1972)

        A special issue on women and film.

ART 4   Miner, Dorothy
        ANASTASE AND HER SISTERS: WOMEN ARTISTS OF THE MIDDLE AGES (Baltimore, MD.: Walters Art Gallery, 1971)

        Miner describes the specific and differing conditions of women's practices. She relates women's use of art forms to particular historical factors like definitions of amateur and professional work and attitudes to women's membership of professional bodies.

ART 5 Skiles, Jacqueline and McDevitt, Janet (eds.)
A DOCUMENTARY HISTORY OF WOMEN ARTISTS IN REVOLUTION (New York: Know, 1971)

This includes reprints of Muriel Castanis 'Behind Every Artist There is a Penis', *Village Voice* (March 1970) and 'Forum: Women in Art', *Art Magazine* (February 1971). It describes the New York demonstrations against museum sexism which were a focal point for activism on the part of American women artists.

ART 6 *Women and Art* (Winter 1971)

The predecessor of the *Feminist Art Journal*. It was edited by Pat Mainardi, Marjorie Kramer and Irene Peslikis. This issue contained articles about Alice Neel and Rosa Bonheur, among others.

ART 7 Chmaj, Betty (ed.)
IMAGE, MYTH AND BEYOND (Pittsburgh: Know, 1972)

Examines star roles in movies and in comic books, together with images of women in rock music and assesses the implications for popular culture.

ART 8 Edwards, Lee et al. (eds.)
WOMAN: AN ISSUE (Boston, Mass.: Little, Brown, 1972)

A brilliantly diverse exploration into just what it means to be a woman artist. Contains self-portraits of fifteen women painters.

ART 9 Fiske, Betty et al. (eds.)
SEX DIFFERENTIALS IN ART EXHIBITION REVIEWS: A STATISTICAL STUDY AND SELECTED PRESS REACTION (Los Angeles, CA.: Tamarind Lithography Workshop, 1972)

Arts, Film, Theatre, Media, Music

This is a landmark study documenting the vast discrimination against women artists in the reviews of their shows by the art press and other media.

ART 10   Babhart, Ann and Brown, Elizabeth
'Old Mistresses, Women Artists of the Past', *The Walters Art Gallery Bulletin* 24: 7 (April 1972) 1–8

The article concerns an exhibition of women artists and Romaine Brooks, Artemisia Gentileschi and Mary Cassatt are discussed. An excellent introduction to the entire topic of women artists and their problems. The authors demonstrate how numbers of women have successfully dealt with social obstacles but also touch on the irony of misattributions and the conflicts involved in assuming the male role.

ART 11   Hess, Thomas and Nochlin, Linda (eds.)
WOMAN AS SEX OBJECT: STUDIES IN EROTIC ART 1730–1970 (New York: Newsweek Inc., 1972)

About the difficulty of role reversal in representation.

ART 12   Krasilovsky, Alexis Rafael
WEST COAST WOMEN ARTISTS CONFERENCE (Valencia, CA.: California Institute of the Arts, 1972)

An account of feminist art history, paintings, sculpture, film and feminist aesthetics.

ART 13   Nemser, Cindy
'Art Criticism and the Gender Prejudice', *Arts Magazine* 46 (March 1972) 44–6

Nemser deals with the question of whether there are recognisable feminine characteristics in art created by women. She confronts the critical vocabulary that is rife with sexual connotations.

ART 14   Nemser, Cindy
'Stereotypes and Women Artists', *The Feminist Art Journal* 1: 1 (April 1972) 22–3

An article exploring the characteristics of 'phallic criticism' from the nineteenth century to the present-day in reviews of women artists.

ART 15 'Women and Film', *Take One* III: 2 (February 1972)

A special issue.

ART 16 'Women and Film', *The Velvet Light Trap* (Fall 1972)

A special issue devoted to this topic.

ART 17 'Special Issue', *Art Magazine* 5 (Fall 1973)

Published in Toronto: this is a special issue devoted to women in art. Included are essays by Fleisher and Graeme on 'Woman as an Art Viewer'.

ART 18 Cole, Doris
FROM TIPI TO SKYSCRAPER: A HISTORY OF WOMEN'S ARCHITECTURE (Boston: I Press, 1973)

This is a description of women's contributions to architecture and an analysis of why there have been so few women architects. Cole discusses women's contributions in native American culture, in the Utopian communes of the Shakers, in the nineteenth century and into the present.

ART 19 Duncan, Carol
'Virility and Domination in Early Twentieth Century Vanguard Painting', *Art Forum* 12 (December 1973) 30–9

A good example of how a feminist analysis can offer valuable new insights. This explores male sexuality, in both imagery and style, of the Fauve and the Brücke artists. Duncan briefly discusses how this imagery was an especially pernicious obstacle for women artists.

ART 20 Haskell, Molly
FROM REVERENCE TO RAPE: THE
TREATMENT OF WOMEN IN THE MOVIES (New
York: Holt, Rinehart and Winston, 1973)

She shows how film represents the male artist's point of view and how women's images plunged in importance, centrality and worth. Crediting the early strong images of women to a decentralised control of the industry and to charismatic, strong-willed women (Bette Davis) Haskell describes the devolution of the female image to the non substantive sex symbols and rape victims of contemporary film.

ART 21 Hess, Thomas B. and Baker, Elizabeth C. (eds.)
ART AND SEXUAL POLITICS: WOMEN'S
LIBERATION, WOMEN ARTISTS AND ART
HISTORY (New York: Macmillan, 1973)

First published in the special issue of *Arts News* 69: 9 (January 1971). A collection of essays on women as artists and the social forces they contend with and express in their work. There are articles by Linda Nochlin and Rosalyn Drexler among others.

ART 22 Johnston, Claire (ed.)
NOTES ON WOMEN'S CINEMA (London: SEFT, 1973)

A crucial account of a feminist shift in film criticism away from criticism being about the discovery of meaning to criticism uncovering the means of production. Gives a greater attention to the specificities of artistic production, particularly how character is produced by textual operations such as narration or *mis-en-scène*.

ART 23 Mainardi, Patricia
'Quilts: The Great American Art', *Feminist Art Journal* 2: 1 (1973) 18–23

Mainardi criticises the view that quiltmakers are precursors of modern abstract painters and insists that this values their art and aesthetic largely in terms of a male aesthetic.

Her writings have helped feminists to appreciate quilts as a formerly ignored artistic heritage.

ART 24 Mellen, Joan
WOMEN AND THEIR SEXUALITY IN THE NEW FILM (New York: Horizon Press, 1973)

Using a literary approach, Mellen concentrates on characters and stereotypes in essays about contemporary American and European films.

ART 25 Minault, Denise
WOMAN AS HEROINE: EXHIBITION CATALOGUE (Worcester: Worcester Art Museum, 1973)

The first exhibition to examine the role of women in seventeenth-century Italian Baroque painting.

ART 26 Rosen, Marjorie
POPCORN VENUS: WOMEN, MOVIES AND THE AMERICAN DREAM (New York: Coward McCann and Geoghegan, 1973)

Rosen describes movie stars, their narrative placing and their development in terms both of their own control over their sexuality (for example, Rita Hayworth) and that created for them by the media.

ART 27 Schwartz, Therese
'They Built Women a Bad Art History', *Feminist Art Journal* 2: 3 (Fall 1973) 10–11, 22

Schwartz rebukes several nineteenth-century writers for their extreme misogyny toward women artists. She believes them instrumental in the near eradication of women from art history.

ART 28 Tucker, Anne (ed.)
THE WOMAN'S EYE (New York: Alfred A. Knopf, 1973)

A survey of important women photographers, including Kasebier, Johnston, Bourke-White, Lange, Abbott, Morgan, Arbus, Wells, Dater and Nettles. It includes reproductions.

ART 29 'Women and the Arts', *Arts in Society* XI: 1 (Spring/Summer 1974)

A special issue including essays by Glueck on making cultural institutions more responsive to women and by Elizabeth Janeway on images of women.

ART 30 Hill, Vicki Lynn
FEMALE ARTISTS: PAST AND PRESENT
(Berkeley, CA.: Women's History Research Center Inc., 1974)

Hill lists artists in all media, galleries, critics, women working on research projects, teachers, museum and slide registers and some annotated references to books and articles.

ART 31 Janz, Mildred
'Ours is a Theater of and by Men: And Now We Need a Theater of Women', PLAYWRIGHTS, LYRICISTS, COMPOSERS ON THEATER, ed. O. L. Guernsey, Jr. (New York: Dodd, Mead and Co., 1974)

An example of the way women might have written a tragedy in the classical repertoire. She uses feminist work in linguistics to show that imagery and language would need to be radically altered.

ART 32 Kaplan, Ann E.
'The Feminist Perspective in Film Studies', *University Film Association Journal* (1974) 26–31

A proposed methodology for a feminist criticism which could reveal the extent of women's dehumanisation in film.

ART 33 Orloff, Katherine
ROCK AND ROLL WOMEN (Los Angeles, CA.: Nash, 1974)

Women in rock music are too often dismissed as simply groupies or single performers. Orloff counters this in interviews with twelve female rock performers discussing the influence of the women's movement on their careers.

ART 34 Schapiro, Miriam (ed.)
ANONYMOUS WAS A WOMAN: DOCUMENTATION OF THE WOMEN'S ART FESTIVAL AND A COLLECTION OF LETTERS TO YOUNG WOMAN ARTISTS (Valencia, CA.: California Institute of the Arts, 1974)

A premise of this festival is the need to separate from male teachers and students because feminine experience is devalued in traditional settings. The section of letters is about the lack of role models for female art students.

ART 35 Tufts, Eleanor
OUR HIDDEN HERITAGE: FIVE CENTURIES OF WOMEN ARTISTS (London: Paddington Press, 1974)

Tufts readdresses the neglect and omission of women artists by providing 22 mini-monographs. Although Tufts represents a reformist trend in feminist art criticism by still using traditional aesthetic modes, her book is one of the most important anthologies of forgotten women artists.

ART 36 Vogel, Lise
'Fine Arts and Feminism: The Awakening Consciousness', *Feminist Studies* 2: 1 (1974) 3–37

A thoughtful discussion of feminist art criticism to date.

ART 37 Acuff, Betty (ed.)
'Special Issue', *Art Education* (November 1975)

Contains scholarly articles about women in art, on art education and sexual stereotyping.

ART 38 Benton, Suzanne
THE ART OF WELDED SCULPTURE (New York: Van Nostrand Reinhold, 1975)

A feminist book on technique in a field often considered 'masculine'. There is a personal commentary about the problems of women in the art world and how those problems approach on personal life. The book uses female pronouns throughout.

ART 39 Butler-Paisley, Matilda
IMAGE OF WOMEN IN ADVERTISEMENTS: A PRELIMINARY STUDY OF AVENUES FOR CHANGE (Stanford, CA.: Stanford University Press, 1975)

Based on interviews with feminists and advertisers it suggests changes through national women's organisations, nationwide boycotts and the Federal Trade Commission.

ART 40 Chicago, Judy
THROUGH THE FLOWER: MY STRUGGLE AS A WOMAN ARTIST (New York: Anchor/Doubleday, 1975)

An autobiographical account of her training and teaching. Includes descriptions of and responses to women artists of the past and present and an account of the relationship between feminism and art.

ART 41 Hollander, A.
SEEING THROUGH CLOTHES (New York: Viking, 1975)

Useful resource for feminists analysing the history of theatre costume. A good study of the changing images of men and women in theatre.

ART 42 Johnston, Claire and Cook, Pat
THE WORK OF DOROTHY ARZNER: TOWARDS
A FEMINIST CINEMA (London: BFI, 1975)

The authors develop feminist readings of the classic decades of Hollywood in the 1940s and 1950s, and examine the contradictions surrounding the position of women (such as Arzner's) in relation to production.

ART 43 McGarry, Eileen
'Documentary, Realism and Women's Cinema', *Women and Film* 7 (Summer 1975)

A Barthesian approach about sexist codes. McGarry reveals how in film social codes are overlaid with codes of appearances for the actress.

ART 44 Millum, Trevor
IMAGES OF WOMEN: ADVERTISING IN WOMEN'S MAGAZINES (Totowa, N.J.: Rowman and Littlefield, 1975)

Millum looks at major forms of stereotyping in terms of production and mode. This is useful as a source book for feminist critiques.

ART 45 Mulvey, Laura
'Visual Pleasure and Narrative Cinema', *Screen* 16: 3 (1975)

A pioneering argument that the eroticisation of women on the screen comes about through the way cinema is structured around three explicitly male looks or the 'gaze': the look of the camera, the look of men within the narrative and the look of the male spectator.

ART 46 Nemser, Cindy
ART TALK: CONVERSATIONS WITH TWELVE WOMEN ARTISTS (New York: Scribner's, 1975)

The editor of the *Feminist Art Journal* is in discussion with Nancy Grossman, Alice Neel and Audrey Flack among others. Issues discussed are stereotypes of male and female beauty; symbols of sexual fantasy and uses of realism. The book contains photographs of the artists and their work.

ART 47   Orenstein, Gloria
'Art History', *Signs* 1: 2 (Winter 1975) pp. 505–25

A good overview of feminist art history of the 1970s.

ART 48   Smith, Sharon
WOMEN WHO MAKE MOVIES (New York: Hopkinson and Blake, 1975)

A historical account of women film makers beginning with the French woman Alice Guy Blaché in 1896. It includes new film-makers in America working outside Hollywood and a directory of 725 women film makers in the United States.

ART 49   'Special Issue', *Visual Dialog* 1: 2 (Winter 1975/1976) and 2: 3 (Winter 1976/1977)

Two issues devoted to women in the visual arts. They include articles by Brodsky on the Women's Art Movement, by Loeb, and Packard among others.

ART 50   Adams, C. and Laurikietis, R. (eds.)
THE GENDER TRAP: BOOK THREE: MESSAGES AND IMAGES (London: Virago, 1976)

This looks at male and female stereotypes presented by the mass media, through both the printed word and visual image.

ART 51   'Women in Art', *Art Journal* XXXV: 4 (Summer 1976)

This includes articles by Lucy Lippard and Lise Vogel among others.

ART 52 Cadogan, Mary and Craig, Patricia
YOU'RE A BRICK, ANGELA! A NEW LOOK AT GIRLS' FICTION FROM 1839 TO 1975 (London: Gollancz, 1976)

Shows how much of girls' fiction has been written by men leading to stereotypes of passive, domesticated women.

ART 53 Jackson, Irene
'Black Women and Afro-American Tradition', *Sing Out* 25: 2 (1976) 10–13

She discusses the contributions of Afro-American women to American traditional music in such genres as lullabies and work songs.

ART 54 Lippard, Lucy
FROM THE CENTER (New York: E. P. Dutton, 1976)

Thirty essays delineate the growth of Lippard's feminism and the present status of women's art. She covers contemporary art, film and women's art groups setting out feminist criteria for evaluating aesthetics.

ART 55 Lippard, Lucy
EVA HESSE (New York: New York University Press, 1976)

Lippard describes how Hesse's search for self-knowledge included a close involvement with psychoanalysis which provided her with a theoretical framework with which to understand the conflicting identities of women.

ART 56 Nemser, Cindy
'Towards A Feminist Sensibility: Contemporary Trends in Women's Art', *Feminist Art Journal* 5 (Summer 1976) 19–23

Nemser discusses the diversity of women's art as well as some of the commonalities such as frequent autobiographical content, documentation of the immediate experience of a woman, art with political statements and art with sexual imagery.

ART 57 Petersen, Karen and Wilson, J. J.
WOMEN ARTISTS: RECOGNITION AND REAPPRAISAL FROM THE EARLY MIDDLE AGES TO THE TWENTIETH CENTURY (New York: Harper and Row, 1976; London: The Women's Press, 1978)

A chronological account of women's art giving a good historical overview of women artists working in the Western tradition. The authors accumulate information, biographies and reproductions in a search for an obliterated history. They consider themes and imagery specific to women and stimulated a general reconsideration of assumptions in art history.

ART 58 Whitworth, Sarah
'The Lesbian Image in Eve', THE LAVENDER HERRING: LESBIAN ESSAYS FROM THE LADDER, eds. Grier, Barbara and Reid, Coletta (Baltimore, MD.: Diana Press, 1976) pp. 284–357

An important section of eight essays showing the significance of cultural studies in the depiction of lesbianism.

ART 59 Wiesenfeld, Cheryl et al. (eds.)
WOMEN SEE WOMEN (New York: Thomas Y. Cromwell, 1976)

An excellent collection of photographs by contemporary women photographers. There are brief biographies of the photographers.

ART 60 Beasley, M. and Gibbons, S. (eds.)
WOMEN IN MEDIA: A DOCUMENTARY SOURCE BOOK (Washington, D.C.: Women's Institute for Freedom of the Press, 1977)

A very useful resource.

ART 61 *Chrysalis: A Magazine of Women's Culture*

The first issue 1: 1 and 2 (1977) included articles by Ruth

Iskin 'Joan Snyder: Toward A Feminist Imperative', and Dolores Hayden, 'Redesigning the Domestic Workplace'. The second had Lucy Lippard 'Quite Contrary: Body, Nature and Ritual in Women's Art' and a catalogue of feminist publishers.

ART 62 Cowie, Elizabeth
'Women, Representation and the Image', *Screen Education* 23 (Summer 1977)

Cowie argues that sexist stereotyping is not because sexism resides in the image but because feminism enables us to read new connotations.

ART 63 *Feminist Art Journal*

A quarterly begun in the spring of 1972 that ceased publication with 6: 2 (Summer 1977). With its editor Cindy Nemser the journal consistently combined controversy with scholarship.

ART 64 Harrison, Margaret
'Notes on Feminist Art in Britain 1970–1977', *Studio International* 193: 987 (1977)

A full account of initiatives taken during the 1970s by women artists. They established a viable context for the viewing and serious discussion of their work by opening galleries, staging exhibitions and publishing magazines.

ART 65 Hayes, Danielle
WOMEN PHOTOGRAPH MEN (New York: William Morrow, 1977)

A humanistic collection of images of men, as seen by women. The introduction is by Molly Haskell.

ART 66 *Heresies: A Feminist Publication On Art and Politics*

The first issue (1977) includes articles about women in the community, the mural movement, feminist abstract art

Arts, Film, Theatre, Media, Music

and Lucy Lippard on mobility in the art world. Subsequent issues continued this important criticism.

ART 67   Kay, Karen and Peary Gerald (eds.)
WOMEN AND THE CINEMA: A CRITICAL ANTHOLOGY (New York: E. P. Dutton, 1977)

The first anthology of criticism about women and film. It deals with all aspects of women and film: imagery, actresses, women in production, feminist politics and theory.

ART 68   Moore, H.
THE NEW WOMEN'S THEATRE (New York: Vintage, 1977)

The first scholarly criticism about women and theatre. A description and anthology of the feminist theatre movement.

ART 69   Pool, Jeannie C.
WOMEN IN MUSIC HISTORY: A RESEARCH GUIDE (Ansonia Station, N.Y.: Pool, 1977)

Pool has written an excellent introduction and research guide to women in music history. Her aim is to retrieve information about ignored women musicians and she includes an essay on the history of women in music along with bibliographies and discographies.

ART 70   Ruddick, Sara and Daniels, Pamela (eds.)
WORKING IT OUT: TWENTY-THREE WOMEN WRITERS, ARTISTS, SCHOLARS THINK ABOUT THEIR LIVES AND WORK (New York: Pantheon, 1977)

With a foreword by Adrienne Rich. This contains accounts by Miriam Shapiro among others on the relationship between art, feminism and technique and the uses of alternative strategies by artists of the past and present.

ART 71   Swan, Susan Burrows
PLAIN AND FANCY: AMERICAN WOMEN AND THEIR NEEDLEWORK, 1700–1850 (New York: Holt, Rinehart and Winston, 1977)

A profusely illustrated social history of American women and a discussion of their needlework.

ART 72   Synder-Ott, Joelynn
WOMEN AND CREATIVITY (Millbrae, CA.: Les Femmes, 1977)

Synder-Ott is both a teacher and artist. She includes two chapters on women's art pedagogy and women's studies at Moore College, Philadelphia and a Feminist Art Program at community level.

ART 73   Torre, Susanna (ed.)
WOMEN IN AMERICAN ARCHITECTURE: A HISTORIC AND CONTEMPORARY PERSPECTIVE (New York: Watson Gupthill, 1977)

This includes essays by Dolores Hayden, among others, on the historic roots of the associations in culture between single-family housing, the nuclear family and women's roles. It looks at increasing privatisation in the home with the introduction of home appliances and documents the exhibition held at the Brooklyn Museum in 1977.

ART 74   Wilding, Faith
BY OUR OWN HANDS: THE WOMEN ARTISTS' MOVEMENT, SOUTHERN CALIFORNIA, 1970–1976 (Santa Monica, CA.: Double Y, 1977)

This important book traces the genesis and development of the Women's Art Movement and feminist groups such as the Feminist Studio Workshop, Woman Space, the Feminist Art Programs at Fresno and CalArts.

ART 75   Feinberg, Jean et al.
'Political Fabrications: Women's Textiles in Five Cultures', *Heresies* 4 (1978) 28–37

An attempt to relate the social and political position of women to the status of their textile-making in several societies.

ART 76   Fine, Elsa Honig
WOMEN AND ART: A HISTORY OF WOMEN PAINTERS AND THEIR WORK FROM THE FIFTEENTH TO THE TWENTIETH-CENTURY (Montclair, N.J.: Allenheld and Schramm, 1978)

Fine does not accept that the established notion of 'fine arts' is a proper object of study for understanding the role of women in a given period. She suggests that social conditions influence the creative process.

ART 77   French, Brandon
ON THE VERGE OF REVOLT: WOMEN IN AMERICAN FILMS OF THE FIFTIES (New York: Ungar, 1978)

French finds an ambiguous representation of women, one in which marriage, sex roles, motherhood, were not clearly defined or synchronised with social mores of the 1950s. The text has a bibliography and photographs.

ART 78   Hollister, Valerie and Weatherford, Elizabeth
' "By the Lakeside There is An Echo": Towards a History of Women's Traditional Arts', *Heresies* 4 (1978) 119–23

They note the absence of information about women's ritual art and call for further research in this area.

ART 79   Kaplan, Ann E. (ed.)
WOMEN IN *FILM NOIR* (London: BFI, 1978)

The authors see *film noir* as the exception to the standard Hollywood portrayal of sexual stereotypes. Examining films such as *Gilda* and *Double Indemnity* they show how women's sexuality is posed as a threat which the films can only with difficulty contain.

ART 80   Nochlin, Linda and Harris, A.
WOMEN ARTISTS: 1550–1950 (Los Angeles, CA.: Los Angeles County Museum of Art and Alfred A. Knopf, 1978)

The catalogue of a huge exhibition held in Los Angeles documenting the extensive range of women's art.

ART 81   Tuchman, Gaye et al.
HEARTH AND HOME: IMAGES OF WOMEN IN THE MASS MEDIA (New York: Oxford University Press, 1978)

Shows in concrete detail how women are 'erased' from view in the media or are creatures whose identity rests on their male relationships.

ART 82   Walters, Margaret
THE NUDE MALE (London: Paddington Press, 1978)

The male nude from a female perspective. It offers a new way of assessing the male in art from classical times to present-day. Walters also tests cultural assumptions, and shows how art history assumes that 'nude' as applied to male and female has quite different meanings. Art history, Walters reveals, portrays the male as symbol of order and harmony, and less subject to the vagaries of fashion than the female.

ART 83   Williamson, Judith
DECODING ADVERTISEMENTS: IDEOLOGY AND MEANING IN ADVERTISING (London: Marian Boyers, 1978)

A feminist and structuralist analysis of current advertising. Williamson uses Lacanian analysis to deconstruct the language and uses of specific examples giving a clear exposition of terms such as 'absence' and 'interpellation'.

ART 84   Bank, Mirra
ANONYMOUS WAS A WOMAN (New York: St Martin's Press, 1979)

Reproductions of American women's folk art—including quilts and needlework. The accompanying essay describes this work as real art.

ART 85 Brown, Janet
FEMINIST DRAMA: DEFINITION AND CRITICAL ANALYSIS (Metuchen, N.J.: Scarecrow Press, 1979)

Using paradigms from Kenneth Burke, Brown gives accounts of feminist plays and theatre groups. Shange, Childress and Drexler, among others, are considered.

ART 86 Chicago, Judy
THE DINNER PARTY (Garden City, N.Y.: Anchor/ Doubleday, 1979)

The story of the sculpture and history of her epic work *The Dinner Party*. There are short biographies of all the figures and accounts of the studio work and techniques. Many women worked with Chicago to create a feminist last supper recreating women's history and our contribution to civilisation.

ART 87 Erens, P. (ed.)
SEXUAL STRATAGEMS: THE WORLD OF WOMEN IN FILM (New York: Horizon Press, 1979)

Includes articles on the problems for women of production, exhibition and distribution as well as the social and political context for feminist films. With essays on films directed by men, feminist criticism and films directed by women. There is also an annotated bibliography.

ART 88 Greer, Germaine
THE OBSTACLE RACE: THE FORTUNES OF WOMEN PAINTERS AND THEIR WORK (London: Secker and Warburg, 1979)

A chronological survey of women painters with a useful case study of Gentileschi and discussion about the notion of the exceptional woman.

ART 89   *Jump/Cut*

In general the journal has focused more than others on the social and political context for feminist film. Special issues include: The Cuban Cinema, N20 (May 1979) and N22 (May 1980); Lesbians and Film, N24/25 (March 1981) and Film and Feminism in Germany, N27 (July 1982).

ART 90   Munro, Eleanor
ORIGINALS: AMERICAN WOMEN ARTISTS (New York: Simon and Schuster, 1979)

Munro interviewed contemporary women artists and discusses their work and the origins of their art.

ART 91   Perkins, T.
'Rethinking Stereotypes', IDEOLOGY AND CULTURAL PRODUCTION, ed. M. Barrett et al. (London: Croom Helm, 1979)

Perkins makes a feminist critique of the material realities in patriarchal film discourse. She argues that stereotypes are produced out of social practices which they are then, in a reversal of cause and effect, taken to explain.

ART 92   Berger, John
WAYS OF SEEING (London: Writers and Readers, 1980)

Shows how male artists have traditionally created imagery and compositions which express the power of the male patron over women. He explains how, historically, the primary viewer of a painting of a nude woman has been its male owner which led to a tradition of the objectification of the female nude.

ART 93   Chicago, Judy and Hill, S.
EMBROIDERING OUR HERITAGE: THE DINNER PARTY NEEDLEWORK (New York: Anchor/ Doubleday, 1980)

An account of the techniques, collective work and

historical research involved in creating the textile work for *The Dinner Party*.

ART 94 Goreau, A.
RECONSTRUCTING APHRA: THE SOCIAL BIOGRAPHY OF APHRA BENN (New York: Dial, 1980)

Adding a feminist slant to recent biographical and sociological study of women of the theatre.

ART 95 Rich, Ruby
'In the Name of Feminist Film Criticism', *Heresies* 9 (Spring 1980) 74–81

An earlier version of this article was published as 'The Crisis of Naming in Feminist Film Criticism', *Jump/Cut*, 19 (December 1978) 9–12. Rich shows feminist film criticism tends to accept feminist film as an area of study rather than as a sphere of action.

ART 96 Chinoy, H. K. and Jenkins, L. W.
WOMEN IN AMERICAN THEATRE (New York: Crown, 1981)

A crucial collection of essays and original writings on women playwrights and forms of cultural expression such as pageants hitherto regarded as 'extra-literary'.

ART 97 French, M.
SHAKESPEARE'S DIVISION OF EXPERIENCE (New York: Summit, 1981)

A feminist perspective which by using a thematic and character analysis follows the tradition of English literary criticism in which the text is primary.

ART 98 Hayden, Dolores
THE GRAND DOMESTIC REVOLUTION: A HISTORY OF FEMINIST DESIGNS FOR AMERICAN HOMES, NEIGHBORHOODS AND CITIES (Cambridge, Mass.: MIT Press, 1981)

Hayden shows how women have become trapped in the role of caretaker of the domestic economy and reviews recent historical literature on changes in housing form, domestic technology and women's attitude to domestic roles. A crucial example of feminist architectural criticism.

ART 99   Holledge, Julie
INNOCENT FLOWERS: WOMEN IN THE
EDWARDIAN THEATRE (London: Virago, 1981)

Discusses the work of women actresses, production and writers. Holledge gives a useful account of theatre's relation to the Women's Rights Movement, the Actresses Franchise League and the Women's Theatre Company.

ART 100 Morgan, Fidelis
THE FEMALE WITS: WOMEN PLAYWRIGHTS IN
THE RESTORATION (London: Virago, 1981)

This is a book of modern editions of five stageworthy plays, therefore it is not a fully feminist criticism as such but along with biographical sketches Morgan includes introductory notes discussing the relationship of gender and genre in each writer.

ART 101 Parker, R. and Pollock, G.
OLD MISTRESSES (London: Routledge & Kegan Paul, 1981)

A searching analysis of women's position in culture. The book is about the misrepresentation of women's art and what this treatment reveals about the ideological basis of art history. It shows how art history has privileged male notions of creativity, and examines the specific ways women have made art in different periods; how they contribute to, as well as sometimes oppose, dominant styles and images; and women's relation to art practice as well as to the institutions of art. The book also contains a survey of twentieth-century avant-garde movements.

Arts, Film, Theatre, Media, Music

ART 102   Wandor, Michelene
UNDERSTUDIES: THEATRE AND SEXUAL POLITICS (London: Methuen, 1981)

An important history of feminist and gay theatre in the 1970s in Britain written by one of its playwrights. Wandor describes the work of women playwrights such as Pam Gems and Caryl Churchill; the work of feminist collectives such as Monstrous Regiment; and offers an interesting comparison of the male Left and feminism. Wandor has also made significant collections of women's plays also published by Methuen.

ART 103   Wolff, Janet
THE SOCIAL PRODUCTION OF ART (London: Macmillan, 1981)

She argues that art is the complex construction of history and society, and reviews recent developments including feminism and semiotics, hermeneutics and marxism. Wolff compares examples from art as well as literature. Her major theme is the problem of the 'author' and her subsidiary theme is women's participation in artistic production or their exclusion from it.

ART 104   Broude, N. and Garrard, M.D. (eds.)
FEMINISM AND ART HISTORY (New York: Harper and Row, 1982)

These essays reconsider, from a feminist perspective, some of the standing assumptions of the discipline of art history and hold out the possibility of the alteration of art history itself, its methodology and theory. A full range of historical periods, figures and themes are included.

ART 105   Ewen, Stuart and Ewen, Elizabeth
CHANNELS OF DESIRE: MASS IMAGERY AND THE SHAPING OF THE AMERICAN CONSCIOUSNESS (New York: McGraw-Hill, 1982)

Describes the way oppositional styles in art attempt to subvert dominant ideologies.

ART 106　　Kuhn, Annette
　　　　　　WOMEN'S PICTURES: FEMINISM AND THE
　　　　　　CINEMA (London: Routledge & Kegan Paul, 1982)

　　　　　　Kuhn asks how counter is counter cinema. She explains terminology and examines real alternatives for feminist film analysis and for feminist film-making comparing mainstream and alternative cinema. Using Lacanian psychoanalytic theory she argues that feminist cinema can be a new form of expression.

ART 107　　Neuls-Bates, Carol
　　　　　　WOMEN IN MUSIC: AN ANTHOLOGY OF
　　　　　　SOURCE READINGS FROM THE MIDDLE AGES
　　　　　　TO THE PRESENT (New York: Harper and Row, 1982)

　　　　　　A key collection of articles, interviews, biographies and letters all describing the lack of scope for women musicians in performance and the role of education and musical training.

ART 108　　Banner, Lois
　　　　　　AMERICAN BEAUTY (New York: Alfred A. Knopf, 1983)

　　　　　　An attempt to retrieve fashion for feminism. Banner argues that women's creativity in dress is underrated like other feminine skills and argues that the pursuit of beauty has bound together women of different classes and ethnic groups.

ART 109　　Ferguson, Marjorie
　　　　　　FOREVER FEMININE: WOMEN'S MAGAZINES
　　　　　　AND THE CULT OF FEMININITY (London:
　　　　　　Heinemann, 1983)

　　　　　　This lays the foundation for a sociology of women's magazines. Ferguson compares British and American magazines looking at the interaction of their messages to women with the impact of social, cultural and economic change upon their female audiences. She makes an institutional analysis of magazine production using a combination of methods and sources: content analysis, interviews, observations, documentations, statistics.

ART 110 Kaplan, Ann E.
WOMEN AND FILM (New York: Methuen, 1983)

An account of, and introduction to, film theory and how it applies to the representation of women. She summarises the debate about realism in feminist film criticism very well and gives interesting accounts of the work of contemporary European, British and American women filmmakers.

ART 111 Kelly, Mary
POST-PARTUM DOCUMENT (London: Routledge & Kegan Paul, 1983)

'Conceived' as an exhibition in the late 1970s. There are six documents and an introduction by Lucy Lippard, together with a reprinted selection of review articles. Kelly documents her experience of childbirth and child care and the formation of the unconscious, in an attempt to break with a traditional iconography of madonna and child.

ART 112 'Woman: The Arts 1 and 2', *Massachusetts Review* XXIV 1 and 2 (Spring/Summer 1983)

Two special issues which contain a huge range of contemporary women's art and literature. There are introductions to Latin American writing, Native American art, photodocumentaries of Shaker women, theatre pieces; essays on Ethel Smyth and women's music; on feminist theatre, women's sculpture; portraits by women and feminist criticism.

ART 113 Reinhardt, N. S.
New Directions for Feminist Criticism in Theatre and the Related Arts', A FEMINIST PERSPECTIVE IN THE ACADEMY, eds. Langland, E. and Gore, W. (Chicago: University of Chicago Press, 1983)

A thorough account of the different uses of theatre by men and women in terms of imagery, space and costume.

ART 114 Rosenberg, Jan
WOMEN'S REFLECTIONS: THE FEMINIST FILM MOVEMENT (Ann Arbor: University of Michigan Press, 1983)

A history and documentation of the feminist movement largely in terms of the realist and documentary film.

ART 115 Rubinstein, Charlotte Streifer
AMERICAN WOMEN ARTISTS: FROM EARLY INDIAN TIMES TO THE PRESENT (Boston, Mass.: G. K. Hall and Co., 1983)

Rubinstein describes the relation between women's art and their social and cultural circumstances. It is arranged chronologically with chapters on native American women, the 1960s feminist art movement and a bibliography.

ART 116 Anscombe, Isabelle
A WOMAN'S TOUCH: WOMEN IN DESIGN FROM 1860 TO THE PRESENT DAY (London; Virago, 1984)

This describes the history of design focusing in particular on the work of the constructivist Stepanova and examining the influence of feminism on designers such as Poiret.

ART 117 Brundsdon, Charlotte
FILMS FOR WOMEN (London: BFI, 1984)

Films discussed range from *Julia*, *Coma* and other Hollywood products to avant-garde and political films. Topics included are sexual stereotyping, pornography, fiction vs. documentary and strategies for distribution.

Arts, Film, Theatre, Media, Music

ART 118   Doane, Mary Ann et al. (eds.)
RE-VISION: ESSAYS IN FEMINIST FILM
CRITICISM (Los Angeles, CA.: University
Publications of America, 1984)

Issues range from the problem of determining the woman's time and place within the cinematic apparatus to an investigation into, and reclamation of genres, traditionally attributed to the female. Other questions explored include the relations between sound and image; the implication of the representation of female desire and the female 'look' in the horror film.

ART 119   Keyssar, Helene
FEMINIST THEATRE (London and New York: Macmillan, 1984)

Looks at definitions of realism, documentary and fantasy for their relevance to feminism. A useful account of the work of contemporary feminist writers such as Shange, Churchill, Gems, Wandor, O'Malley among others.

ART 120   de Lauretis, Teresa
ALICE DOESN'T: FEMINISM, SEMIOTICS, CINEMA (London: Macmillan, 1984)

An introduction to theoretical writing about semiotics with particular application to the films *Presents* and *Bad Timing*. de Lauretis addresses several issues of feminist theory including the relation between meaning and experience.

ART 121   Matrix
MAKING SPACE: WOMEN AND THE MAN-MADE ENVIRONMENT (London: Pluto Press, 1984)

A collection of essays about the new feminist architecture showing how sexist assumptions about family life and the role of women have been built into the design of our homes and cities. Seven women architects and designers set out strategies for public recognition and describe the history of past struggles.

ART 122   Parker, R.
          THE SUBVERSIVE STITCH (London: The Women's Press, 1984)

          She traces shifting notions of femininity and roles ascribed to women, through embroidery, from medieval times to today. Parker uses household accounts, women's magazines, letters, novels and art works to look at the way embroidery is used by women to negotiate the constraints of the feminine role. 100 photographs.

ART 123   Todd, Susan (ed.)
          WOMEN AND THEATRE: CALLING THE SHOTS (London: Faber and Faber, 1984)

          First-hand accounts of aspects of women's work in the theatre from British actresses, directors and writers. It contains many descriptions and critiques, from a feminist perspective, of acting roles, contemporary and Shakespeare's plays, lighting production and stage design.

ART 124   Ecker, G. (ed.)
          FEMINIST AESTHETICS (London: Women's Press, 1985)

          A collection of current feminist work in Germany. There are essays on feminist architecture, writing, photography, art, music and theoretical discussion of concepts of essentialism, matriarchal mythology and the conditions for women's independent artistic development.

ART 125   Gentile, Mary C.
          FILM FEMINISMS: THEORY AND PRACTICE (Westport, CT.: Greenwood Press, 1985)

          An introduction to a range of theories including Eisenstein and Bazin applied to mainstream and feminist films. Discussion of Mészàros, Sander, Rainer, Gorris among others. An interesting mixture of linguistic and feminist ideas.

ART 126   Kent, Sarah and Morreau, Jacqueline (eds.)
WOMEN'S IMAGES OF MEN (London: Writers and Readers, 1985)

Based on an exhibition of women's work at the ICA gallery in London in 1980. There are interviews and articles with women artists and critics on three issues: the rebirth of figurative art; the use of art for political comment; and the emergence of women artists as an important force in the art world. They look at themes such as the potential of the male nude, uses of anthropology and feminism and photography.

ART 127   Kuhn, Annette
THE POWER OF THE IMAGE: ESSAYS ON REPRESENTATION AND SEXUALITY (London: Routledge & Kegan Paul, 1985)

Kuhn looks at the construction of femininity and masculinity in cross-dressing films such as *Some Like It Hot*; the relationship of text and sexuality in *The Big Sleep*; and VD propaganda films of the turn of the century.

ART 128   Warner, Marina
MONUMENTS AND MAIDENS: THE ALLEGORY OF THE FEMALE FORM (London: Wiedenfeld and Nicolson, 1985)

Warner draws on myth, poetry, painting and sculpture to pose questions about the use of images of women such as Britannia or the Statue of Liberty. She describes the legacy of Greek culture and myth to the female presence today and current political and movie imagery. This text builds on Warner's early work on Joan of Arc and the Virgin Mary.

ART 129   Wilson, Elizabeth
ADORNED IN DREAMS: FASHION AND MODERNITY (London: Virago, 1985)

Fashion and beautification of the self have been seen by some feminists as expressions of subordination, and Wilson argues that this simple moralising misses the richness of fashion's cultural and political meanings—that fashion can be used in liberating ways even if it remains ambiguous. She describes the history of fashion, surveys theoretical writings, the fashion industry, the influence of popular culture and the role of fashion and sub-cultures.

Psychology

This section introduces the major psychologists, psychoanalytic theories and paradigms of most interest to current feminist readers. The reference points are concepts of 'difference', 'nature', sex and gender role critiques as well as re-evaluations of the discipline.

PSY 1   Deutsch, Helene
         THE PSYCHOLOGY OF WOMEN: A PSYCHOANALYTIC INTERPRETATION (New York: Grune and Stratton, 1944/1945)

         Written by a disciple of Freud the work is important in the history of theory about the psychology of women. The themes are feminine passivity, masochism, psychology of motherhood and menopause and Deutsch believes that feminine passivity is a universal characteristic.

PSY 2   Carlson, E. R. and Carlson, R.
         'Male and Female Subjects in Personality Research', *Journal of Abnormal and Social Psychology* 61 (1961) 482–3

         The first in a subsequent series of critiques about the well-known bias against using female subjects in psychology research. They describe how men and women are treated differently in apparently objective research.

PSY 3   Horney, Karen
         FEMININE PSYCHOLOGY (New York: Norton, 1967)

         This is a reprint of *New Ways in Psychoanalysis* (New York: Norton, 1939). Known primarily for her theoretical differences with Freud and for her essay 'The Dread of Women', *International Journal of Psychoanalysis XIII* (1932), Horney writes about frigidity, monogamy, and feminine masochism. She describes the resentment harboured by all men toward women which expresses itself in phallocentric thinking; in the devaluation of motherhood and in a generally misogynist civilisation.

PSY 4   Bernard, Jessie
THE SEX GAME (Englewood Cliffs, N.J.: Prentice-Hall, 1968)

Bernard describes technological changes in the structure of sex relationships and concludes that each generation has to live out its own sex destiny.

PSY 5   Lewis, E. C.
DEVELOPING WOMAN'S POTENTIAL (Ames, Iowa: Iowa State University Press, 1968)

Lewis describes the biased interpretation of biased data in past psychology which was trying to prove that career women are maladjusted.

PSY 6   Bardwick, Judith et al. (eds.)
FEMININE PERSONALITY AND CONFLICT (Belmont, CA.: Brooks/Cole, 1970)

Descriptions of biological and social factors together with psychoanalysis that contribute to definitions of femininity. Includes discussion of adolescence and psychological conflict and reproduction.

PSY 7   Broverman, Inge et al.
'Sex-role Stereotypes and Clinical Judgements of Mental Health', *Journal of Consulting and Clinical Psychology* 34 (February 1970), 1–7

The authors show how women are socialised into mental illness and conclude that a paradigm of 'adjustment' is inappropriate to women.

PSY 8   Chasseguet-Smirgel, Janine (ed.)
FEMALE SEXUALITY: NEW PSYCHOANALYTIC VIEWS (Ann Arbor: University of Michigan Press, 1970)

The author challenges Millett's account of penis envy and argues a convincing case for seeing female penis envy as a manifestation of a little girl's need to establish her own identity as separate from the mother. A process which the author claims is essential for female creativity. This represents the French mode of psychoanalysis and contains a historical review of the main studies of femininity by Freud, his followers and his opponents.

PSY 9 Bardwick, J. M.
THE PSYCHOLOGY OF WOMEN: A STUDY OF BIO-CULTURAL CONFLICTS (New York: Harper and Row, 1971)

Describes the psychodynamics of middle-class American women. The topics examined include motivation in work; arguments with traditional psychology and sex differences in personality.

PSY 10 Sherman, J. A.
ON THE PSYCHOLOGY OF WOMEN: A SURVEY OF EMPIRICAL STUDIES (Springfield, Ill.: C. C. Thomas, 1971)

A review of literature about the psychology of women collected before the new emphasis inspired by the women's movement shifted the direction of research toward motivational theory. Sherman's book emphasises biology because the author feels that the reproductive cycle is inexorably connected to psychological response.

PSY 11 Ulanov, Ann Belford
THE FEMININE: IN JUNGIAN PSYCHOLOGY AND CHRISTIAN THEOLOGY (Evanston, Ill.: Northwestern University Press, 1971)

The author explores various aspects of the feminine as a style of consciousness not restricted to women alone, but common to men as well. She feels that the suppression of the female has been detrimental to Western modes of thought for both sexes and suggests that the androgynous psyche is the next step toward a psychological ideal.

PSY 12   Weisstein, N.
'Psychology Constructs the Female', ROLES WOMEN PLAY: READING TOWARDS WOMEN'S LIBERATION (Belmont, CA.: Brooks/Cole, 1971) ed. M. H. Garskof.

The first phase of research about the depiction of woman as victim. The author shows how in the division of characteristics that governed sex-role stereotyping women have received the worst of the deal. This follows on from Weisstein's work 'Kinder, Kuche, Kirche' in *Sisterhood is Powerful* ed. R. Morgan.

PSY 13   Bardwick, J. M. (ed.)
READINGS ON THE PSYCHOLOGY OF WOMEN (New York: Harper and Row, 1972)

This is a collection of 47 theory and research papers divided into seven sections: the development of sex differences; socialisation; the women's liberation movement; inter-cultural comparisons; criteria of mental health and theories of psychoanalysis.

PSY 14   Chesler, Phyllis
WOMEN AND MADNESS (New York: Doubleday, 1972)

The classic text of feminist psychoanalysis. Chesler argues that psychotherapy and hospitalisation are forms of patriarchal control. She discusses the psychological dimensions of female personality in our culture and the patient careers of 60 women together with analysis of mental illness statistics from 1950 to 1969. She concludes that sex-role stereotypes are the cause of so-called mental illness.

PSY 15   Horner, Matina S.
'Toward an Understanding of Achievement-Related Conflicts in Women', *Journal of Social Issues* 28: 2 (1972), pp. 157–75

A new account of achievement motivation and fear of success in women. Horner's work catalysed and changed this whole area of research in her refocusing of the field.

PSY 16   Sherfey, Mary Jane
         THE NATURE AND EVOLUTION OF FEMALE
         SEXUALITY (New York: Random House, 1972)

         This has new information about female biology and sexuality and their relation to psychology, based on Sherfey's discovery of the inductor theory in medical literature (i.e. that the mammalian male is derived from the female). Since all embryos start from the female this has significant implications for psychiatry and it directly contradicts Freudian theory that the clitoris is a vestigial organ.

PSY 17   Weinberg, Martin and Bell, Man
         HOMOSEXUALITY: AN ANNOTATED
         BIBLIOGRAPHY FROM THE KINSEY
         INSTITUTE (New York: Harper and Row, 1972)

         Some references to psychiatric studies of lesbians usually by men. None explicitly points in a feminist direction or are undertaken by feminists but the findings establish that where lesbian groups are assessed for personality disorders—very few were found. The articles assessed are mainly psychometric and physiological, but do pay attention to a wide range of homosexual adjustment.

PSY 18   Miller, Jean Baker (ed.)
         PSYCHOANALYSIS AND WOMEN:
         CONTRIBUTIONS TO NEW THEORY AND
         THERAPY (New York: Brunner/Mazal, 1973;
         Harmondsworth: Penguin, 1973)

         An anthology of writings on women by psychoanalysts. Articles include Horney's 'The Flight from Womanhood', Sherfey's 'On the Nature of Female Sexuality' among others.

PSY 19   Denmark, Florence (ed.)
         WHO DISCRIMINATES AGAINST WOMEN?
         (Beverley Hills, CA.: Sage, 1974)

         This book grew out of the American Psychological Association Conference in 1972. The paper deals with some sources of discrimination against women, for example by parents, by men, by social institutions and by other women.

PSY 20   Maccoby, Eleanor and Jacklin, Carol Nagy
THE PSYCHOLOGY OF SEX DIFFERENCES (Palo Alto, CA.: Stanford University Press, 1974)

A landmark book bringing together current scholarship on male/female differences in social behaviour, intellectual abilities, motivation and aspiration. A summary of 1400 pieces of research which concludes that there are few sex differences.

PSY 21   Mitchell, Juliet
PSYCHOANALYSIS AND FEMINISM (London: Allen Lane, 1974; New York: Pantheon, 1974)

This reassesses Freudian psychology to develop an understanding of the psychology of femininity and its ideological oppression of women. By analysing sexuality, femininity and the family as treated in the works of Freud, Reich and Laing, she demonstrates that Freud's theories have much to offer women in understanding their sexuality. The book shows a movement in feminist criticism to a concern with meanings and the human psyche.

PSY 22   Strouse, Jean (ed.)
WOMEN AND ANALYSIS: DIALOGUES ON PSYCHOANALYTIC VIEWS OF FEMININITY (New York: Grossman Publishers, 1974)

A group of writings by well-known members of the psychoanalytic movement on women's issues. The Freudian articles are each followed by an essay with critical or dissenting viewpoints. There is also an essay by Barbara Gelpi on the androgyne.

PSY 23   Breen, D.
THE BIRTH OF A FIRST CHILD: TOWARDS AN UNDERSTANDING OF FEMININITY (London: Tavistock, 1975)

Breen specifically concentrates on women's reactions to birth and definitions of women's experience rather than describing the evolution of childhood.

PSY 24 Hammer, Signe
DAUGHTERS AND MOTHERS: MOTHERS AND DAUGHTERS (New York: Quadrangle Books, 1975)

A study of the psychology of the mother–daughter relationship using interviews with over 75 women.

PSY 25 Mander, Anica Vesel, and Rush, Anne Kent
FEMINISM AS THERAPY (New York: Random House, 1975)

This is an important statement by pioneers who used women's groups to create personal changes. It attempts to deprofessionalise therapy and to show women that political understanding and peer support can bring about personal change.

PSY 26 Unger, Rhoda Kesler and Denmark, Florence L. (eds.)
WOMAN: DEPENDENT OR INDEPENDENT VARIABLE (New York: Psychological Dimensions, 1975)

This collection defines the new psychology of women with research pieces on all aspects of women's psychology.

PSY 27 Chesler, Phyllis and Goodman, E. J.
WOMEN, MONEY AND POWER (New York: W. W. Morrow, 1976)

This deals with the taboo topic of how women can redefine their attitudes to power and directly confront male supremacy.

PSY 28 Dinnerstein, Dorothy
THE MERMAID AND THE MINOTAUR: SEXUAL ARRANGEMENTS AND HUMAN MALAISE (New York: Harper and Row, 1976)

Dinnerstein gives an explanation of men's fear of women which she argues is due to women's monopoly of mothering. This makes men find their need for women too overwhelming. She concludes that the fateful symbiosis of minotaur and mermaid should end so that all human beings, male and female, could embody all aspects of the human.

PSY 29   Kaplan, Alexandra and Bean, Joan (eds.)
BEYOND SEX-ROLE STEREOTYPES: READINGS TOWARD A PSYCHOLOGY OF ANDROGYNY
(Boston: Little, Brown, 1976)

Essays critiquing mental health and therapy. It includes Sandra Bem's 'Sex-Role Inventory (BSRI)' a design for an androgynous test. Bem discovers that the brightest people tested were the most androgynous and argues that problems of sex-role stereotyping could be eliminated by androgyny.

PSY 30   Laws, J. L.
'Work Aspiration of Women', *Signs* I (1976), 33–49

This documents the effect of bias in the area of work and work motivation. Laws notes that women who work outside the home are assumed to be deviant.

PSY 31   Maccoby, Eleanor (ed.)
THE DEVELOPMENT OF SEX DIFFERENCES
(Palo Alto, CA.: Stanford University Press, 1976)

An excellent collection of essays by psychologists concerned with the theory of sex differences. There are essays on intellectual functioning, cultural institutions and a standard reference bibliography.

PSY 32   Miller, Jean Baker (ed.)
TOWARD A NEW PSYCHOLOGY OF WOMEN
(Boston, Mass.: Beacon Press, 1976)

Miller's key term is 'affiliation'—the acquisition of a sense of self through relationships derived from early symbolic bonds between mother and female infant. Psychoanalysis itself, Miller argues, only became necessary because aspects of affiliation were dissociated from culture. In a better society facts about women's psychology that are treated as aspects of their inferiority would become the building blocks of a more humane culture—autonomy for example could be part of affiliation with others. The first important expression of a woman-centred analysis.

PSY 33 Roberts, J. I. (ed.)
BEYOND INTELLECTUAL SEXISM: A NEW WOMAN, A NEW REALITY (New York: McKay, 1976)

An analysis of the intellectual establishment, guided by the feminist view that we must examine behaviour in a socio-political context.

PSY 34 Williams, Elizabeth Friar
NOTES OF A FEMINIST THERAPIST (New York: Praeger, 1976)

A personal account which argues that a feminist therapist must be supportive rather than an expert. She sees two major outcomes of feminist therapy: that women should see themselves and other women as being as worthy as men and that women should experience self-esteem in the roles that they have chosen.

PSY 35 Donelson, Elaine and Gullahorn, Jeanne (eds.)
WOMEN: A PSYCHOLOGICAL PERSPECTIVE (New York: John Wiley, 1977)

This anthology is intended as a text for undergraduates in psychology and women's studies. Topics include sex-typed behaviour, the quest for androgyny as well as those from biology.

PSY 36 Friday, Nancy
MY MOTHER/MY SELF: THE DAUGHTER'S SEARCH FOR IDENTITY (New York: Delacorte Press, 1977)

The thesis of this book is that daughters reflect in their own lives many aspects of their mothers. A populist text, it is interesting for its autobiography and because Friday consulted women such as Pauline Bart, Helene Deutsch and Fuchs Epstein. Friday's earlier work, *My Secret Garden: Women's Sexual Fantasies* (Trident Press, 1973) is a compilation of women's fantasies.

PSY 37   O'Leary, Virginia
TOWARD UNDERSTANDING WOMEN (Monterey, CA.: Brooks/Cole, 1977)

This is designed as an introductory text in the psychology of women with a particular focus on biology, psychology and sex roles. It is interesting because O'Leary combines extensive discussion of the empirical literature with references to her personal experiences.

PSY 38   Rawlings, Edna and Carter, Dianne (eds.)
PSYCHOTHERAPY FOR WOMEN: TREATMENT TOWARD EQUALITY (Springfield, Ill.: C.C. Thomas, 1977)

Papers seeking to incorporate the theoretical frameworks of feminism and radical therapy into psychotherapy. Readings include non-sexist psychotherapy; assertion training; psychotherapy for lesbians; social activism as therapy. There is a feminist bibliography.

PSY 39   Roy, Maria (ed.)
BATTERED WOMEN: A PSYCHOSOCIOLOGICAL STUDY OF DOMESTIC VIOLENCE (New York: Van Nostrand Reinhold, 1977)

An anthology of articles by psychiatrists, sociologists, criminologists and others collected by the director of Abused Women's Aid in Crisis Inc., a New York City organisation helping battered women. Included are articles on the history of wife-beating, demography and legal solutions and future trends.

PSY 40   Sherman, J. A. and Denmark, F. L. (eds.)
THE PSYCHOLOGY OF WOMEN: FUTURE
DIRECTIONS FOR RESEARCH (New York:
Psychological Dimensions, 1977)

This contains essays such as one by M. Parke attacking psychology as a discipline; by R. Nelson 'Creativity in Women' a trenchant critique of creativity research; by Denmark and others on achievement motivation; by S. Bem on psychological sex-typing and by P. Schwarz on the social psychology of female sexuality.

PSY 41   Tauvis, Carol and Offir, Carole
THE LONGEST WAR: SEX DIFFERENCES IN
PERSPECTIVE (New York: Harcourt, Brace
Jovanovich, 1977)

This surveys the sociological and psychological research on sex role socialisation. The authors have a moderate feminist perspective.

PSY 42   Troll, Israel J. and Israel K.
LOOKING AHEAD: A WOMEN'S GUIDE TO THE
WOMEN'S PROBLEMS AND JOYS OF GROWING
OLDER (Englewood Cliffs, N.J.: Prentice-Hall, 1977)

This sparked a resurgence of interest in studies about the psychology of older women by dispelling some myths.

PSY 43   Williams, Juanita
PSYCHOLOGY OF WOMEN: BEHAVIOR IN A
BIOSOCIAL CONTEXT (New York: W. W. Norton,
1977)

An introductory text for courses in the psychology of women it covers the topics of myths, stereotypes, sex differences, childbirth, sexuality, deviance and ageing. The aim is to understand psychology within its social context.

PSY 44 Chodorow, Nancy
THE REPRODUCTION OF MOTHERING: PSYCHOANALYSIS AND THE SOCIOLOGY OF GENDER (Berkeley, CA.: University of California Press, 1978)

A highly influential account of female identity. Chodorow shows the failure of psychoanalytic theories to account for the reproduction of mothering. Using the theory of object-relations from Freud Chodorow describes the divergent experiences of girls and boys in the pre-Oedipal period. Female core gender identity comes from an unresolved relationship with the mother while boys define the masculine as that which is not the mother. This explains why the feminine has been repressed in our culture.

PSY 45 Frieze, Irene H. et al. (eds.)
WOMEN AND SEX ROLES: A SOCIAL PSYCHOLOGICAL PERSPECTIVE (New York: W. W. Norton, 1978)

Intended as a text for courses in psychology, sociology and women's studies the topics are sex roles, theories of feminine personality, cognitive-development theories, life decisions and others.

PSY 46 Keller, Evelyn Fox
'Gender and Science', *Psychoanalysis and Contemporary Thought* I (1978)

Keller attacks the commonplace of western culture which associates 'maleness' with science and scientific inquiry. She argues that this is a distortion and becoming outdated, and that there is a fundamental congruence between maleness, as culturally defined and the scientific worldview which dominates western thought. Dissociating herself from some feminists, Keller argues that scientific research should be separated from its genderised impulse to domination.

PSY 47 Leeson, Joyce and Gray, Judith
WOMEN AND MEDICINE (London: Tavistock, 1978)

About the treatment women receive from the medical professions. Authors describe the relation doctors make between women's psychology and women's 'complaints'; and how natural events such as menstrual pain are seen as deviant.

PSY 48 Orbach, Susie
FAT IS A FEMINIST ISSUE (London: Paddington Press, 1978)

Orbach is co-founder of the Women's Therapy Centre, London. She gives case histories and analysis of existing psychiatric theories on diet and women from a feminist perspective. There are practical exercises.

PSY 49 Sherman, J. A.
SEX-RELATED COGNITIVE DIFFERENCES: AN ESSAY ON THEORY AND EVIDENCE (Springfield, Ill.: C. C. Thomas, 1978)

A comprehensive review and evaluation of the theory that women's and men's brains are different in psychologically important ways. Sherman carefully shows that this is unsupportable on scientific grounds.

PSY 50 Balmary, M.
PSYCHOANALYZING PSYCHOANALYSIS: FREUD AND THE HIDDEN FAULT OF THE FATHER (Baltimore, MD.: Johns Hopkins Press, 1979)

Balmary argues that Freud was wrong to stop believing his patients and gives a feminist redress of Freud's morphology and case histories.

PSY 51 Gullahorn, Jeanne (ed.)
PSYCHOLOGY AND WOMEN: IN TRANSITION (New York: John Wiley, 1979)

This contains essays by D. P. Waber, M. Komarovsky, E. Douvan and R. Kulka, E. Mavis Hetherington, Marthe Cox and Roger Cox, Eleanor E. Maccoby, Janet T. Spence, Martha Mednick. It is based on the premise that one of the goals of the psychology of women is the development of a non-sexist psychology. Encompassing many aspects of women's social relationships, it contains critiques of sociobiology, divorce research, personality research.

PSY 52 MacLeod, Sheila
THE ART OF STARVATION (London: Virago, 1981)

An account of anorexia nervosa explored in psychology, autobiography, myth and literature. McLeod's is an interesting analysis of recent psychiatric theories which she compares to her own autobiographical responses.

PSY 53 Eichenbaum, L. and Orbach, S.
OUTSIDE IN . . . INSIDE OUT: WOMEN'S PSYCHOLOGY, A FEMINIST PSYCHOANALYTIC APPROACH (Harmondsworth: Penguin, 1982)

The authors describe new developmental models of women's psychology together with a radical reappraisal of the mother–daughter relationship and its impact on gender. The book is invaluable for its first-hand accounts of feminist therapy and counselling and its strategies for feminist psychotherapy.

PSY 54 Fliegel, Zenia Odes
'Half a Century Later: Current Status of Freud's Controversial Views on Women', *Psychoanalytic Review* 69: 1 (1982), 7–28

Fliegel shows that Freud was mistaken about the formation of female gender identity and about the formation of the desire to mother since he underestimated the pre-Oedipal. The article includes a full bibliography.

PSY 55 Gallop, Jane
THE DAUGHTER'S SEDUCTION: FEMINISM AND PSYCHOANALYSIS (London: Macmillan, 1982; Ithaca, N.Y.: Cornell University Press, 1982)

The book examines the relation between contemporary feminism and the psychoanalytic theories of Jacques Lacan. Through readings of the major texts of French theory, Gallop addresses such topics as sexual difference, desire, reading, writing, power, family, phallocentrism.

PSY 56 Gilligan, Carol
IN A DIFFERENT VOICE: ESSAYS ON PSYCHOLOGICAL THEORY AND WOMEN'S DEVELOPMENT (Cambridge, Mass.: Harvard University Press, 1982)

A full analysis of female moral development which converges in part with the theories of Chodorow and Jean Baker Miller. Gilligan, relying on Chodorow's view of female gender identity, describes a female perception of morality as one connected with responsibilities to others while males' relate primarily to the balancing of rights. Unlike Chodorow, however, Gilligan speaks of a 'marriage' between male and female styles of moral development and is therefore closer to the androgyny school of feminist psychology than to a woman-centred perspective.

History

Works listed here are works on the United States and Britain clustering around family history, suffrage, socialist and labour movements, prostitution, education history and the history of women's work. Feminist historiography and revisionist feminist history is a particularly fruitful area in feminist criticism.

HIST 1   Beard, Mary Ritter
WOMEN AS A FORCE IN HISTORY: A STUDY IN TRADITIONS AND REALITIES (New York: Macmillan, 1946; Reprint New York: Octagon Books, 1976)

A classic example of early feminist historiography. Beard examines the subjugation of women in the light of historical reality and of women's actual participation in work. She proves that women have made a much greater contribution to the economy than simply by producing children.

HIST 2   Hewitt, Margaret
WIVES AND MOTHERS IN VICTORIAN INDUSTRY (London: Rockliff, 1958; Westport, Conn.: Greenwood Press, 1975)

Hewitt documents the mid-nineteenth-century exploitation of women, in particular noting the influence of changes in the factory system on the homes and families of those employed in the mills and factories.

HIST 3   Flexner, Eleanor (ed.)
CENTURY OF STRUGGLE: THE WOMEN'S RIGHTS MOVEMENT IN THE UNITED STATES (Cambridge, Mass.: Harvard University Press, 1959)

There are three substantial sections: women in the colonial era, the first steps towards education and reform and the Seneca Falls Convention of 1848; women's organisations including the suffrage movement and women's role in early labour unions; the crusade for the right to vote 1900-1920. Among other ideas, the authors discuss the use of anti-slavery campaigns by women to enable them to speak publicly and show how the possibility of power for women has historically been befogged by sentimentality.

HIST 4   Banks, J. A. and Olive
FEMINISM AND FAMILY PLANNING IN VICTORIAN ENGLAND (Liverpool: Liverpool University Press, 1964; New York: Schocken, 1964)

The authors' aims are to be of value to population policy-makers and revitalise feminism. They study changes in middle-class life; the relationship of feminism to the birth rate, and give reasons for the fall in fertility. There is a pertinent case study of the relationship between social movements and social change.

HIST 5   Davies, Stella
LIVING THROUGH THE INDUSTRIAL REVOLUTION (London: Routledge & Kegan Paul, 1966)

Davies describes the change in women's relationship to productivity from their monopolies (particularly in brewing) and home factories to family labour.

HIST 6   Benston, M.
THE POLITICAL ECONOMY OF WOMEN'S LIBERATION (New York: Monthly Review Press, 1970)

Benston is a Marxist-feminist who uses the tools of class analysis to reveal the differences between Marxism and women's history.

HIST 7   Rover, C.
LOVE, MORALS AND THE FEMINISTS (London: Routledge & Kegan Paul, 1970)

This discusses divorce, prostitution and sexual morality, examining Victorian codes and their relation to women's emancipation. The works of J. Butler, Annie Besant, Marie Stopes and Victoria Woodhull are considered.

HIST 8   Scott, Anne Firor
THE SOUTHERN LADY: FROM PEDESTAL TO POLITICS 1830–1930 (Chicago: University of Chicago Press, 1970)

Scott describes the stereotype of the Southern woman as the submissive homemaker but asserts that the reality was quite different. She relates the changes brought about by the Civil War and increasing education and notes the struggle for the right to vote and the changing image of the 1920s. The book contains an excellent bibliographical essay on sources.

HIST 9   Chmaj, Betty E. (ed.)
AMERICAN WOMEN AND AMERICAN STUDIES (Pittsburgh: Know, 1971)

Shows how even leading historical theories such as Turner's theory of the frontier and American character deal only with males.

HIST 10   Fussell, G. E. and Fussell, K.
THE ENGLISH COUNTRY WOMAN: A FARMHOUSE SOCIAL HISTORY A.D. 1500–1900 (New York: Benjamin Blom, 1971)

The work is profusely illustrated and the authors give specific attention to folk life.

HIST 11   Greenwald, Maurine
'On Teaching Women's History', AMERICAN WOMEN AND AMERICAN STUDIES ed. B. E. Chmaj (Pittsburgh: Know, 1971)

Greenwald demonstrates that a male bias not only determines what is selected for study but how it is interpreted. She feels that the particularly unexplored areas of history are descriptions of women slaves, servants and immigrants buried in court records and travelogues.

HIST 12   Hole, J. and Levine, E.
THE REBIRTH OF FEMINISM (New York: Quadrangle, 1971)

A study of the resurgence of feminism—its history, origins, development, philosophy, issues and activities. The authors analyse the roots of the contemporary women's movement and include a chronology from 1961–1971 of representative events and activities concerning women's issues. They focus on particular areas of concern to contemporary feminism such as abortion, child care, education, the image of women, and entry into the professions.

HIST 13   Lerner, Gerda
THE WOMEN IN AMERICAN HISTORY (Menlo Park, CA.: Addison-Wesley, 1971)

Lerner divides the history of women into four chronological periods, analysing their role in the home, as citizens and as employees. She contends that despite discrimination women have been a major force in history.

HIST 14   Lerner, Gerda (ed.)
BLACK WOMEN IN WHITE AMERICA: A DOCUMENTARY HISTORY (New York: Pantheon Books, 1972)

An early attempt to include the experience of black women in American history. Lerner shows that black women were given greater educational opportunities than black men.

HIST 15   Smith-Rosenberg, Carroll
'The Hysterical Woman: Sex Roles and Role Conflict in Nineteenth Century America', *Social Research* XLIX (Winter 1972) 652–78

A stimulus to the history of sexuality and the history of

families. The author describes lesbianism as part of women's culture and equates domesticity with subordination as a source of women's illness and frustration.

HIST 16   Bullough, Vern and Bullough, Bonnie
THE SUBORDINATE SEX: A HISTORY OF ATTITUDES TOWARDS WOMEN (Urbana, Ill.: University of Illinois Press, 1973)

The authors trace attitudes to women in a variety of cultures from the ancient Near East to modern America paying special attention to Islam, China and India.

HIST 17   Davidoff, Leonore
THE BEST CIRCLES: WOMEN AND SOCIETY IN VICTORIAN ENGLAND (London: Croom Helm, 1973; Totowa, N.J.: Rowman and Littlefield, 1973)

Davidoff amalgamates history with sociology to examine bourgeois controls over women's mobility and to show how patterns of London society contributed to Victorian ideas of the family. Victorian bourgeois ideology attributed ancillary roles to women as decorative guardians of the home and social order.

HIST 18   Ehrenreich, Barbara and English, Deirdre
WITCHES, MIDWIVES AND NURSES: A HISTORY OF WOMEN HEALERS (Old Westbury: Feminist Press, 1973; London: Writers and Readers, 1973)

This presents a valid history of women as healers, as 'good' witches in anthropology, offering a new perspective on women's health and skills.

HIST 19   O'Faolain, Julia and Martines, Lauro (eds.)
NOT IN GOD'S IMAGE: WOMEN IN HISTORY FROM THE GREEKS TO THE VICTORIANS (New York: Harper and Row, 1973)

The focus is on women in European societies. The authors collate testimonies to present a close-up picture of the lives of ordinary women from different classes.

HIST 20   Rowbotham, Sheila
          HIDDEN FROM HISTORY: 300 YEARS OF
          WOMEN'S OPPRESSION AND THE FIGHT
          AGAINST IT (London: Pluto Press, 1973)

          One of the first contemporary feminist historians in
          Britain, Rowbotham's book is a product of her involve-
          ment in the women's liberation movement. Examining
          material on birth control, abortion and female sexuality;
          on the relationship of women's oppression and class
          exploitation Rowbotham concludes that 'a socialist
          feminism is again possible in the world'.

HIST 21   Thonnessen, W.
          THE EMANCIPATION OF WOMEN: THE RISE
          AND DECLINE OF THE WOMEN'S MOVEMENT
          IN GERMAN SOCIAL DEMOCRACY 1863–1933
          (London: Pluto Press, 1973)

          An original edition first published in 1969 which describes
          phases in political attitudes to the women's movement,
          theories of women and emancipation and changes in state
          and party ideologies.

HIST 22   Vicinus, Martha (ed.)
          SUFFER AND BE STILL: WOMEN IN THE
          VICTORIAN AGE (Bloomington: Indiana University
          Press, 1973)

          This examines class stereotypes and femininity in
          Victorian England, the rise of domestic ideology and the
          depiction of working women in Victorian painting.
          Contributors include Kate Millett, Elaine Showalter
          among others.

HIST 23   Altbach, E. H.
          WOMEN IN AMERICA (Lexington, Mass.: D. C.
          Heath, 1974)

          Intended as a general introduction to the history of
          American women the text is divided into four sections:
          domestic history; women at work; the women's move-
          ment; and the new feminism. Altbach concentrates on

what she calls 'ordinary female lives' rather than the exceptional women.

HIST 24　　Banner, L. W.
WOMEN IN MODERN AMERICA: A BRIEF HISTORY (New York: Harcourt Brace Jovanovich, 1974)

Banner divides the modern history of women into three parts: 1890–1920 a period of active feminism; 1920–1960 a period of inactive feminism; 1960 to the present with radical feminism. She situates her analysis of women's activity in the social history of each period.

HIST 25　　Hartmann, Mary S. and Banner, Louis W. (eds.)
CLIO'S CONSCIOUSNESS RAISED: NEW PERSPECTIVES ON THE HISTORY OF WOMEN (New York: Harper and Row, 1974)

These papers were given at the Berkshire Conference of Women Historians held in 1973 and avoid the biographical approach of the first feminist historians to deal with women in groups. The collection includes essays by Judith Walkowitz on the Contagious Diseases Act, P. Branca on Victorian household incomes and Laura Oren on the welfare of working-class women in Britain.

HIST 26　　Kelly, Joan
WOMEN'S HISTORY (Bronxville, N.Y.: Sarah Lawrence College, 1974)

As an early collection of references the study is, by necessity, short but Kelly provides useful background ranging from antiquity through to the industrial society.

HIST 27　　Sochen, June
HERSTORY: A WOMAN'S VIEW OF AMERICAN HISTORY (New York: Alfred A. Knopf, 1974)

Looks at information generally omitted from standard American histories in particular examining the white American male's denigration of blacks, native Americans and the natural environment.

HIST 28   Thompson, R.
WOMEN IN STUART ENGLAND AND AMERICA:
A COMPARATIVE STUDY (London: Routledge &
Kegan Paul, 1974)

A monograph dealing with specific aspects of women's history.

HIST 29   Branca, P.
SILENT SISTERHOOD: MIDDLE-CLASS WOMEN
IN THE VICTORIAN HOME (London: Croom
Helm, 1975)

Branca demonstrates that gentility and leisure were typical only of women of the *upper* middle classes and she analyses the physical and emotional burdens placed on the majority of women of middling rank by three events: the rising standard of living; the shock of modernisation; and the loneliness of new urban and suburban communities.

HIST 30   DuBois, Ellen
'The Radicalism of the Women's Suffrage Movement: Notes Toward the Reconstruction of Nineteenth-Century Feminism', *Feminist Studies* 3 (Fall 1975) 63–71

DuBois shows, by looking at the whole question of the historical meaning of suffrage, how radical the vote was for women in the context of women's roles in nineteenth-century society. Gaining the vote called into question women's traditional activities as individuals in the family.

HIST 31   Morewedge, R. T.
THE ROLE OF WOMEN IN THE MIDDLE AGES
(London: Hodder and Stoughton, 1975)

Diverse representations of women's roles in literature, visual arts, oral, illiterative communities and Renaissance society. Morewedge examines the representation of women in Gothic manuscripts and courtly romances.

HIST 32   Power, Eileen
          MEDIEVAL WOMEN (Cambridge: Cambridge
          University Press, 1975)

          Power describes the exclusion of women from guild
          membership although there is evidence of women's
          presence at all levels of production. As the division
          between amateur and professional work developed in
          the Reformation women were relegated to an amateur
          area.

HIST 33   Ryan, Mary P.
          WOMANHOOD IN AMERICA: FROM COLONIAL
          TIMES TO THE PRESENT (New York: New
          Viewpoints, 1975)

          Ryan describes historical male-conceived views of
          women. She shifts the periodisation of women's history
          into a feminist orientation.

HIST 34   Smith-Rosenberg, Carroll
          'The Female World of Love and Ritual: Relations
          Between Women in Nineteenth-Century America',
          Signs 1: 1 (Autumn 1975) 1–29

          An influential essay which contributed to the development
          of a woman-centred perspective in history with her
          emphasis on the world of women and the culture of
          domesticity. Creates a new tradition of feminist scholar-
          ship by replacing male homogeneity with female
          complexity.

HIST 35   Baxandall, Rosalyn et al. (eds.)
          AMERICA'S WORKING WOMEN (New York:
          Random House, 1976)

          The text looks at women in American history and the
          work they have done. There are good accounts of Indian
          women, women factory workers, women slaves, women
          in the industrial period and women in the labour move-
          ment up to 1975.

HIST 36   Boulding, E.
THE UNDERSIDE OF HISTORY: A VIEW OF
WOMEN THROUGH TIME (Boulder, Col.:
Westview Press, 1976)

A macro-history of the evolution of women's roles from the Paleolithic period to modern times. Boulding focuses on western history in her account of changes in agriculture, urban life and the codification of law. She gives weight to the crucial force of religion.

HIST 37   Carroll, Berenice A. (ed.)
LIBERATING WOMEN'S HISTORY:
THEORETICAL AND CRITICAL ESSAYS
(Urbana, Chicago: University of Illinois Press, 1976)

A crucial collection of 23 essays on the new feminist historiography. Contributors describe the inappropriate evolutionist stance towards women taken by male historians, the interactions between the different 'spheres' of women and argue for a more sophisticated and feminist use of single forms of historiography such as demography. Historians include Gerda Lerner, Juliet Mitchell and Sarah Pomeroy.

HIST 38   Conrad, Susan Phinney
PERISH THE THOUGHT: INTELLECTUAL
WOMEN IN ROMANTIC AMERICA 1830–1860
(New York: Oxford University Press, 1976)

Conrad believes that women of the generation of Margaret Fuller, Lydia Maria Child and Elizabeth Cady Stanton represent the first female intellectuals in America. She asserts that this was due to the stimulus of the romantic revolution.

HIST 39   Davin, Delia
WOMAN-WORK: WOMEN AND THE PARTY IN
REVOLUTIONARY CHINA (Oxford: Clarendon
Press, 1976)

An assessment of changes in the social relations of the sexes in China during the course of the twentieth century.

Davin's definitions of feminism, revolutionary history and orthodox Marxist solutions are particularly interesting.

HIST 40 Evans, R. J.
THE FEMINIST MOVEMENT IN GERMANY 1894–1933 (London and Beverly Hills: Sage, 1976)

This is the first scholarly study of the movement. It contributes to a comparative study of feminism by showing that feminism cannot be properly understood unless it is seen as an integral part of the social and political system. It describes the relationship of liberalism to feminism and attempts to delineate what radicalises women.

HIST 41 Gadol, Joan Kelly
'The Social Relation of the Sexes: Methodological Implications of Women's History', *Signs* 1 (Summer 1976) 809–23

An excellent discussion of the conceptual problems involved in periodising women's history.

HIST 42 Gordon, Linda
WOMAN'S BODY, WOMAN'S RIGHTS: A SOCIAL HISTORY OF BIRTH CONTROL IN AMERICA (New York: Grossman Publishers, 1976; Harmondsworth: Penguin, 1977)

The control of reproduction is introduced as a crucial feminist issue and Gordon demonstrates how it has always been essentially a political struggle over the right of women to win self-determination.

HIST 43 McBride, Theresa
THE DOMESTIC REVOLUTION: THE MODERNIZATION OF HOUSEHOLD SERVICES IN ENGLAND AND FRANCE 1820–1920 (London: Croom Helm, 1976; New York: Holmes and Meier, 1976)

This attempts to write the servant class into history since McBride regards the neglect of this class to come from the fact that servants were female. She shows how demographers have overlooked the contribution of servants to the formation of modern urban populations. Social and economic historians ignored servants because they had no 'exchange' value. Domestic service McBride considers to have a pivotal role in the modernisation of women.

HIST 44 Mitchell, Juliet and Oakley, Anne (eds.)
THE RIGHTS AND WRONGS OF WOMEN
(Harmondsworth: Penguin, 1976)

Including contributions from sociologists and literary critics as well as historians this provides a body of empirical knowledge on which to base the case against sexism. In essays by Leonora Davidoff and others writers reinterpret the social world from the perspective of women.

HIST 45 Bridenthal, R. and Kooz, C. (eds.)
BECOMING VISIBLE: WOMEN IN EUROPEAN HISTORY (Boston, Mass.: Houghton Mifflin, 1977)

This is a classic collection of the new feminist historiography with an essay by Joan Kelly on the methodological implications of women's history in Renaissance studies. The authors erase distorted and derogatory information about women and construct useful new models with which to give accounts of women's history.

HIST 46 Cantor, Milton and Laurie, Bruce (eds.)
CLASS, SEX AND THE WOMAN WORKER
(Westport, CT.: The Greenwood Press, 1977)

This is a collection of scholarly articles about the history of American working women. They range through the rise of class consciousness among Lowell factory girls, the work of immigrant women, to women in trade unions. The articles centre on the theme of how immigrant women, in particular, handled divided allegiances. The collection comes from a conference held at Radcliffe College in 1974.

HIST 47   Cott, Nancy F.
THE BONDS OF WOMANHOOD: 'WOMAN'S SPHERE' IN NEW ENGLAND 1780–1835 (New Haven, CT.: Yale University Press, 1977)

A radical feminist reinterpretation of the concepts of sexual repression and domesticity. Using diaries, and manuscripts as well as the sermons of ministers Cott shows that domesticity was a comfortable occupation for middle-class women not a frustration. Victorian women were able to use their 'sexual repression' as a source of power and a means of control over reproduction.

HIST 48   Fischer, Christiane (ed.)
LET THEM SPEAK FOR THEMSELVES: WOMEN IN THE AMERICAN WEST 1849–1900 (Hamden, CT.: Archon Books, 1977)

An anthology with interesting details of the folklife of American pioneer women.

HIST 49   Gluck, Sherna
'What's so Special About Women?: Women's Oral History', *Frontiers* 2: 2 (1977) 3–17

Gluck argues that oral history is a necessary part of women's history because other documentary sources often do not exist for women. The essay is in a special issue of *Frontiers* on oral history which includes articles about black women in Colorado, Chinese women immigrants and folk groups of the American Northwest.

HIST 50   Lerner, Gerda (ed.)
THE FEMALE EXPERIENCE: AN AMERICAN DOCUMENTARY (Indianapolis: Bobbs-Merrill, 1977)

A reconstruction of female experience in personal accounts of work, childhood, marriage and politics combined with a conceptual discussion of female culture.

HIST 51   Lewenhak, S.
　　　　　WOMEN AND TRADE UNIONS: AN OUTLINE
　　　　　HISTORY OF WOMEN IN THE BRITISH TRADE
　　　　　UNION MOVEMENT (London: Benn, 1977)

The author shows how nineteenth-century trade unions were male-dominated and how women were isolated and divided as workers, for example, as domestic workers. She gives examples of where trade unionism was strong amongst women and how women in factories were able to assert their rights as workers in the Lancashire cotton industry.

HIST 52   Llewelyn, Davies (ed.)
　　　　　LIFE AS WE HAVE KNOWN IT BY CO-
　　　　　OPERATIVE WORKING WOMEN (London:
　　　　　Virago, 1977; first published by Hogarth Press in 1931)

A reprint of a classic anthology of working class autobiographies which carries an introduction by Virginia Woolf. It reveals the role of the Co-operative Guild as an agent in the education of women and provides a moving first-hand record of the lives, experiences and aspirations of working women.

HIST 53   Rowbotham, Sheila
　　　　　A NEW WORLD FOR WOMEN: STELLA
　　　　　BROWNE: SOCIALIST FEMINIST (London: Pluto Press, 1977)

A case study of the relationship between a feminist ideology of sexual liberation and economic and social history. Rowbotham uses Browne to bring a debate about reproduction into the socialist arena and focuses on the relationship of feminism to the Left.

HIST 54   Vicinus, Martha (ed.)
　　　　　A WIDENING SPHERE: CHANGING ROLES OF
　　　　　VICTORIAN WOMEN (Bloomington: Indiana
　　　　　University Press, 1977)

A companion to *Suffer and Be Still* this volume includes: Walkowitz on prostitution; Holcombe on wives and property; Johansson on sex and death, wih a select bibliography by Barbara Kanner.

HIST 55   Wertheimer, Barbara Mayer
WE WERE THERE: THE STORY OF WORKING WOMEN IN AMERICA (New York: Pantheon Books, 1977)

The author finds that women from colonial times have worked in nearly every kind of job, usually in the face of opposition by men. She describes labour unions for women in particular the International Ladies Garment Workers Union.

HIST 56   Branca, P.
WOMEN IN EUROPE SINCE 1750 (London: Croom Helm, 1978)

Using data from a wide variety of sources including census figures, labour reports and personal accounts, Branca demonstrates that women from different classes, cultures and nationalities have many experiences in common. She gives a prominence to woman's place in the family.

HIST 57   Delamont, Sara and Duffin, Lorna
THE NINETEENTH-CENTURY WOMAN: HER CULTURAL AND PHYSICAL WORLD (London: Croom Helm, 1978; New York: Barnes and Noble, 1978)

The text focuses on a new area of Victorian female experience—the relationship between women's bodies and minds in nineteenth-century thought. Using insights from social anthropology to illuminate historical material, the authors examine education, medicine and mental illness, and feminist and anti-feminist attempts to challenge prevailing concepts of illness, health and social convention.

HIST 58   Donegan, Jane B.
WOMEN AND MEN WIDWIVES: MEDICINE, MORALITY AND MISOGYNY IN EARLY AMERICA (Westport, CT.: Greenwood Press, 1978)

This describes the takeover of midwifery by men. Donegan believes that the history of midwifery is closely related to the history of feminism and the topic (and threat) are very relevant to contemporary medicine.

HIST 59   DuBois, Ellen Carol
FEMINISM AND SUFFRAGE: THE EMERGENCE OF AN INDEPENDENT WOMEN'S MOVEMENT IN AMERICA, 1848–1869 (Ithaca, N.Y.: Cornell University Press, 1978)

DuBois believes that the women's suffrage movement should not be seen as simply a reformist movement but that the fight for the vote, although unsuccessful, led to a rise in social consciousness.

HIST 60   Ehrenreich, Barbara and English, Deirdre
FOR HER OWN GOOD: ONE HUNDRED AND FIFTY YEARS OF THE EXPERT'S ADVICE TO WOMEN (Garden City, N.Y.: Anchor Doubleday, 1978; London: Pluto Press, 1979)

The authors introduced the new area of women's health to feminist history. The medical system is strategic to women's oppression, they show, because it was medical science which defined female difference as strange, pathological and sick.

HIST 61   Liddington, J. and Norris, J.
ONE HAND TIED BEHIND US: THE RISE OF THE WOMEN'S SUFFRAGE MOVEMENT (London: Virago, 1978)

Using much unpublished material—from diaries, newspaper accounts, and interviews with the last surviving descendants of the suffragists—the authors create a vivid portrait of grass-roots radicalism, the Co-op, and socialist periodicals.

HIST 62   Saffioti, H. I. B.
WOMEN IN CLASS SOCIETY (New York: Monthly Review Press, 1978)

This contains an account of feminist activity in Latin America. It distinguishes between bourgeois and socialist feminism and their contributions to women's organisations, describing the marginalisation of women in production and the development of capitalism.

HIST 63 Stites, R.
THE WOMEN'S LIBERATION MOVEMENT IN RUSSIA: FEMINISM, NIHILISM AND BOLSHEVISM 1860–1930 (Princeton, N.J.: Princeton University Press, 1978)

The first narrative history of the Russian women's movement. The author examines the relationship of feminist ideas to political events, and the impact of urbanisation and industrialisation on women and their ideas. He ends with a discussion of Marxist theories about the woman question.

HIST 64 Tilly, Louise and Scott, J.
WOMEN, WORK AND THE FAMILY (New York: Holt, Rinehart and Winston, 1978)

A new women's history, building onto the social history developed since the 1960s but correcting it for gender. This is a feminist analysis of women's work in England and France from 1500 to 1700 which challenges the traditional view that industrialisation separated the family from work by demonstrating the family's continued role in production.

HIST 65 Wohl, A. (ed.)
THE VICTORIAN FAMILY (London: Croom Helm, 1978; New York: St Martin's Press, 1978)

An examination of the Victorian family using the new social history created by feminism. Essays about the Victorian novel, nannies, mills and reform focus on two groups largely repressed and exploited in Victorian society—women and children—and look at material influences on child-rearing and domesticity.

HIST 66 Berkin, C. R. and Norton, M. B. (eds.)
WOMEN OF AMERICA: A HISTORY (Boston, Mass.: Houghton Mifflin, 1979)

A chronological picture of women's lives which covers education, economic status, ideology and legal status. By using biography, legal analysis, quantitive data, organisational studies and demography the authors reveal the extent of this new feminist scholarship.

HIST 67 Burman, S. (ed.)
FIT WORK FOR WOMEN (London: Croom Helm, 1979)

A collection of essays which discuss the impact of domestic ideology on women's waged work and also the 'unwaged' work of women as landladies or at home. Contributors include Davidoff, Liddington and Hall.

HIST 68 Cott, Nancy F. and Pleck, E. H. (eds.)
A HERITAGE OF HER OWN: TOWARDS A NEW SOCIAL HISTORY OF AMERICAN WOMEN (New York: Simon and Schuster, 1979)

The contributors argue that women's history goes beyond social history because it establishes sex as a fundamental category. Describing the lives of women in the United States from the seventeenth century onwards Gerda Lerner, Eugene Genovese, Linda Gordon, and Carroll Smith-Rosenburg, among others utilise the experimental methods of the new feminist social history.

HIST 69 Evans, R. J.
THE FEMINISTS (London: Croom Helm, 1979)

Examining a variety of theories, Evans discusses the issues of sex ratios, surplus women and the relation of both to the entry of women into the professions. It is this, she demonstrates, which helps to explain the emergence of feminism in the late nineteenth century.

HIST 70 Evans, Sara
PERSONAL POLITICS: THE ROOTS OF WOMEN'S
LIBERATION IN THE CIVIL RIGHTS
MOVEMENT AND THE NEW LEFT (New York:
Alfred A. Knopf, 1979)

Evans examines the origins of contemporary feminism in other left movements of the 1960s. She finds a significant connection between the two social forces, suggesting that some contemporary feminism is more a reaction to the oppressive attitudes of men on the left.

HIST 71 *Frontiers* 4 (Fall 1979)

A special issue on lesbian history with essays by Judith Schwartz and Josephine Donovan.

HIST 72 Hollis, Patricia
WOMEN IN PUBLIC: THE WOMEN'S MOVEMENT
1850–1900 (London: George Allen and Unwin, 1979)

A thorough account of campaigns for legal changes in divorce, child custody and the Married Women's Property Act.

HIST 73 Lerner, Gerda
THE MAJORITY FINDS ITS PAST: PLACING
WOMEN IN HISTORY (New York: Oxford
University Press, 1978)

These are essays written while Lerner was developing a theory of women's history. They represent an invaluable account of personal growth and the growth of a new field. In describing mill girls, black women and American feminism, Lerner tackles the problems of conceptualisation, periodisation, interdisciplinary approaches in a comprehensive historiography of the new social history. Most importantly, Lerner locates specific virtues in the historical and psychological experience of women's difference and takes the view that female experience ought to be the major focus of study and a source of dominant values for culture as a whole. The key to women's history is to accept it as the *majority* of mankind.

HIST 74   McCrindle, J. and Rowbotham, S. (eds.)
DUTIFUL DAUGHTERS: WOMEN TALK ABOUT
THEIR LIVES (Harmondsworth: Penguin, 1979)

A social history of interviews with working-class or lower middle-class British women. Oral accounts centre on processes of puberty, sexuality, education, with first-hand evidence of medical histories, family relationships, housing, and describe the impact of the Education Act 1944. An attempt to show that shared individual experience is an important part of the social discovery of a common condition.

HIST 75   Schramm, Sarah
PLOW WOMEN RATHER THAN REAPERS: AN INTELLECTUAL HISTORY OF FEMINISM IN THE UNITED STATES (Metuchen, N.J.: Scarecrow Press, 1979)

Schramm describes the current of feminist thought which runs through the history of the United States. She believes that feminism is more tactical than ideological.

HIST 76   Trescott, M. M. (ed.)
DYNAMOS AND VIRGINS REVISITED: WOMEN AND TECHNOLOGICAL CHANGE IN HISTORY (Metuchen, N.J.: Scarecrow Press, 1979)

This is the first synthesis of material about women in technological history. It shows the participation of women in technological change and its impact on them; class disparities in women's use of technology and the stability of sex roles *within* a changing technological environment.

HIST 77   Boston, S.
WOMEN WORKERS AND THE TRADE UNION MOVEMENT (London: Davis Poynter, 1980)

Using first-hand accounts as well as records, Boston describes the experiences of women as trade union members. She documents the rise in female membership at the beginning of the century; the increased industrial employment of women during the First World War and their unemployment immediately after.

HIST 78   Bryant, M.
           THE UNEXPECTED REVOLUTION: A STUDY OF
           THE EDUCATION OF WOMEN AND GIRLS IN
           THE NINETEENTH CENTURY (London: University
           of London, 1980)

           An account of the challenges by middle-class women to
           the useless and decorative roles allocated to them in the
           nineteenth century.

HIST 79   Burstyn, Joan N.
           VICTORIAN EDUCATION AND THE IDEAL OF
           WOMANHOOD (London: Croom Helm, 1980)

           Burstyn draws an interesting analogy between the indus-
           trialisation of teaching and the industrialisation of other
           occupations. She shows that just as small-scale workshops
           initiated and maintained by women were replaced by
           men's organisations so in education women, similarly, lost
           control over education content and teaching methods.

HIST 80   *Feminist Studies* 6: 1 (1980) 28–54

           A symposium on politics and culture in women's history.
           Contributors, Mary Jo Buhle, Ellen DuBois and Gerda
           Lerner among others, debate the historical significance
           and character of a distinct 'woman's culture'. They call
           for historians to integrate knowledge of women's culture
           into their theories and argue that feminist scholarship
           must clarify terminology like 'women's rights' and
           'women's emancipation' in order for theory to contribute
           to political feminism.

HIST 81   Fletcher, S.
           FEMINISTS AND BUREAUCRATS: A STUDY IN
           THE DEVELOPMENT OF GIRLS' EDUCATION
           IN THE NINETEENTH CENTURY (Cambridge:
           Cambridge University Press, 1980)

           Describes feminist efforts to give girls the benefits of a
           male curriculum and the battering down of barriers to
           women's entry into higher education.

HIST 82 John, Angela V.
BY THE SWEAT OF THEIR BROW: WOMEN
WORKERS AT VICTORIAN COAL MINES
(London: Croom Helm, 1980)

John points to a dichotomy between the fashionable ideal of womanhood and the necessity and reality of female manual labour. She views the problems of pit women both from their perspective and from their position in the class struggle. It is a helpful micro and macro study of the exclusion campaigns of the 1880s.

HIST 83 Kerber, Linda
WOMEN OF THE REPUBLIC: INTELLECT AND
IDEOLOGY IN REVOLUTIONARY AMERICA
(Chapel Hill: University of North Carolina Press, 1980)

As a period of spiritual revival and social change, the Revolution, Kerber claims, was the most exciting period for American women. She reads letters, court records and diaries not as a source of local colour but as where the 'real' story of those years might be located. Kerber treats women's history both as a subject in its own right and as a strategy to test too-long held generalisations about the past.

HIST 84 Maclean, Ian
THE RENAISSANCE NOTION OF WOMEN
(Cambridge: Cambridge University Press, 1980)

An examination of theology, medicine, ethics, politics and law for their attitudes to women. He provides a context for understanding European Renaissance feminism and its connections with humanist scholarship, religion and the problems of language.

HIST 85 Norton, Mary Beth
LIBERTY'S DAUGHTERS: THE
REVOLUTIONARY EXPERIENCE OF AMERICAN
WOMEN 1750–1800 (Boston: Little, Brown, 1980)

Norton takes the revolution to be a turning point in the history of women in America. Their experience in the Revolution helped women to achieve a new and better place in the family and a sense of having a political—if private—role to play in the new Republic.

HIST 86   Walkowitz, Judith R.
PROSTITUTION AND VICTORIAN SOCIETY: WOMEN, CLASS AND THE STATE (Cambridge: Cambridge University Press, 1980)

This is a major contribution to women's history, working-class history and the social history of medicine and politics. Walkowitz demonstrates how feminists mobilised over sexual questions, how public discourse on prostitution redefined sexuality in the late nineteenth century, and how the state helped to recast definitions of social deviance.

HIST 87   Widdowson, Frances
GOING UP INTO THE NEXT CLASS (London: WRRC, 1980)

She describes the relationship between education and social mobility and between the state control of elementary schools and colleges and women's role as teachers. A subtle analysis of the interaction of class and gender in pressures affecting middle-class women in the nineteenth century.

HIST 88   Wilson, Elizabeth
ONLY HALFWAY TO PARADISE: WOMEN IN POST-WAR BRITAIN 1945–1968 (London: Tavistock, 1980)

Wilson includes culture, literature, social policy and the activities of feminists in her description of contemporary women's liberation. The text cuts across conventional academic disciplines to examine the construction of discourses of 'femininity'.

HIST 89   Banks, Olive
FACES OF FEMINISM (Oxford: Martin Robinson, 1981)

An authoritative survey of feminist history. Banks identifies three intellectual traditions in feminism: the Enlightenment; Evangelical Christianity and socialism. She describes feminism's alliances with other social movements such as moral reform, anti-slavery and social welfare and raises interesting questions about the part played by feminists in the development of the Welfare State. A particularly helpful section is Bank's account of the feminist movements in Britain and America in the 1960s.

HIST 90   Dyhouse, Carol
GIRLS GROWING UP IN LATE VICTORIAN AND EDWARDIAN ENGLAND (London: Routledge & Kegan Paul, 1981)

A historical survey of curricula and theories of education in relation to social Darwinism. Dyhouse points to the importance of domestic subjects in engendering ideas of femininity.

HIST 91   Hall, Catherine
'Gender Divisions and Class Formation in the Birmingham Middle Class 1780–1830', PEOPLE'S HISTORY AND SOCIALIST THEORY, ed. Ralph Samuel (London: Routledge & Kegan Paul, 1981)

Although this is a case study of one urban area, Hall deftly situates it in a feminist theory of the rise of domestic ideology. She examines English middle-class anxieties about the French Revolution and how that class sought stability through strengthening the role of the bourgeois family.

HIST 92   Hellerstein, E. O., Hume, L. P. and Offen, K. M. (eds.)
VICTORIAN WOMAN: A DOCUMENTARY ACCOUNT OF WOMEN'S LIVES IN NINETEENTH-CENTURY ENGLAND, FRANCE AND THE UNITED STATES (Stanford, CA.: Stanford University Press, 1981; Brighton: Harvester Press, 1981)

A collection of historical documents which contains short

accounts of feminist history by Barbara Gelpi, Marilyn Yalom and the authors.

HIST 93   Pinchbeck, Ivy
WOMEN WORKERS IN THE INDUSTRIAL REVOLUTION 1750–1850 (London: Virago, 1981)

A reprint of the original edition (1930) with a new introduction by Kerry Hamilton. An early feminist account of employment and pay practices and attitudes to women workers.

HIST 94   Stuard, Susan Mosher
'The Annales School and Feminist History: Opening Dialogue with the American Stepchild', *Signs* 7: 1 (Autumn 1981) 135–43

A revisionist account of the work of Annales historian F. Braudel. Stuard claims that an emphasis on the material conditions of life does not necessarily yield insights into the experience of women.

HIST 95   Boyd, N.
JOSEPHINE BUTLER, OCTAVIA HILL, FLORENCE NIGHTINGALE: THREE VICTORIAN WOMEN WHO CHANGED THEIR WORLD (London: Macmillan, 1982)

These are case studies of the interaction between women's ideology and social policy. Boyd examines the families, class and society of each woman and the impact of these on professional careers.

HIST 96   Gorham, D.
THE VICTORIAN GIRL AND THE FEMININE IDEAL (London and Canberra: Croom Helm, 1982)

Through the biographies of Victorian women such as Florence Nightingale and Marie Stopes, Gorham considers ways in which gender roles are learned and accepted and reveals the tensions between the assumptions of Victorian education and women's actual experiences.

HIST 97   Kessler-Harris, A.
OUT TO WORK: A HISTORY OF WAGE-
EARNING WOMEN IN THE UNITED STATES
(New York: Oxford University Press, 1982)

This is an overview of the history of American working women from the colonial era up to the present-day and an analysis of their experience in relation to the family, sexuality and feminism. The author's central thesis is that the transformation of women's work into wage labour has undermined the ideology of 'woman's place', in the contradiction it set up between an economic need for women employees and the cultural definition of femaleness.

HIST 98   Smith, Hilda
REASON'S DISCIPLES: SEVENTEENTH
CENTURY ENGLISH FEMINISTS (Urbana, Ill.:
University of Illinois Press, 1982)

A detailed inspection from a sociological perspective of the texts of Makin, Woolley, Elstob and Astell among others. Smith uses a group-centred understanding of women as a key to understanding the period.

HIST 99   Spender, Dale
WOMEN OF IDEAS AND WHAT MEN HAVE
DONE TO THEM: FROM APHRA BENN TO
ADRIENNE RICH (London: Routledge & Kegan Paul, 1982)

Spender describes 150 women of the past and shows how they have been devalued as creative intellectual thinkers.

HIST 100   Whitelegg, G. et al. (eds.)
THE CHANGING EXPERIENCE OF WOMEN
(Oxford: Martin Robertson, 1982)

Twenty-six articles collected as a teaching text for the British Open University Women's Studies course. They examine the relationship between women's position in the family and employment from the Industrial Revolution, and the textile and retail trades of the nineteenth century.

All focus on the interaction of ideology, work and family in women's experience.

HIST 101 Beddoe, Deirdre
DISCOVERING WOMEN'S HISTORY: A PRACTICAL MANUAL (London: Pandora Press, 1983)

A very useful introduction to feminist historiography. Beddoe shows how to locate and use sources describing ordinary women's lives in Britain from 1800 to 1945. There are sections on work, family, sexuality, home and education.

HIST 102 Cameron, Avril and Kuhrt, Amelie (eds.)
IMAGES OF WOMAN IN ANTIQUITY (London: Croom Helm, 1983)

The authors cover a wide geographical and chronological range from the ancient Hittite kingdom to the early Celts, and from the Achaemenid to the Byzantine Empire. Women's roles as witches, as priestesses, as mothers, and as courtesans are examined in an amalgam of approaches including religion, art, biology and economics. Contributors include Susan Pomeroy.

HIST 103 Clark, Alice
THE WORKING LIFE OF WOMEN IN THE SEVENTEENTH CENTURY (Re-issue London: Routledge & Kegan Paul, 1983)

A pioneering and influential early feminist historian, Clark compares the housewife in pre-industrial Britain organising self-sufficient economic units with the later removal of women from production into the home.

HIST 104 Eisenstein, Sarah
GIVE US BREAD BUT GIVE US ROSES (London: Routledge & Kegan Paul, 1983)

This is a series of essays about late Victorian ideas towards women and work, advice books and working-class women's critical responses. Eisenstein describes the growing consciousness of wage-earning women in the United States between 1890 and the First World War. She defines 'consciousness' as a negotiated response to work and ideology.

HIST 105 London Feminist History Group
THE SEXUAL DYNAMICS OF HISTORY (London: Pluto Press, 1983)

Eleven essays cover a range of topics from female emigration to the New World, sexual violence and nineteenth-century attitudes towards rape, abortion and domestic ideology, to women in public life.

HIST 106 Lucas, A. M.
WOMEN IN THE MIDDLE AGES: RELIGION, MARRIAGE AND LETTERS (Brighton: Harvester Press, 1983)

By examining wills, charters, medical, theological and philosophic treatises Lucas is able to prove that women had a significant role to play in the social and intellectual life of the period. Lucas makes a very useful conjunction of historical and literary material when describing the topic of marriage and there is a full bibliography.

HIST 107 Marshall, R. K.
VIRGINS AND VIRAGOS: THE HISTORY OF WOMEN IN SCOTLAND FROM 1080 TO 1980 (London: Collins, 1983)

This describes the roles of women in marriage, the court and at home. An example of the newer historiography in its use of letters, and private archives as well as census reports and government records. Marshall aims to eradicate stereotypes of Victorian women and the notion that active women are exceptional.

HIST 108 Newton, J. L. et al. (eds.)
SEX AND CLASS IN WOMEN'S HISTORY (London: Routledge & Kegan Paul, 1983)

Essays which initially appeared in *Feminist Studies* reflect developments in feminist history of nineteenth-century Britain and America. They describe women's networks, the tailoring trade, family history and the relation of gender to working-class life and male domination.

HIST 109   Riley, Denise
WAR IN THE NURSERY (London: Virago, 1983)

An historical examination of post-war attitudes to pre-school children in Britain and America. Riley examines the influential psychologies of John Bowlby and Donald Winnicott. Riley also includes a full history of child psychology and the Child Study Movement from the nineteenth century and examines socialist and feminist thinking about the period.

HIST 110   Sarah, E. (ed.)
REASSESSMENT OF 'FIRST WAVE' FEMINISM (Oxford: Pergamon Press, 1983)

A rich collection of articles about feminism in Europe and America, including accounts of feminist sexuality campaigns 1880–1914.

HIST 111   Spender, Dale
THERE'S ALWAYS BEEN A WOMEN'S MOVEMENT THIS CENTURY (London: Pandora Press, 1983)

In interviews with, and accounts of, twentieth-century feminists Spender describes the continuity of women's ideas in her attempt to construct a contemporary tradition of feminist thought.

HIST 112   Taylor, Barbara
EVE AND THE NEW JERUSALEM: SOCIALISM AND FEMINISM IN THE NINETEENTH CENTURY (London: Virago, 1983)

This brings to attention the least acknowledged aspect of Owenism—its theoretical and practical commitment to women's liberation. Taylor shows that the development of socialism displaced Owenite ideas about sexuality. Owenite feminism laid some of the ideological foundations for the Victorian women's movements and Taylor re-addresses the orthodox representation of pre-suffrage feminism as a middle-class movement.

HIST 113 Kelly, Joan (ed.)
WOMEN, HISTORY AND THEORY (Chicago: University of Chicago Press, 1984)

A socialist-feminist collection of essays which extends a critique of the state to include gender as well as class domination.

HIST 114 Newman, L. M.
MEN'S IDEAS/WOMEN'S REALITIES: POPULAR SCIENCE 1870–1915 (Oxford: Pergamon Press, 1984)

This offers a historical perspective on feminism by bringing together a collection of articles first published between these dates and analysing them in the light of contemporary arguments.

HIST 115 Roberts, E.
A WOMAN'S PLACE: AN ORAL HISTORY OF WORKING-CLASS WOMEN 1890–1940 (Oxford: Basil Blackwell, 1984)

This is based on women's memories of their day-to-day worlds in three Lancashire towns. Roberts describes a range of experiences from mill work to child care and the roles of mothers. She challenges some assumptions about the status of women and family relationships.

HIST 116 Heron, Liz (ed.)
TRUTH, DARE OR PROMISE: GIRLS GROWING UP IN THE FIFTIES (London: Virago, 1985)

A collection of twelve autobiographical accounts from women, both gay and heterosexual, who grew into feminism in the 1970s. Sheila Rowbotham, Alison Fell and others illustrate features of post-war British history like the 1944 Education Act which transformed many British girls' lives and possibilities.

HIST 117 Rendell, Jane
THE ORIGINS OF MODERN FEMINISM: WOMEN IN BRITAIN, FRANCE AND THE UNITED STATES 1780–1860 (London: Macmillan, 1985)

A history of modern feminism, its language of religious enthusiasm and separate spheres. Rendell locates its intellectual foundations in the re-working of Enlightenment ideals and the feminising of evangelical religion.

Anthropology and Myth

The focus of this chapter is on cultural feminism and its explorations of mystical, pre-industrial and cross-cultural studies together with folk literature, contemporary ethnography and classic and contemporary theory.

ANTH 1   Landes, Ruth
THE OJIBWA WOMAN (New York: Columbia University Press, 1938)

A pioneering work which provides a very full description of the lives of women in the culture Landes studied.

ANTH 2   Mead, Margaret
MALE AND FEMALE: A STUDY OF THE SEXES IN A CHANGING WORLD (New York: William Morrow, 1949)

This represents the development in Mead's thinking from the publication of *Sex and Temperament* in 1935 to the late 1940s. She discusses the relation between biological sex differences and cultural conceptions of sex roles, drawing on data from the seven South Sea cultures she studied extensively. She moves into a broader anthropological analysis by including a consideration of sexual relations in the United States.

ANTH 3   Benedict, Ruth Fulton
AN ANTHROPOLOGIST AT WORK: WRITINGS OF RUTH BENEDICT (New York: Houghton Mifflin, 1959)

A collection of Benedict's published and unpublished papers, dealing with her humanist and poetic aims together with a short study of Mary Wollstonecraft.

ANTH 4   Lurie, Nancy O. (ed.)
MOUNTAIN WOLF WOMAN (Ann Arbor: University of Michigan Press, 1961)

The book revitalises native traditions and promotes an awareness of the traditional role of women in religion and culture. There are examples of women's dance, healing and life-styles.

ANTH 5   Schneider, David and Gough, Kathleen (eds.)
MATRILINEAL KINSHIP (Berkeley, CA.: University of California Press, 1962)

Discusses the power of women (or their lack of power) in matrilineal and patrilineal orders. The authors find women and children to be under male authority in both except for specially qualifying conditions applicable to a minority. In both, emotional bonds between a mother and her children are subject to a father's kinship group.

ANTH 6   Harrison, Jane
MYTHOLOGY (New York: Harcourt, Brace and World, 1963)

A classic study first published in 1924. Harrison's search for a way women might exert power differently from men led directly to the 'matriarchal' controversy and served as a catalyst for the reaction against 'biology' which was necessarily an early stage in feminist thought. A classical anthropological account showing that myths are responses to environment.

ANTH 7   Levy, Rachel G.
RELIGIOUS CONCEPTIONS OF THE STONE AGE AND THEIR INFLUENCE ON EUROPEAN THOUGHT (New York: Harper Torchbooks, 1963)

This was originally published in 1948. It shows how caves and tombs were designed to resemble the body of the mother so that spirits could be reborn there. Levy reveals how the idea of the mother was connected to the idea of death—an association which remains powerful in patriarchal thought.

ANTH 8   Paulme, Denise (ed.)
WOMEN OF TROPICAL AFRICA (Berkeley:
University of California Press, 1963)

Originally published in France in 1960 as *Femmes d'Afrique noir*, the six essays are by female anthropologists departing from male patterns of ethnographic research. They examine the roles of mothers, and marriage and the family.

ANTH 9   Hays, H. R.
THE DANGEROUS SEX (New York: C. Putnam, 1964)

According to Adrienne Rich, Hays has written the least misogynist account of myths. He summarises the idea that myths are projective expressions of a male fear of women in anthropological, historical and psychological studies.

ANTH 10   Douglas, Mary
PURITY AND DANGER: AN ANALYSIS OF CONCEPTS OF POLLUTION AND TABOO
(London: Routledge & Kegan Paul, 1966)

The classic text of feminist anthropology about men's fear of menstruation and their uses of naming as a means of gaining control. Men's manipulation of a socially defined 'dangerous' state points paradoxically to the positive, creative aspects of menstruation.

ANTH 11   Culver, Elsie Thomas
WOMEN IN THE WORLD OF RELIGION (Garden City, N.Y.: Doubleday, 1967)

Culver surveys the extent of women's participation in the church from pre-Christian times to the present to illustrate the long history of a male monopoly of religious leadership. She finds that women have been uniformly discriminated against in the past and documents the new trends which are leading to ordination for women within some religious dominations.

ANTH 12　Young, Frank W. and Bacdayan, Albert
'Menstrual Taboos and Social Rigidity', CROSS-CULTURAL APPROACHES: READINGS IN COMPARATIVE RESEARCH, ed. Clellan S. Ford (New Haven, CT.: HRAF Press, 1967) pp. 95–110

Examines menstrual taboos cross-culturally, in terms of men's need to restrict women and assert dominance.

ANTH 13　Fischer, Ann and Golde, Peggy
'The Position of Women in Anthropology', *American Anthropologist* 70 (April 1968) 337–44

An essay evaluating the situation of women in anthropology—their numbers, contributions and opportunities for employment.

ANTH 14　Suhr, Elmer G.
THE SPINNING APHRODITE: THE EVOLUTION OF THE GODDESS FROM EARLIEST PRE-HELLENIC SYMBOLISM THROUGH LATE CLASSICAL TIMES (New York: Melios, 1969)

This describes the art of spinning in ancient Greece in relation to its symbolism and its connection with the goddess Aphrodite.

ANTH 15　Diamond, Norma
'Fieldwork in a Complex Society: Taiwan', BEING AN ANTHROPOLOGIST IN ELEVEN CULTURES, ed. George Spindler (New York: Holt, Rinehart and Winston, 1970) pp. 113–41

A feminist account of the problems of working in a male-oriented society.

ANTH 16　Doely, S. B. (ed.)
WOMEN'S LIBERATION AND THE CHURCH: THE NEW DEMAND FOR FREEDOM (New York: Association Press, 1970)

Each contributor describes the subordinate position of

women within organised religion. An overview of ways in which Christian feminism can identify and then work to correct the historic relegation of women.

ANTH 17 Eermath, M. S.
ADAM'S FRACTURED RIB: OBSERVATIONS ON WOMEN IN THE CHURCH (Philadelphia: Fortress, 1970)

The author juxtaposes the question of the role of women in the Church against the activities of the women's movement.

ANTH 18 Gale, Fay (ed.)
WOMAN'S ROLE IN ANTHROPOLOGICAL SOCIETY (Canberra: Australian National Institute of Aboriginal Studies, 1970)

A collection of diverse essays from one symposium.

ANTH 19 Golde, Peggy (ed.)
WOMEN IN THE FIELD: ANTHROPOLOGICAL EXPERIENCES (Chicago: Aldine, 1970)

This is a collection of the experiences of twelve women anthropologists undertaking fieldwork, who describe not only their memorable field trips, but also the subjective impact of these experiences. They discuss how they felt as women working in a foreign culture. A most comprehensive and thoughtful study of sex and gender in fieldwork.

ANTH 20 Gonzales, Nancie
'Cakchiquetos and Caribs: The Social Context of Fieldwork', MARGINAL NATIVES: ANTHROPOLOGISTS AT WORK, ed. M. Freilich (New York: Harper and Row, 1970) pp. 153–84

A description of how the relationship between men and women in the host society affects fieldwork.

ANTH 21   Borun, Minda, et al.
WOMEN'S LIBERATION: AN ANTHROPOLOGICAL VIEW (Pittsburgh: Know, 1971)

This discusses myth, folklore and matriarchy, and attempts to mediate between extreme anthropological positions. A short monograph presents a balanced and readable feminist introduction to how anthropology views women and to the relevance of the field to the women's liberation movement.

ANTH 22   Davis, Elizabeth Gould
THE FIRST SEX (New York: G. P. Putnam, 1971)

Gould Davis contends that women are more heroic than men since they are superior to them biologically and emotionally and that the word 'hero' was originally feminine—*hera*. Her text omits oriental, pre-colonial African and American myths but had a great impact because she exhumed a wealth of materials—from myths, history and archaeology. A genesis for speculations about the possibility and nature of female power.

ANTH 23   Goodale, J.
TIWI WIVES: A STUDY OF THE MELVILLE ISLAND, NORTH AUSTRALIA (Seattle: University of Washington Press, 1971)

An ethnography of marriage among the Tiwi. This looks at the marriage system from a feminist perspective and therefore clarifies certain features of kinship.

ANTH 24   Harding, Esther M.
WOMEN'S MYSTERIES: ANCIENT AND MODERN (New York: Harper and Row, 1971)

Harding suggests that male puberty rites are attempts by men to achieve women's power which we obtain through menstruation. Harding further suggests that women use menstruation as a time for reaching into subjectivity.

Anthropology and Myth

ANTH 25 von Franz, Marie-Louise
PROBLEMS OF THE FEMININE IN FAIRY TALES
(New York: Spring Publications, 1972)

She surveys the association between spinsters, witchcraft and womanhood and argues that women's confrontation with her animus = her 'masculine' as in Man In The Moon, separates a woman from emotional, intellectual and spiritual life. Franz uses notions of anima and animus from Jungian psychology.

ANTH 26 Morgan, Elaine
THE DESCENT OF WOMAN (New York: Stein and Day, 1972)

Morgan attempts to restore womankind to the history of evolution by attacking the androcentric evolutionary theory of the primacy of the male of the species.

ANTH 27 Diner, Helen
MOTHERS AND AMAZONS (Garden City, N.Y.: Anchor, 1973)

First published in the 1920s this shows how masculine intellect and spirit have dominated social interpretations and culture in the shape of moral and intellectual history. Diner envisioned a prehistoric civilisation centred on the female both as mother and head of family, and as deity.

ANTH 28 Ehrenreich, Barbara and English, Deirdre
WITCHES, MIDWIVES AND NURSES: A HISTORY OF WOMEN HEALERS (Old Westbury, N.Y.: Feminist Press, 1973)

The authors suggest that women healers in the western tradition were called witches by the authorities and describe how this 'birthright' of medicine has been usurped by male professionals. These profound, ambivalent attitudes toward women's wisdom persist in folk, popular and élite western traditions.

ANTH 29 Fee, Elizabeth
'The Sexual Politics of Victorian Social Anthropology', *Feminist Studies* (Winter/Spring 1973) pp. 23–9

The author finds in Victorian culture studies an attempt to counter feminist challenges to the institution of marriage.

ANTH 30 Nelson, C. (ed.)
THE DESERT AND THE SOWN (Berkeley: University of California Press, 1973)

Essays unveil assumptions about women in societies where stress is laid on the separate worlds of the sexes. They use ethnographic literature to show that a male control of political activity does not exclude women from influence.

ANTH 31 Romero, Joan Arnold (ed.)
WOMEN AND RELIGION (Tallahassee, Fla.: Florida State University, 1973)

A history of attitudes toward menstruation from ancient times to the present which demonstrates male fear, envy and hatred of women.

ANTH 32 Stevens, Evelyn P.
'*Marianismo*: The Other Face of *Machismo* in Latin America', FEMALE AND MALE IN LATIN AMERICA, ed. Ann Pescatello (Pittsburgh: University of Pittsburgh Press, 1973) pp. 89–101

Stevens details the Latin ideology of *marianismo* which asserts the female spiritual superiority of women over men and which she sees as complementing the male ideal of *machismo*.

ANTH 33 Van Vuran, Nancy
THE SUBVERSION OF WOMEN AS PRACTICED BY CHURCHES, WITCH-HUNTERS AND OTHER SEXISTS (Philadelphia: Westminster Press, 1973)

A self-explanatory title. Van Vuran deals with the whole question of gender selection in witch-hunts.

ANTH 34   Hageman, Alice L. (ed.)
SEXIST RELIGION AND WOMEN IN THE
CHURCH: NO MORE SILENCE! (New York:
Association Press, 1974)

These essays grew out of the Lentz Lectures at the Harvard Divinity School delivered in 1972–1973. Contributors are theologians who explore sexism in religion as it occurs throughout the Protestant, Catholic and Jewish religions. It includes an essay by Mary Daly.

ANTH 35   Matthiasson, C. J. (ed.)
MANY SISTERS: WOMEN IN CROSS-CULTURAL
PERSPECTIVE (New York: Free Press, 1974)

A useful collection of articles dealing with Egypt, Guatemala, India, Cambodia, Eskimos, China and the Middle East. They look at residence patterns; descent, inheritance and kinship and argue that the stereotype of the submissive woman has no basis in fact.

ANTH 36   Murphy, Y. and Murphy, R. F.
WOMEN OF THE FOREST (New York: Columbia
University Press, 1974)

The authors investigate a women's subculture and determine whether it functions to support or to challenge the society's dominant values. A penetrating study of the world of women in a South American tribe describing how women's folklore may project an 'ideology' at variance with a male view of things.

ANTH 37   Rosaldo, M. Z. and Lamphere, L. (eds.)
WOMEN, CULTURE AND SOCIETY (Stanford,
CA.: Stanford University Press, 1974)

The best and most crucial collection of key feminist articles: Bridget O'Laughlin, 'Meditation of Contradictions: Why Mbum women do not eat chicken' shows how patrilineal descent systems appropriate the fruits of women's labour in reproduction and socialisation. Most important and controversial: Sherry Ortner, 'Is Female to Male as Nature is to Culture?'. This develops Lévi-Strauss to show that 'women as nature/male as culture' is an ideological construct which encouraged women's devaluation by connecting women to nature. She argues that this allocation of female to nature, child rearing and domesticity is one of the prime sources of women's oppression. The essay provoked much debate among feminists.

ANTH 38   Ruether, Rosemary R. (ed.)
RELIGION AND SEXISM: IMAGES OF WOMEN IN THE JEWISH AND CHRISTIAN TRADITIONS (New York: Simon and Schuster, 1974)

Essays show how Old Testament parables and other fables describe women's sexuality as the husband's property.

ANTH 39   Ardener, S.
PERCEIVING WOMEN (London: Dent, 1975; New York: John Wiley, 1975)

A social anthropology of different women's groups—nuns, gypsies, diplomats' wives and African tribeswomen. The collection reveals how males control modes of symbolic production and ties this to the problem of bias in ethnography by proposing that models male informants provide are understandable to social anthropologists socialised within a male-oriented intellectual tradition.

ANTH 40   Douglas, Mary
IMPLICIT MEANINGS (London: Routledge & Kegan Paul, 1975)

Building on her work in *Natural Symbols* and *Purity and Danger* Douglas writes about human belief systems—especially the relation between the sacred and the profane. She suggests that ideas about order and disorder must be placed in a more complex theory in order to explain why human being impose order and institute cults like virginity.

ANTH 41   Farrar, Claire (ed.)
WOMEN AND FOLKORE (Austin: University of Texas Press, 1975)

This discusses contributions to folklore as well as omissions. An important contribution to the advancing study of women and folklore. It surveys some of the scholarship of the past and introduces such issues as women's genres, women's groups and their folklore and the image of women held by a society and the relation of such images to folklore.

ANTH 42   Friedl, E.
WOMEN AND MEN: AN ANTHROPOLOGIST'S VIEW (New York: Holt, Rinehart and Winston, 1975)

An explanation of cross-cultural differences and similarities using economic theory. An overview of sex roles in foraging and horticultural societies. The book accounts for the relative power of men and women in terms of who controls production and extra-domestic exchange. It is very sensitive to the importance of ritual and ceremonial as symbolic statements of sex role differences.

ANTH 43   Martin, M. and Voorhies, Barbara
FEMALE OF THE SPECIES (New York: Columbia University Press, 1975)

This studies women in a range of societies including gathering and horticultural groups and the socialist and capitalist organisations of industrial society.

ANTH 44   Pomeroy, Sarah B.
GODDESSES, WHORES, WIVES AND SLAVES: WOMEN IN CLASSICAL ANTIQUITY (New York: Schocken, 1975)

Pomoroy distinguishes between behavioural science's version of myths and myths' original cult activities which paid attention to the fulfilment of women's needs.

ANTH 45   Raphael, D. (ed.)
BEING FEMALE: REPRODUCTION, POWER AND CHANGE (The Hague: Mouton, 1975)

A useful collection of anthropological articles about

women cross-culturally. They show how viewing the world from a male vantage point has distorted our understanding and slowed our science.

ANTH 46   Reed, Evelyn
WOMAN'S EVOLUTION: FROM MATRIARCHAL CLAN TO PATRIARCHAL FAMILY (New York: Pathfinder Press, 1975)

Reed uses orthodox Marxist theory to show how the advent of women's oppression within the family was coincident with the emergence of class.

ANTH 47   Reiter, Rayna R. (ed.)
TOWARD AN ANTHROPOLOGY OF WOMEN (New York: Monthly Review Press, 1975)

Contains seminal essays: S. Slocum 'Woman the Gatherer: Male Bias in Anthropology' which argues that social organisations did not stem from male bonding and hunting but from mother/infant relations and food-sharing; Gayle Rubin 'The Traffic in Women: Notes on the Political Economy of Sex' which explains gender difference in terms of social structure; and Paula Webster 'Matriarchy: A Vision of Power' on how matriarchy can encourage women to create new images.

ANTH 48   Reuss, Richard A. and Lund, Jane (eds.)
ROADS INTO FOLKLORE: *FESTSCHRIFT* IN HONOR OF RICHARD M. DOBSON (Bloomington, Ind.: Folklore Forum, 1975)

Twelve women are among the contributors in a collection of autobiographical essays in which folklorists explain how they became interested in the field.

ANTH 49   Rohrlich-Leavitt, Ruby
PEACEABLE PRIMATES AND GENTLE PEOPLE: ANTHROPOLOGICAL APPROACHES TO WOMEN'S STUDIES (New York: Harper and Row, 1975)

Shows how the idea that woman is universally inferior reflects Western cultural bias.

ANTH 50 Rohrlich-Leavitt, Ruby (ed.)
WOMEN CROSS-CULTURALLY: CHANGE AND CHALLENGE (The Hague: Mouton, 1975)

A collection of important essays including E. Leacock 'Class Commodity and the Status of Women' an argument that family organisation is an intrinsic part of capitalist production; and Rohrlich-Leavitt's own 'Aboriginal Women: Male and Female Anthropological Perspectives' suggesting that women are superior ethnographers since their double consciousness is the same as that which characterises economically exploited and stigmatised groups.

ANTH 51 Stack, C. B. et al.
'Review Essay: Anthropology', *Signs* 1 (1975) 147–59

A good account of recent research.

ANTH 52 Wolf, Margery and Witke, Roxane (eds.)
WOMEN IN CHINESE SOCIETY (Stanford, CA.: Stanford University Press, 1975)

Written by scholars of history, literature, anthropology and Asian studies. There is work on marriage resistance; suicide; pollution and village life.

ANTH 53 Delaney, J. et al.
THE CURSE: A CULTURAL HISTORY OF MENSTRUATION (New York: E. P. Dutton, 1976)

This suggests that taboos of menstruation are practices to help men void the power of the menstruating woman and that men attempt to recreate for themselves in culture what biology has assigned exclusively to women.

ANTH 54 Hafkin, Nancy J. and Bay, Edna (eds.)
WOMEN IN AFRICA: STUDIES IN SOCIAL AND ECONOMIC CHANGE (Stanford, CA.: Stanford University Press, 1976)

A project of the Women's Committee of the African Studies Association, this is an anthology of articles representing the results of recent fieldwork in Africa south of the Sahara by scholars in the fields of history, economics, political science, anthropology, sociology and women's studies.

ANTH 55   Hammond, Dorothy and Jablow, Alta
WOMEN IN THE CULTURES OF THE WORLD
(Menlo Park, CA.: Cummings, 1976)

This suggests feminists must scavenge for information about women in parenthetical remarks, footnotes and addenda. The authors organise their work by dealing with women in the family in chronological order in traditional societies; discussing the theory of matriarchy and then dealing with women and the economy.

ANTH 56   Kessler, Evelyn
WOMEN: AN ANTHROPOLOGICAL VIEW (New York: Holt, Rinehart and Winston, 1976)

Areas surveyed include biology, puberty rites, women in the context of the archaeological record, technology and economics. Particularly interesting are the chapters drawing on life histories and ethnographies.

ANTH 57   Rush, Anne Kent
MOON, MOON (New York: Random House, 1976)

An exploration of lunar myths, rites and symbols with research on witchcraft.

ANTH 58   Shapiro, J.
'Sexual Hierarchy Among the Yanomama', SEX AND CLASS IN LATIN AMERICA, eds. Nash, J. and Safa, H. (New York: Praeger, 1976)

Discusses differences in women's and men's work patterns, their different access to public status and control of the marriage system by men.

ANTH 59 Singer, June
ANDROGYNY: TOWARD A NEW THEORY OF
SEXUALITY (Garden City, N.Y.: Anchor Press,
1976)

Singer examines past and present mythology to find out how the rigid definitions of male and female can be transcended. She claims Edenic Adam is a hermaphrodite and basically asexual.

ANTH 60 Stone, Merlin
THE PARADISE PAPERS: THE SUPPRESSION OF
WOMEN'S RITES (London: Virago, 1976)

Stone describes the possibilities of woman power and explains how and why it was taken over. She claims that scholars simply project their own assumptions when analysing ancient cultures. Reprinted as *When God Was a Woman* (New York: Harcourt, Brace and Jovanovich, 1978).

ANTH 61 Trible, Phyllis
'Depatriarchalising in Biblical Interpretation', THE
JEWISH WOMAN: NEW PERSPECTIVES, ed.
Elizabeth Koltun (New York: Schocken Books, 1976)
pp. 217–40

A feminist exegesis claiming that terms can be read as androgynous and used generically for all humankind. Trible shows that the creation of women was not secondary and claims that modern assertions that God is masculine are misleading.

ANTH 62 Warner, Marina
ALONE OF ALL HER SEX: THE MYTH AND
CULT OF THE VIRGIN MARY (London:
Wiedenfeld and Nicolson, 1976; New York: Alfred A.
Knopf, 1976)

Warner describes the disturbing effect on women of an unobtainable virgin image which creates acknowledged female inferiority.

ANTH 63 Weideger, Paula
MENSTRUATION AND MENOPAUSE: THE PHYSIOLOGY AND PSYCHOLOGY, THE MYTH AND THE REALITY (New York: Alfred A. Knopf, 1976)

A very full discussion of the physiology and psychology of menstruation and menopause which also touches on related social issues.

ANTH 64 Weiner, Annette
WOMEN OF VALUE, MEN OF REKNOWN (Austin: University of Texas Press, 1976)

Weiner's promise is that Malinowski failed to accord sufficient importance to women in his accounts, misrepresenting for example their social and symbolic significance in systems of exchange. She reanalyses Trobriand society and charges that social anthropologists have commonly taken too narrow a view of social order.

ANTH 65 Cassell, Joan
A GROUP CALLED WOMEN: SISTERHOOD AND SYMBOLISM IN THE FEMINIST MOVEMENT (New York: David McKay, 1977)

Cassell uses a feminist anthropological approach to describe becoming a feminist and the new systems of meaning that occur in women once radicalised.

ANTH 66 Lamphere, Louise
'Review Essay: Anthropology', *Signs* 2 (1977) 612–27

Survey of recent anthropological work on and by women.

ANTH 67 Niethammer, Carolyn
DAUGHTERS OF THE EARTH: THE LIVES AND LEGENDS OF AMERICAN INDIAN WOMEN (New York: Collier Books, 1977)

An attempt to reconstruct the lives of American Indian women prior to the penetration of their culture and society by Europeans. Niethammer utilises early anthropology writings as well as feminist anthropology.

ANTH 68　Ochs, Carol
BEHIND THE SEX OF GOD: TOWARD A NEW CONSCIOUSNESS: TRANSCENDING MATRIARCHY AND PATRIARCHY (Boston, Mass.: Beacon Press, 1977)

A rejection of the dualism of mind and body.

ANTH 69　Schlegal, Alice (ed.)
SEXUAL STRATIFICATION: A CROSS-CULTURAL VIEW (New York: Columbia University Press, 1977)

The book examines male-dominated as well as egalitarian societies. The point made is that a correct assessment of sexual power relations requires examination of the informal strategies utilised by women, not just formal positions of authority.

ANTH 70　Washbourn, Penelope
BECOMING WOMAN: THE QUEST FOR WHOLENESS IN FEMALE EXPERIENCE (New York: Harper and Row, 1977)

Washbourn suggests that rituals of menstruation create symbolic, interpretive frameworks for women to negotiate life crisis. These rituals show woman is not isolated but part of a community.

ANTH 71　Zelman, Elizabeth
'Reproduction, Ritual and Power', *American Ethnologist* 4 (1977) 714–33

A cross-cultural study of 60 groups which describes female pollution-avoidance rituals and male rituals associated with female reproduction in terms of the social need to maximise or minimise sex differences.

ANTH 72   Ardener, S. (ed.)
DEFINING FEMALES: THE NATURE OF WOMAN IN SOCIETY (London: Croom Helm, 1978)

This collection is about the significance of categories men and women make to codify and confront their worlds and the problems that arise from those boundaries. (For example how women in public life without children lack definition as female.)

ANTH 73   Caplan, P. and Bujra, J. (eds.)
WOMEN UNITED, WOMEN DIVIDED: COMPARATIVE STUDIES OF TEN CONTEMPORARY CULTURES (London: Tavistock, 1978)

A cross-cultural collection of articles from the London Women's Anthropology Group on aspects of female solidarity, sexual division, sexual segregation, kinship and spirituality.

ANTH 74   'Great Goddess Issue', *Heresies* 5 (Spring 1978)

A collection of contemporary feminist responses to theories about goddess-worshipping cultures and their influence. Considers specifically the ideas of J. J. Bachofen and Robert Briffault.

ANTH 75   Hoch-Smith, Judith and Spring, Anita (eds.)
WOMEN IN RITUAL AND SYMBOLIC ROLES (New York: Plenum Press, 1978)

This contains an essay by Marigene Arnold about her fieldwork in Mexico on spinsters and virginity and also an account by Lois Paul on the careers of midwives in Mayan communities.

ANTH 76   Holzberg, Carol
'Anthropology: The Science of Man?', *International Journal of Women's Studies* 1 (1978) 438–44

Surveys anthropological work relating to women to date.

ANTH 77 Matalene, Carolyn
'Women as Witches', *International Journal of Women's Studies* 1 (1978) 473–587

A long study of the persecution of witches during the great European witch-hunts. Matalene relates this, along with the courtly love ethic, to a male view of women as passive.

ANTH 78 Shuttle, Penelope and Redgrove, Peter
THE WISE WOUND: EVE'S CURSE AND EVERYWOMAN (Harmondsworth: Penguin, 1978)

A radical reinterpretation of the rites of the menarche which can create a universal power for women by encouraging recognition of their mothers and the passion in that relationship. An exhaustive study of the myths and stories of menstruation.

ANTH 79 Christ, Carol P. and Plaskow, J. (eds.)
WOMANSPIRIT RISING: A FEMINIST READER IN RELIGION (San Francisco, CA.: Harper and Row, 1979)

This contains Elaine Pagels 'What Became of God the Mother? Conflicting Images of God in Early Christianity' and Elizabeth Fiorenza on 'Feminist Spirituality, Christian Identity and Catholic Vision'. The book revises figures like Mary Magdalene and gives a critical delegitimation of culturally sacred narratives.

ANTH 80 Fisher, Elizabeth
WOMAN'S CREATION (Garden City, N.Y.: Anchor Press, 1979)

Fisher discusses the feminist implications of the Great Goddess tradition. A reinterpretation of dominant theories of evolution which discusses the issue of women's actual political and cultural power in the pre-Judeo-Christian period.

ANTH 81   Goldenberg, Naomi
CHANGING OF THE GODS: FEMINISM AND THE END OF TRADITIONAL RELIGIONS (Boston, Mass.: Beacon Press, 1979)

An attempt to salvage some of Freud's and Jung's ideas for a feminist iconography. At the moment Goldenberg feels the animal/animus model works better for men than for women by supporting stereotypes in its guard against change.

ANTH 82   Kolbenschlag, Madonna
KISS SLEEPING BEAUTY GOOD-BYE: BREAKING THE SPELL OF FEMININE MYTHS AND MODELS (Garden City, N.Y.: Doubleday, 1979)

The author finds the story's symbolism to be passive but also dynamic in calling women forth to an 'awakening' and spiritual maturity. She examines the theme in American popular novels, films and fairy tales.

ANTH 83   Pagels, Elaine H.
THE GNOSTIC GOSPELS (New York: Random House, 1979)

Pagels links gnostic sources which describe God in both masculine and feminine terms with similar descriptions of human nature described as a dyadic entity consisting of two equal male and female components. She finds that the androgyne in early works indicates a state of autonomy, describes the original unity of humankind, and the fullness of the divine, and describes how Gnostic texts were labelled heretical by orthodox Christianity.

ANTH 84   Rapp, Rayna
'Review Essay: Anthropology', *Signs* 4 (1979) 497–513

Good survey of recent anthropological work on women.

ANTH 85   Rowe, Karen
'Feminism and Fairy Tales', *Feminist Studies* 6 (1979) 237–57

Rowe thinks fairy tales make female subordination seem romantically desirable and promote the paradigm of the passive woman as a negative model.

ANTH 86   Stone, Merlin
ANCIENT MIRRORS OF WOMANHOOD: OUR GODDESS AND HEROINE HERITAGE (New York: New Sibylline, 1979)

Stone describes how men suppressed women's rites connected with goddess worship.

ANTH 87   Washbourn, Penelope
SEASONS OF WOMAN: SONG, POETRY, RITUAL, PRAYER, MYTH, STORY (New York: Harper and Row, 1979)

An anthology of writing from various literary genres which provides women with accounts of our spiritual sensibility. Most describe stages in the fertility cycle because women's spiritual and religious experience revolved around female sexuality. A diversity of cultural accounts of Ukrainian to native American women show the close relationship between the female body and spirit.

ANTH 88   Falk, Nancy and Gross, Rita (eds.)
UNSPOKEN WORLDS: WOMEN'S RELIGIOUS LIVES IN NON-WESTERN CULTURES (New York: Harper and Row, 1980)

A collection of essays giving a wide overview of the roles that women play in the religious life of non-western cultures. It argues that women's striving for identity can, in many parts of the world, be achieved only through their contributions to religious life, either through the domestic rites in the home or through their contributions and experiences as diviners, visionaries and religious leaders. The authors describe cultures from Australia to India and ancient China to present-day South America. They conclude that women's contributions are as important as men's although less obvious because they are concentrated on life, home and nature.

ANTH 89   Green, Rayna
'Review Essay: Native American Women', *Signs* 6 (1980)

Green describes a vigorous tradition of writing since 1960 which has not yet developed as a body of literature.

ANTH 90   Hall, N.
THE MOON AND THE VIRGIN: REFLECTIONS ON THE ARCHETYPAL FEMININE (New York: Harper and Row, 1980)

Information about myth goddesses bearing the author's name; about witches, fairy tales, mirror imagery and paradigms of psychological depression, this text is written by a Jungian therapist.

ANTH 91   Hillman, James (ed.)
FACING THE GODS (Irving, Texas: Spring Publications, 1980)

This contains several feminist essays by Kirksey and Malamud on psychological femininity and the Amazon problem.

ANTH 92   Lacks, Roslyn
WOMEN AND JUDAISM: MYTH, HISTORY AND STRUGGLE (Garden City, N.Y.: Doubleday, 1980)

An attack on the sexist etiology of Judaic ritual.

ANTH 93   MacCormack, Carol and Strathern, Marilyn (eds.)
NATURE, CULTURE AND GENDER (Cambridge: Cambridge University Press, 1980)

This book argues that symbolic analyses of gender constitute a particularly fertile field for anthropological research. It challenges the viability of structuralist models which neglect folk models and actual statistical descriptions of real societies. It claims social anthropology should be not semiology but the study of the actual behaviour of human beings.

ANTH 94 O'Flaherty, Wendy Doniger
WOMEN, ANDROGYNES AND OTHER
MYTHICAL BEASTS (Chicago: University of
Chicago Press, 1980)

This deals with Hindu mythology, in an interesting consideration of sexual metaphors and animal symbols as indicative of male-female relationships.

ANTH 95 Rosaldo, M. Z.
'The Use and Abuse of Anthropology: Reflections on Feminism and Cross-cultural Understanding', *Signs* 5: 3 (1980) 389–417

Rosaldo cautions against an oversimplified use of her original concept or generalisations about women's universal oppression, arguing that women's status is a complex product of a variety of social forces. She asks why, if women-gathering was important, was it not celebrated?

ANTH 96 Starr, Elizabeth
'On Sexism in Folklore Scholarship', *Folklore Women's Communication* 20 (1980) 16–22

An important redress of male perspectives in anthropology.

ANTH 97 Thorsten, Geraldine
GOD HERSELF: THE FEMININE ROOTS OF
ASTROLOGY (Garden City, N.Y.: Doubleday, 1980)

Thorsten looks for positive associations in horoscopes throughout the world describing symbols of serpents, eggs and circles.

ANTH 98 Ardener, S. (ed.)
WOMEN AND SPACE: GROUND RULES AND
SOCIAL MAPS (London: Croom Helm, 1981)

These essays contain ethnographic evidence from actresses, politicians, and farmers which examine space in its physical and social and symbolic dimensions as experienced by women. The text stresses the positive aspects of women and space as well as describing restrictive practices in the rules governing sexual segregation and taboo.

ANTH 99   Downing, Christine
THE GODDESS: MYTHOLOGICAL REPRESENTATIONS OF THE FEMININE (New York: Crossroads, 1981)

Downing reconsiders the role of Athene as the woman artist in relation to Zeus, the owl and the serpent, in order to give a Jungian, feminist interpretation of myth.

ANTH 100   Sanday, Peggy Reeves
FEMALE POWER AND MALE DOMINANCE (New York: Cambridge University Press, 1981)

As part of her cross-cultural study anthropologist Sanday examined 112 creation stories world-wide, noting that origin myths feature a female creator. She discusses Iroquoian and Senecan versions of female power.

ANTH 101   Spretnak, Charlene
LOST GODDESSES OF EARLY GREECE: A COLLECTION OF PRE-HELLENIC MYTHS (Boston, Mass.: Beacon Press, 1981)

First published in 1978 by Moon Books of California this text tries to remove a culturally imposed bias which refuses to see the deity as originally female. Spretnak's goal, when considering Pandora, Hera, Athena, is not the reinstatement of prehistoric cultural structures but the transmission of possibilities.

ANTH 102   Warner, Marina
JOAN OF ARC: THE IMAGE OF FEMALE HEROISM (London: Weidenfeld and Nicolson, 1981)

Warner describes Joan's image as a type of miraculous liberator like the early virgin but with the subversive power of the armed maiden. Warner's studies contribute significantly to the illumination of legendary models of heroic women.

ANTH 103 Spretnak, Charlene
THE POLITICS OF WOMEN'S SPIRITUALITY: ESSAYS ON THE RISE OF SPIRITUAL POWER WITHIN THE FEMINIST MOVEMENT (Garden City, N.Y.: Anchor Press, 1982)

A feminist collection about spirituality in the women's movement. Essays by Kay Turner and E. M. Broner, among others, discuss female ritual and honour in women's ceremonies.

ANTH 104 Weigle, Marta
SPIDERS AND SPINSTERS: WOMEN AND MYTHOLOGY (Albuquerque: University of New Mexico, 1982)

A major trove of information on women and mythology. As an anthology of texts of various kinds it skilfully weaves together commentary, many illustrations and an extensive bibliography. Marta Weigle draws on a variety of sources, both visual and verbal, from religion, psychology, literature, folklore and anthropology to examine goddess, spinster, heroines, and matriarchy figures as symbols of power.

ANTH 105 Jordan, Rosan and Kalcik, Susan (eds.)
WOMEN'S FOLKLORE, WOMEN'S CULTURE (Philadelphia: University of Pennsylvania Press, 1983)

Contains essays on life histories as exemplary patterns of folklore and also work on sex role changes in Muslim communities.

Education and Women's Studies

The field of education has seen a great deal of activity since 1970 and the scope of this chapter is therefore broad: sex discrimination in schools and higher education, anti-sexist and affirmative action, women's studies theory and practice, education as an economic and ideological institution and accounts by women of their teaching experiences.

ED 1 Dolan, Eleanor
'Higher Education for Women', *Higher Education* 20 (September 1963) 5–13

An early study on higher education for women discussing what women want from higher education, what they are actually receiving and what a re-examination of curriculum trends would do.

ED 2 Bernard, Jessie
ACADEMIC WOMEN (University Park, Penn.: Pennsylvania State University Press, 1964)

The author describes the history of women in academic pursuits and their contributions as teachers and scholars. This is a sociological study evaluating motivations, backgrounds and career patterns.

ED 3 Mattfield, Jacquelyn and Van Aken, Carol (eds.)
WOMEN AND THE SCIENTIFIC PROFESSIONS: THE MIT SYMPOSIUM ON AMERICAN WOMEN IN SCIENCE AND ENGINEERING (Cambridge, Mass.: MIT Press, 1965)

This contains essays by Alice Rossi on careers, Jessie Bernard on engineering and other contributors cover women and the medical profession, women in government and private industry.

ED 4   *Female Studies* (Westbury, N.Y.: Feminist Press, from 1967)

A useful series giving an overview each year of Women's Studies courses and criticism, together with aspects of student work. Editors have included Elaine Showalter, Deborah Rosenfelt and Nancy Hoffman among others.

ED 5   Harris, Ann S.
'The Second Sex in Academe', *American Association of University Professors Bulletin* 56 (September 1970) 283-95

This is part of a testimony given to the House Committee on Education. Harris documents many examples of sex discrimination for example in admissions and pay. There is a good bibliography on the status of women in higher education.

ED 6   Reeves, Nancy (ed.)
WOMANKIND BEYOND THE STEREOTYPES (Chicago: Aldine, Atherine, 1971)

With essays by Eleanor Flexner on women in labour; and by Charlotte Perkins Gilman on women and education.

ED 7   Sandler, Bernice
A FEMINIST APPROACH TO THE WOMAN'S COLLEGE (Washington, D.C.: Association of American Colleges, 1971)

An early study promoting the benefits of going to a woman's college.

ED 8   Scott, Anne
THE AMERICAN WOMAN: WHO WAS SHE? (Englewood Cliffs, N.J.: Prentice-Hall, 1971)

Scott explores the relationship between the changing role of women in American society and changes in women's education, patterns of work and views of the family.

ED 9   Theodore, A. (ed.)
        THE PROFESSIONAL WOMAN (Cambridge, Mass.:
        Schenkman, 1971)

        This brings together recent research about professional women in America within a sociological framework. It contains essays by Cynthia Epstein and Alice Rossi on science.

ED 10   Anderson, Scarvia B. (ed.)
        SEX DIFFERENCES AND DISCRIMINATION IN EDUCATION (Worthington, Ohio: Charles A. Jones, 1972)

        This includes content analysis of children's books and essays and argues for changes in sex-role portrayals.

ED 11   Chmaj, Betty E. and Gustafson, Judith (eds.)
        IMAGE, MYTH AND BEYOND: AMERICAN WOMEN AND AMERICAN STUDIES, VOL. TWO (Pittsburgh, PA.: Know, 1972)

        This is the updated version of Chmaj's *American Women and American Studies* (1971) and similarly includes syllabi relevant to women's studies, reprints of articles on Women's Studies and an exploration of the status of academic women.

ED 12   Burstyn, Joan
        'Women and Education: A Survey of Recent Historical Research', *Educational Leadership* 31 (November 1973)

        A good evaluation of studies to that date in the field of the history of women in higher education.

ED 13   Carnegie Commission on Higher Education
        OPPORTUNITIES FOR WOMEN IN HIGHER EDUCATION: THEIR CURRENT PARTICIPATION, PROSPECTS FOR THE FUTURE AND RECOMMENDATIONS FOR ACTION (New York: McGraw-Hill, 1973)

This is a good summary and analysis of the status of women in higher education covering students, faculty and non-faculty and its arguments for change are equipped with statistical data.

ED 14 'Special Issue', *Educational Leadership* 31 (November 1973)

A special number on women and education with articles on sexism in textbooks, sex roles and sex bias.

ED 15 Frazier, Nancy and Sadker, Myra
SEXISM IN SCHOOL AND SOCIETY (New York: Harper and Row, 1973)

This contains an annotated bibliography of the women's movement and sexism in education together with a sex-bias questionnaire. Intended as an in-service text for teachers it shows how the subject could be part of a school's curriculum.

ED 16 Harrison, Barbara Grizzuti
UNLEARNING THE LIFE: SEXISM IN SCHOOL (New York: William Morrow, 1973)

An account of one school's efforts to come to terms with sexism in education. It contains an action blueprint and an agenda for changing biased education. Anecdotal but stimulating as a piece of pioneer feminism.

ED 17 Robinson, Lora H.
WOMEN'S STUDIES: COURSES AND PROGRAMS FOR HIGHER EDUCATION (Washington, D.C.: American Association for Higher Education, 1973)

An excellent bibliography on the genesis and development of Women's Studies as a discipline.

ED 18 Rosenfelt, Deborah Silverton (ed.)
GOING STRONG: NEW COURSES/NEW PROGRAMS (Old Westbury, N.Y.: Feminist Press, 1973)

Describes the content and bibliographies of Women's Studies courses and focuses particularly on innovative approaches with a comprehensive cover of race, culture, class and nationality. Organised into: Interdisciplinary; Humanities and Arts; Social Sciences; Sciences; Vocational/Professional/Applied and Miscellaneous (consciousness-raising, for example).

ED 19   Rossi, Alice and Calderwood, Ann (eds.)
ACADEMIC WOMEN ON THE MOVE (New York: Russell Sage Foundation, 1973)

Essays surveying women's options in entering and participating in academia and what actions are being taken towards change. The book brings together the findings of numerous studies about the status of women in higher education.

ED 20   Furniss, W. Todd and Graham, Patricia A. (eds.)
WOMEN IN HIGHER EDUCATION (Washington, D.C.: American Council on Education, 1974)

Papers from a conference which covered topics such as higher education, academic programmes, affirmative action and contexts for decisions. There are papers by well-known specialists including Juanita Kreps, Helen Austin and Catherine Stimpson.

ED 21   Richardson, Betty
SEXISM IN HIGHER EDUCATION (New York: Seaburg Press, 1974)

Richardson looks at many facets of discrimination against women at university level.

ED 22   Stacey, Judith et al. (eds.)
AND JILL CAME TUMBLING AFTER: SEXISM IN AMERICAN EDUCATION (New York: Dell Press, 1974)

A comprehensive collection of essays by Horner, Howe, Rossi, among others, showing how sexism operates at all levels of education. It suggests how schools can eradicate institutional, cultural, and psychological varieties of sexism.

ED 23 Abramson, Joan
THE INVISIBLE WOMAN: DISCRIMINATION IN THE ACADEMIC PROFESSION (San Francisco: Jossey-Bass, 1975)

Abramson's own academic experience is the starting point for her inquiry into the sex discrimination of universities and colleges. She includes a case-study of her own sex discrimination suits against the University of Hawaii; describes myths of meritocracy and information and gives a critical analysis of methods of appeal available to women who suffer discrimination.

ED 24 Daniels, Arlene Kaplan
A SURVEY OF RESEARCH CONCERNS ON WOMEN'S ISSUES (Washington, D.C.: Association of American Colleges, 1975)

A critical review of research findings to date on topics such as the women's movement, socialisation and education, work, marital status and health. It addresses two major issues: how research will affect social policy and what research questions can provide the information needed to promote positive changes in social policy.

ED 25 Howe, Florence (ed.)
WOMEN AND THE POWER TO CHANGE (New York: McGraw-Hill, 1975)

This looks at the power women actually have and potential changes. It includes now classic essays such as Adrienne Rich 'Toward a Woman-Centered University', essays on law schools, and male careers with contributors describing their lives as feminists in the world of higher education.

ED 26 Maccia, Elizabeth Steiner (ed.)
WOMEN AND EDUCATION (Springfield, Ill.: Charles C. Thomas, 1975)

Twenty-five essays in this collection study the effect of the educational system on American women. Contributors conclude that the system operates in tandem with socialisation, in that women are taught to be subordinate to men. They suggest ways to correct this situation. The book includes essays by such well-known feminist educators as Florence Howe, Alice Rossi, Sheila Tobias and Wilma Scott Heide.

ED 27   Schramm, Sarah Slavin (ed.)
FEMALE STUDIES VIII (Pittsburgh, PA.: Know, 1975)

A pedagogical approach to the strategies involved in getting recognition for Women's Studies. Includes syllabi and bibliographies.

ED 28   Wasserman, Elga et al. (eds.)
WOMEN IN ACADEMIA: EVOLVING POLICIES TOWARD EQUAL OPPORTUNITY (New York: Praeger, 1975)

The editors present a volume of essays on affirmative action progress and policies as they affect academic women.

ED 29   Westervelt, Esther
BARRIERS TO WOMEN'S PARTICIPATION IN POST-SECONDARY EDUCATION: A REVIEW OF RESEARCH AND COMMENTARY AS OF 1973–1974 (Washington, D.C.: United States Government Printing Office, 1975)

This collects evidence of institutional/admission barriers; financial aid; faculty and staff attitudes; deficiencies in curriculum planning and student services. Part II deals with social constraints—of family or class and Part III with psychological attitudes of women and motivation.

ED 30   Adams, Carol and Laurikietis, R. (eds.)
THE GENDER TRAP: A CLOSER LOOK AT SEX
ROLES: BOOK ONE: EDUCATION AND WORK
(London: Virago, 1976)

One in a three-part series of books which analyse the accepted sex roles of men and women in society. Intended as a teaching text it uses cartoons, extracts, poems and interviews on such topics as child-rearing, schools organisation and the exam system.

ED 31   Ahlum, Carol and Fralley, Jacqueline (eds.)
HIGH SCHOOL FEMINIST STUDIES (Old Westbury, N.Y.: Feminist Press, 1976)

This is the first published collection of Women's Studies materials, bibliographies, and syllabi designed for high schools. There is an introduction by Florence Howe and an extensive bibliography. The strength of the collection is the presentation of syllabuses and course outlines for a range of courses.

ED 32   Astin, Helen S. (ed.)
SOME ACTION OF HER OWN: THE ADULT
WOMAN AND HIGHER EDUCATION (Lexington, Mass.: Lexington Books, 1976)

This collection of articles comes out of a study of fifteen continuing education for women programmes looking at the impact of the programmes on students, administrators and families. Articles are by Jessie Bernard and others.

ED 33   Fitzpatrick, Blanche E.
WOMEN'S INFERIOR EDUCATION (New York: Praeger, 1976)

A good study explaining women's minority status in education. It gives a state by state analysis with precise statistics and makes recommendations on how to achieve educational equality.

ED 34   Guttentag, Marcia and Bray, Helen
           UNDOING SEX STEREOTYPES: RESEARCH AND
           RESOURCES FOR EDUCATORS (New York:
           McGraw-Hill, 1976)

           Based on work with 400 children in three school systems, this text answers the question: What can be done to make a classroom non-sexist? Background materials, non-sexist curriculum proposals and bibliographies are included.

ED 35   Howe, Florence
           SEVEN YEARS LATER: WOMEN'S STUDIES
           PROGRAMS IN 1976 (Washington, D.C.: National
           Advisory Council on Women's Educational Programs,
           1976)

           A comprehensive study of fifteen Women's Studies programmes in colleges and universities in the United States. The report discusses curriculum and classroom, students, faculty and administration, the impact of Women's Studies as a strategy for change and issues for the future.

ED 36   Packard, Sandra and Zimmerman, Enid
           'Special Issue', *Studies in Art Education* (Winter 1976)

           This contains research on sexual stereotyping and on women in art education.

ED 37   Sharpe, Sue
           'JUST LIKE A GIRL': HOW GIRLS LEARN TO BE
           WOMEN (Harmondsworth: Penguin, 1976)

           Based on results of a survey at four London schools (involving both English and immigrant girls). This is a descriptive and analytical account of the situation of young girls in Britain set in a historical and social context and illustrated by the girls themselves. Sharpe concentrates on working-class girls and their own experiences of social and school conditioning.

ED 38　　　Berger, G. (ed.)
'Changing Roles of Women: A Symposium', *Journal of Research and Development in Education* 10 (Summer 1977) 1–76

A special cross-cultural issue with articles on female socialisation in America and a feminist approach to the high school curriculum.

ED 39　　　Pottker, Janice and Fishel, Andrew (eds.)
SEX BIAS IN THE SCHOOLS (Rutherford, N.J.: Farleigh Dickinson University Press, 1977)

A collection of accounts of sexist practices in schools from various disciplines including education, sociology, engineering, psychology and political science.

ED 40　　　'Women's Studies Issues', *Radical Teacher* (December 1977 and N17 1980)

The first issue has fifteen articles of personal histories and reviews by instructors of Women's Studies. The second looks at directions in Women's Studies including work on black women and lesbian studies.

ED 41　　　Wolpe, Anne-Marie
SOME PROCESSES IN SEXIST EDUCATION (London: WRRC, 1977)

Based on a study of British comprehensive education, Wolpe discusses the role of the curriculum in the construction of ideology.

ED 42　　　Blumhagen, K. and Johnson, W. (eds.)
WOMEN'S STUDIES (Westport, CT.: Greenwood Press, 1978)

A collection of essays addressing the theoretical, administrative and pedagogical aspects of Women's Studies. Contributors include Schramm, Hoagland and Boneparth.

ED 43   Byrne, E. M.
          WOMEN AND EDUCATION (London: Tavistock, 1978)

          An early account by the future education officer to the UK Equal Opportunities Commission and education consultant to the EEC. Byrne covers issues and research from primary through tertiary education; research on the role of women teachers; strategies for the future and sex-typing of textbooks. A very good chronological study of the post-war period. She shows how the proportion of women in leadership roles in the period between 1965 and 1974 had actually declined. The book challenged the assumption that equal opportunity has been achieved in Britain. Argues that girls suffer from an 'aggregation of inequality'.

ED 44   Crewe, Louie (ed.)
          THE GAY ACADEMIC (Palm Springs, CA.: ETC Publications, 1978)

          A collection of 26 essays representing a variety of fields—history, library science, literature, linguistics, philosophy, psychology, religion and theology, science, sociology, and political science—of scholarship about gay people in academia. It includes essays by Julia Stanley and Barbara Gittings.

ED 45   Deem, Rosemary (ed.)
          WOMEN AND SCHOOLING (London: Routledge & Kegan Paul, 1978)

          This includes essays about every level of British education including material on girls' schools, higher education and careers of women educators. It shows how the treatment of women in education is closely linked to other social policies and prevalent ideology about women's roles.

ED 46   Bristol Women's Studies Group (eds.)
          HALF THE SKY (London: Virago, 1979)

          Two hundred extracts of three centuries of women's thought collected as a basic text for Women's Studies courses. It includes material from history, sociology, fiction, psychology and newspapers organised into themes of childhood, education, sexuality, health, marriage, work and creativity.

ED 47 Rich, Adrienne
ON LIES, SECRETS AND SILENCE (New York: W. W. Norton, 1979)

Contains: 'Toward a Woman-Centered University' an institutional analysis and plea for changing university structures; claiming that feminist culture and politics are inseparable; 'Claiming an Education'—women's colleges as responsible environments; 'Taking Women Students Seriously'—discussing issues which alienate women students. These are perhaps the most significant and moving essays since Virginia Woolf *A Room of One's Own* and *Three Guineas*.

ED 48 Bose, Christine and Priest-Jones, J.
THE RELATIONSHIP BETWEEN WOMEN'S STUDIES, CAREER DEVELOPMENT AND VOCATIONAL CHOICE (Washington, D.C.: National Institute of Education, 1980)

This reviews sociological studies and data sources. It shows that Women's Studies courses are associated with positive attitudes to career choices.

ED 49 Brighton Women and Science Group (eds.)
ALICE THROUGH THE MICROSCOPE: THE POWER OF SCIENCE OVER WOMEN'S LIVES (London: Virago, 1980)

This book argues that scientific rationalism is seen as masculine. There are essays on the technology of contraception, and an exposé of how IQ testing is based on a fallacious psychology of sex differences.

ED 50 Deem, Rosemary (ed.)
SCHOOLING FOR WOMEN'S WORK (London: Routledge & Kegan Paul, 1980)

In essays about British education and the British school system the editor includes interesting material about West Indian girls and their strategies of negotiation through a sexist and racist system.

ED 51   Delamont, S.
SEX ROLES AND THE SCHOOL (London: Methuen, 1980)

The author finds there is a restricted world and range of roles available for girls in school material. She describes the cultural imposition of traditional images of women's roles.

ED 52   Elevson, Allana
WOMEN'S STUDIES IN COMMUNITY COLLEGES (Washington, D.C.: National Institute of Education, 1980)

The re-entry of women has been most dramatic in the community college and this surveys 53 programmes. It shows that the role of Women's Studies can be crucial to women's success.

ED 53   Fowlkes, Martha R. (ed.)
BEHIND EVERY SUCCESSFUL MAN: WIVES OF MEDICINE AND ACADEME (New York: Columbia University Press, 1980)

This uses in-depth interviews with wives of professors on topics of marriage, work and wives' and husbands' careers. It shows that the lives of academic wives are an integral part of a husband's career and that a wife's role enables her husband to work.

ED 54   Hersch, Blanche Glassman
RE-ENTRY WOMEN INVOLVED IN WOMEN'S STUDIES (Washington, D.C.: National Institute of Education, 1980)

This reviews numerous studies and assesses the interaction between returning women and Women's Studies.

It reveals a changing profile of women and includes recommendations for research.

ED 55 Howe, Florence and Lauter, Paul
THE IMPACT OF WOMEN'S STUDIES ON THE CAMPUS AND THE DISCIPLINES (Washington, D.C.: National Institute of Education, February 1980)

The first of eight monographs. The primary impact the authors agree comes from the establishment of a curricular unit. They reveal high productivity ratings for Women's Studies but call for more longitudinal comparisons.

ED 56 Ness, E. and Brooks, K. H.
WOMEN'S STUDIES AS A CATALYST FOR FACULTY DEVELOPMENT (Washington, D.C.: National Institute of Education, 1980)

This reviews literature and reports from Women's Studies programmes. It looks at workshops, conferences and new patterns of faculty government.

ED 57 Porter, Nancy and Eilenchild, Marg.
THE EFFECTIVENESS OF WOMEN'S STUDIES TEACHING (Washington, D.C.: National Institute of Education, 1980)

One of eight monographs reviewing the literature which is assessing changes in attitude towards sex roles and sex role stereotyping.

ED 58 Ruth, Sheila
ISSUES IN FEMINISM: A FIRST COURSE IN WOMEN'S STUDIES (Boston, Mass.: Houghton, Mifflin, 1980)

A Women's Studies text and systematic examination of sources. Ruth believes sex roles limit human choice. What distinguishes the book is a full commentary and bibliography.

ED 59   Spender, Dale and Sarah, Elizabeth (eds.)
LEARNING TO LOSE (London: Women's Press, 1980)

This contains different accounts of the culture, ethos and demands of schooling and their clash with family and home backgrounds. It reveals how different learning environments promote similar concepts of femininity.

ED 60   Dupont, Beatrice (ed.)
UNEQUAL EDUCATION: A STUDY OF SEX-DIFFERENCES IN SECONDARY SCHOOL CURRICULA (New York: UNESCO, 1981)

Published as part of a plan of action adopted by the World Conference of the International Women's Year in Mexico City in 1975. It uses comparative analysis of data throughout the world including material from Afghanistan, Jamaica, Jordon, Madagascar, Mongolia, Portugal and Turkey. Most evidence shows that schooling still perpetuates traditional roles.

ED 61   Kelly, A. (ed.)
THE MISSING HALF: GIRLS AND SCIENCE EDUCATION (Manchester: Manchester University Press, 1981)

This deals with girls' underachievement in science. It covers research and a range of explanations for sex differences in science achievement. Three perspectives are offered: competing theories of the origins of girls' underachievement are evaluated; and short reports of original research, as it presents itself in schools, including the process and determinants of subject choice and teachers' attitudes. It includes first-hand accounts from pupils and teachers and suggests strategies to improve girls' performance.

ED 62   Langland, E. and Gove, W. (eds.)
A FEMINIST PERSPECTIVE IN THE ACADEME (Chicago: University of Chicago Press, 1981)

This covers recent feminist work in all major disciplines, and shows the differences a feminist perspective makes, and how to incorporate feminist materials into a traditional academic course. The collection contains, among other essays: P. Meyer Spacks 'The Difference It Makes', and N. Keohane 'Speaking From Silence' on women's exclusion from political science.

ED 63   Spender, Dale (ed.)
MEN'S STUDIES MODIFIED: THE IMPACT OF FEMINISM ON THE ACADEMIC DISCIPLINES (Oxford: Pergamon Press, 1981)

This collection describes a wide range of male controls in different disciplines and analyses changes brought about in response to feminist challenges. Contributors cover social sciences, medicine, and media studies among fifteen disciplines.

ED 64   'Special Section: Women's Studies', *Change* 14: 3 (April 1982)

With essays from Florence Howe among others, the collection focuses on the issue of teaching Women's Studies from *within* disciplines or as a separate area; and on the role of men in Women's Studies.

ED 65   Cruikshank, Margaret (ed.)
LESBIAN STUDIES: PRESENT AND FUTURE (Old Westbury, N.Y.: Feminist Press, 1982)

A fully comprehensive collection of the new lesbian scholarship incorporating a range of disciplines and areas from literature to sports. There are essays on the pedagogy of lesbian teaching and contributions from most leading lesbian academics.

ED 66   Hull, Gloria T., Scott, Patricia B. and Smith, Barbara (eds.)
ALL THE WOMEN ARE WHITE, ALL THE BLACKS ARE MEN, BUT SOME OF US ARE BRAVE: BLACK WOMEN'S STUDIES (New York: Feminist Press, 1982)

The book is a testament to the existence of a strong black feminist tradition and a response to the invisibility of black female experience in Women's Studies or Black Studies classrooms. The authors see Black Women's Studies as a metaphor for the revolutionary message of Women's Studies—profound social and political change can occur only when the experience of black women is immediately accessible to all women. The text includes theoretical, sociological literary and pedagogical essays, extensive bibliographies, course syllabuses and photographs.

ED 67 'Special Issue: Women and Education', *Off Our Backs* XII (May 1982)

Articles on the theory and practice of Black Women's Studies and on the integration of feminist teaching styles into general curricula. It gives a history of Women's Studies at SUNY Buffalo and accounts of lesbian and Third World women who were fired because of their radical politics.

ED 68 Spender, Dale
INVISIBLE WOMEN: THE SCHOOLING SCANDAL (London: Writers and Readers, 1982)

Spender exposes the myth of equal opportunities in education for women by drawing extensively on studies of classroom interaction. She demonstrates that 'equality' for young women is dependent upon their adjustment to rules and ideas instituted by men for the benefit of men.

ED 69 Abel, Elizabeth and Abel, Emily
THE SIGNS READER: WOMEN, GENDER AND SCHOLARSHIP (Chicago: University of Chicago Press, 1983)

Selections from the first thirty issues of *Signs* indicate salient trends in feminist scholarship since 1975. The text covers theoretical contributions in a variety of disciplines including essays by Smith-Rosenberg, Kelly-Gadol, Fox Keller, Hartmann and Adrienne Rich. The articles are those which have sparked off debates about the traditions of female culture.

ED 70   Bowles, Gloria and Duelli-Klein, Renata (eds.)
THEORIES OF WOMEN'S STUDIES (London:
Routledge & Kegan Paul, 1983)

This examines the assumptions and aims of Women's Studies; its connections with the women's movement; its research and methodologies. A number of disciplines are represented including humanities, social and natural sciences with contributions from several countries describing a range of feminist techniques from quantitive to experiential analysis. The book contains a good bibliography.

ED 71   Bunch, Charlotte and Pollack, S. (eds.)
LEARNING OUR WAY: ESSAYS IN FEMINIST
EDUCATION (New York: The Crossing Press, 1983)

A collection of essays focusing on the New Right's attack on women studies programmes together with a socialist-feminist critique of universities; anti-racism education for white women and writing workshops in prisons. Contributors include Gloria Hull, Florence Howe and Barbara Smith.

ED 72   Dudowitz, R. L. (ed.)
WOMEN IN ACADEME (Oxford: Pergamon Press, 1983)

A collection of articles focusing on how women respond to and experience the academic environment. Essays on black women professors; the role of graduate teaching assistants; lesbian studies and science.

ED 73   Humm, Maggie
'Women Students in Higher Education', *Women's Studies International Quarterly* 6: 1 (1983) 97–105

An analysis of sex discrimination in mixed seminar groups, covering uses of vocabulary, space and sex roles.

ED 74   Purvis, J. and Hales, M.
ACHIEVEMENT AND INEQUALITY IN EDUCATION (London: Routledge & Kegan Paul, 1983)

Together with its companion volume *Education Policy and Society* this covers a range of approaches to the study of education. Key topics: comprehensive education; progressive teaching; gender, race and education; educational policy and ideology; schooling, work and unemployment.

ED 75   Acker, Sandra and Piper, David Warren (eds.)
IS HIGHER EDUCATION FAIR TO WOMEN? (London: Nelson, 1984)

Essays examine the notions of access, equal opportunities and discrimination in particular disciplines. Contributors include Burstyn, Dyhouse on the history of women in higher education and proposals for affirmative action and women's studies from Roberts and Duelli-Klein.

ED 76   Acker, Sandra et al. (eds.)
WOMEN AND EDUCATION (London: Kogan Page, 1984)

Twenty-three essays examine the role of the disciplines, case studies of women and education throughout the world; the education of women in the context of other social institutions; and women, education and social change with policies and strategies. Exemplary coverage of Far East and Third World women.

ED 77   Canadian Research Institute for the Advancement of Women
KNOWLEDGE RECONSIDERED: A FEMINIST OVERVIEW (Ottawa: CRI, 1984)

This discusses feminist thought in relation to different areas of study from literature to anthropology and sociology. Essays by Dorothy Smith and others examine the structure and theoretical framework of each discipline.

ED 78   Fowlkes, Diane and McClure, Charlotte, S. (eds.)
FEMINIST VISION: TOWARDS A
TRANSFORMATION OF THE LIBERAL ARTS
CURRICULUM (University, Ala.: University of
Alabama, 1984)

Taken from a conference of Southern Scholars on Women. There are essays on feminist pedagogy and theory, on androgyny and patriarchy, on feminist art criticism, on racism, history, architecture and sex differences. An essay by Catherine Stimpson looks at theoretical perspectives.

ED 79   Stanworth, M.
GENDER AND SCHOOLING: A STUDY OF
SEXUAL DIVISION IN THE CLASSROOM (London:
Hutchinson, 1983; New Hampshire: Dover, 1984)

Stanworth shows that sexist circumstances surrounding the choice of subjects, curriculum, and teacher/pupil relations systematically undermine girls' abilities and confidence. Stanworth uses her empirical work in mixed classrooms to show that teaching practices serve to reinforce pupils' belief in masculine superiority.

ED 80   Thompson, Jane
LEARNING LIBERATION (London: Croom Helm,
1984)

Thompson dissects the sexism of conventional adult and continuing education for women and argues the case for women-centred education.

ED 81   Culley, Margo and Portuges, Cathy (eds.)
GENDERED SUBJECTS: THE DYNAMICS OF
FEMINIST TEACHING (Boston and London:
Routledge & Kegan Paul, 1985)

A collection of essays by teachers of Women's Studies in America about their work over the past ten years. A mixture of 'classic' statements on feminist pedagogy from Adrienne Rich among others combined with recent work and first hand accounts.

ED 82 Hughes, Mary and Kennedy, Mary (eds.)
NEW FUTURES: CHANGING WOMEN'S
EDUCATION (London: Routledge & Kegan Paul,
1985)

An innovatory series of case studies of British adult and further education, skills workshops and access courses which raises questions about alternative educational practices for women.

ED 83 Weiner, Gaby (ed.)
JUST A BUNCH OF GIRLS: FEMINIST
APPROACHES TO SCHOOLING (Milton Keynes:
Open University Press, 1985)

Essays on girls' experiences of schooling in Britain and reports of feminist teaching initiatives from nurseries to secondary schools. There are clear descriptions of anti-sexist strategies.

Index of Subjects

abortion: TSP 111, HIST 12, HIST 20
absence: LIT 135, LIT 136, ART 83
access: ED 19, ED 75, ED 82
adolescence: SOC 5, SOC 21, SOC 117, SOC 137, ART 52, ED 37
advertising: ART 39, ART 44, ART 83
aesthetics: LIT 3, LIT 12, LIT 43, LIT 47, ART 23, ART 54, ART 101, ART 103, ART 104, ART 124
affirmative action: ED 20, ED 28, ED 75
Africa: LIT 46, ANTH 8, ANTH 39, ANTH 54
Afro-American: LIT 46, LIT 48, LIT 76, LIT 116, ART 53
ageing: PSY 42, PSY 43
Althusser: LIT 42, LIT 84
amateur: ART 4, HIST 32
Amazon: TSP 37, TSP 44, ANTH 27, ANTH 91
androgyny: TSP 41, TSP 87, PSY 11, PSY 29, PSY 35, PSY 56, ANTH 59, ANTH 61, ANTH 83, ANTH 94, ED 78
anti-sexist: SOC 106, SOC 127, PSY 51, ED 34, ED 83
anti-slavery: HIST 3, HIST 89
archaeology: ANTH 56
archetypes: LIT 79
architecture: ART 18, ART 73, ART 98, ART 121, ED 78
Asian: LIT 76, SOC 89, ANTH 52, ED 76
astrology: ANTH 97
autobiography: TSP 129, LIT 3, LIT 43, LIT 50, LIT 60, LIT 67, LIT 91, LIT 96, LIT 106, LIT 110, LIT 118, LIT 121, SOC 29, SOC 101, SOC 119, ART 40, PSY 36, HIST 52, HIST 116, ANTH 48

Barthes: ART 43
biology: TSP 132, PSY 10, PSY 16, PSY 35, PSY 37, ANTH 6, ANTH 49, ANTH 56
birth: PSY 23, PSY 43
black: TSP 7, TSP 20, TSP 24, TSP 64, TSP 103, TSP 108, TSP 109, TSP 129, LIT 32, LIT 46, LIT 57, LIT 60, LIT 80, LIT 81, LIT 90, LIT 114, LIT 117, LIT 121, LIT 132, LIT 150, SOC 10, SOC 21, SOC 111, ART 53, HIST 14, HIST 27, HIST 49, ED 40, ED 66, ED 67, ED 72
bodies: TSP 80, TSP 81, SOC 31, SOC 71, SOC 83, PSY 48, PSY 52, HIST 57, ANTH 68
business: SOC 72, SOC 73

campaigns: ART 5, HIST 3, HIST 72, HIST 110, ED 16, ED 23
careers: ED 3, ED 48
Caribbean: LIT 46
Chicana: LIT 76
child-care: SOC 31, SOC 53, ART 111, HIST 12, HIST 109
children: SOC 6, ED 10
China: HIST 16, HIST 39, HIST 49, ANTH 35, ANTH 88
city: LIT 129, SOC 121, ART 121
class: TSP 46, TSP 92, TSP 103, LIT 77, LIT 101, SOC 58, HIST 108, ANTH 46
community: TSP 57, LIT 35, LIT 68
consciousness-raising: TSP 43, TSP 98
crime: SOC 52, SOC 80, SOC 127
culture: TSP 75, TSP 88, TSP 112, LIT 29, LIT 45, LIT 76, SOC 117, HIST 80, ANTH 37, ANTH 93, ED 69
curriculum: HIST 81, HIST 90, ED 1, ED 15, ED 38, ED 41, ED 55, ED 60, ED 79

daughters: LIT 68, PSY 24, PSY 53, HIST 74
day release: SOC 76
deconstruction: LIT 82, LIT 115, LIT 122
deity: TSP 4, TSP 40, ANTH 27, ANTH 83, ANTH 101
demography: PSY 39, HIST 4, HIST 43
Derrida: LIT 22, LIT 63, LIT 115
design: ART 116
desire: PSY 55
difference: TSP 1, TSP 9, LIT 24, LIT 57,

LIT 61, LIT 66, LIT 82, SOC 33, SOC 56, SOC 118, HIST 73
discrimination: SOC 62, SOC 139, HIST 13, ED 23, ED 75
divorce: SOC 63, PSY 51, HIST 7, HIST 72
documentary: ART 114, ART 119, HIST 14, HIST 50
domestic: ART 73, ART 98, HIST 15, HIST 34, HIST 43, HIST 47, HIST 67

economics: SOC 62, SOC 90, SOC 96, SOC 98, SOC 116, SOC 128, SOC 133
Ecriture: LIT 6
empiricism: SOC 29, SOC 52, ED 79
employment: SOC 93, SOC 112, SOC 133, SOC 139, HIST 93
engineering: ED 3
environment: HIST 27
equal opportunities: ED 28, ED 33, ED 68, ED 75
equal pay: TSP 45, SOC 60, SOC 62, SOC 129, SOC 139
erotic: TSP 78, TSP 125, TSP 134
essentialism: TSP 17, LIT 109, ART 13, ART 124
ethnicity: SOC 82, ART 108
ethnography: SOC 117, ANTH 8, ANTH 23, ANTH 30, ANTH 39, ANTH 50, ANTH 56
evolution: ANTH 26, ANTH 80
experiential: SOC 101, SOC 135, ED 70

fairy tales: ANTH 25, ANTH 82, ANTH 85, ANTH 90
family: TSP 43, TSP 117, TSP 127, SOC 18, SOC 43, SOC 55, SOC 68, SOC 122, SOC 124, SOC 125, ART 121, PSY 55, HIST 4, HIST 15, HIST 17, HIST 30, HIST 56, HIST 64, HIST 65, ANTH 8, ANTH 46, ANTH 50, ANTH 55, ED 8
fantasy: ART 119, PSY 36
fashion: ART 108, ART 129
femininity: LIT 5, LIT 14, LIT 120, SOC 30, SOC 70, ART 127, PSY 6, PSY 21, PSY 22, PSY 23, HIST 88, HIST 90, ANTH 92, ED 59
fertility: TSP 127, SOC 39, HIST 4, ANTH 87
fieldwork: ANTH 19, ANTH 20, ANTH 54

film: ART 3, ART 7, ART 12, ART 15, ART 16, ART 20, ART 22, ART 24, ART 26, ART 32, ART 42, ART 43, ART 45, ART 48, ART 62, ART 67, ART 77, ART 79, ART 87, ART 89, ART 95, ART 106, ART 111, ART 114, ART 117, ART 118, ART 120, ART 125, ART 127, ANTH 82
folk art: ART 84
folklore: ANTH 41, ANTH 48, ANTH 96, ANTH 105
Freud: TSP 12, TSP 79, LIT 58, LIT 100, SOC 70, SOC 97, PSY 1, PSY 3, PSY 8, PSY 16, PSY 21, PSY 22, PSY 44, PSY 50, PSY 54, ANTH 81
future: LIT 76

gaze: ART 17, ART 45, ART 92, ART 118
gender: TSP 120, LIT 15, LIT 21, LIT 42, LIT 62, LIT 69, LIT 77, LIT 101, LIT 105, LIT 118, LIT 134, SOC 25, SOC 50, SOC 56, SOC 64, SOC 81, SOC 85, SOC 126, ART 100, PSY 44, PSY 46, PSY 53, PSY 54, PSY 56, HIST 96, ANTH 93
genres: LIT 34, LIT 49, ANTH 41, ANTH 87
goddess: ANTH 14, ANTH 44, ANTH 74, ANTH 80, ANTH 86, ANTH 90, ANTH 99, ANTH 101, ANTH 104

health: SOC 24, SOC 31, SOC 83, HIST 18, HIST 60, ANTH 28, ED 24
heroine: LIT 3, LIT 53, LIT 78, LIT 83, LIT 86, LIT 106, LIT 123, ART 25, ANTH 22, ANTH 102, ANTH 104
heterosexuality: SOC 36
higher education: ED 1, ED 5, ED 12, ED 13, ED 19, ED 20, ED 21, ED 25, ED 29, ED 32, ED 75
historiography: HIST 37, HIST 45, HIST 73, HIST 101, HIST 107
housework: TSP 54, SOC 6, SOC 22, SOC 42, SOC 43, SOC 66, HIST 103

iconography: ART 111, ART 128, ANTH 62, ANTH 81, ANTH 102
ideology: TSP 115, TSP 118, TSP 135, SOC 91, SOC 97, ART 105, HIST 95, HIST 97, ANTH 36, ED 41
immigrant: HIST 11, HIST 46
India: HIST 16, ANTH 35, ANTH 94

Index of Subjects

industrialisation: HIST 5, HIST 64, HIST 79
interpellation: ART 83
interviews: LIT 116, SOC 117, SOC 119
IQ: ED 49
Islam: SOC 136, HIST 16, ANTH 35, ANTH 105

Jew: LIT 111, ANTH 38, ANTH 61, ANTH 92
Jung: LIT 79, PSY 11, ANTH 25, ANTH 81, ANTH 90, ANTH 99

kinship: SOC 5, ANTH 5, ANTH 23, ANTH 35, ANTH 73

Lacan: LIT 131, ART 83, ART 106, PSY 55
Laing: LIT 44, PSY 21
law: SOC 23, SOC 139, SOC 140, HIST 36
lesbian: TSP 31, TSP 32, TSP 34, TSP 37, TSP 44, TSP 46, TSP 50, TSP 51, TSP 64, TSP 91, TSP 93, TSP 97, TSP 101, TSP 102, TSP 126, TSP 129, TSP 133, LIT 18, LIT 32, LIT 57, LIT 70, LIT 72, LIT 73, LIT 80, LIT 90, LIT 134, LIT 150, SOC 107, ART 58, ART 102, PSY 17, HIST 15, HIST 71, ED 40, ED 44, ED 65, ED 67, ED 72
letters: LIT 16, LIT 65
liberation: TSP 5, TSP 13, TSP 14, TSP 18, TSP 20, TSP 21, TSP 22, TSP 23, TSP 25, TSP 26, TSP 33, TSP 35, TSP 36, TSP 39, TSP 40, TSP 45, TSP 56, TSP 60, TSP 65, TSP 79, TSP 90, TSP 113, LIT 51, SOC 7, SOC 65, SOC 84, HIST 6, HIST 70, HIST 88, ANTH 21
life-cycle: SOC 22

Macherey: LIT 42
madness: LIT 44, LIT 47, PSY 14, PSY 46
marriage: SOC 28, SOC 36, SOC 55, SOC 60, SOC 63, ART 77, HIST 106, ANTH 8, ANTH 23, ANTH 29, ANTH 52, ANTH 58, ED 24, ED 53
Marxism: TSP 14, TSP 92, TSP 110, TSP 132, LIT 59, LIT 90, LIT 103, LIT 126, LIT 150, SOC 14, SOC 64, SOC 70, SOC 84, SOC 97, SOC 105, SOC 120, ART 103, HIST 6, HIST 39, HIST 63, ANTH 46

masochism: PSY 1, PSY 3
maternity: SOC 75, SOC 110
matriarchy: SOC 14, SOC 120, ART 124, ANTH 5, ANTH 6, ANTH 46, ANTH 47, ANTH 55, ANTH 68, ANTH 104
medicine: SOC 4, SOC 35, SOC 40, SOC 45, PSY 47, HIST 57, HIST 58, HIST 60, ED 3, ED 53
media: SOC 37, SOC 74, ART 9, ART 50, ART 60, ART 81, ART 105, ART 109
menopause: PSY 1, ANTH 63
menstruation: LIT 53, PSY 47, ANTH 10, ANTH 12, ANTH 24, ANTH 31, ANTH 53, ANTH 63, ANTH 70, ANTH 78
mental health: PSY 7, PSY 13, PSY 14, PSY 29, HIST 57
middle age: SOC 102
Middle Ages: HIST 31, HIST 32, HIST 106
middle class: TSP 2, PSY 9, HIST 4, HIST 29, HIST 78, HIST 91
midwives: HIST 18, HIST 58, ANTH 28, ANTH 75
miners: HIST 82
minority: SOC 2
mirrors: ANTH 90
misogyny: TSP 12, LIT 1, LIT 21, ART 27, PSY 3, HIST 58
moon: ANTH 57, ANTH 90
mothers: TSP 69, LIT 53, LIT 68, LIT 93, LIT 112, LIT 117, SOC 5, SOC 39, SOC 46, SOC 78, SOC 99, PSY 1, PSY 3, PSY 24, PSY 28, PSY 32, PSY 36, PSY 44, PSY 53, ANTH 7, ANTH 8, ANTH 27
museum: ART 5
music: ART 7, ART 33, ART 53, ART 69, ART 107

native American: LIT 76, ART 18, ART 115, HIST 27, HIST 35, ANTH 4, ANTH 67, ANTH 87, ANTH 89, ANTH 100
nature: TSP 75, SOC 132, ANTH 37, ANTH 93
needlework: ART 71, ART 84, ART 93, ART 122
novels: LIT 3, LIT 5, LIT 8, LIT 9, LIT 11, LIT 14, LIT 18, LIT 19, LIT 21, LIT 26, LIT 28, LIT 31, LIT 33, LIT 35, LIT 36, LIT 38, LIT 39, LIT 41, LIT 44, LIT 47, LIT 51, LIT 53, LIT 54, LIT 55, LIT

64, LIT 65, LIT 75, LIT 77, LIT 79, LIT 84, LIT 85, LIT 86, LIT 89, LIT 91, LIT 92, LIT 94, LIT 97, LIT 98, LIT 100, LIT 101, LIT 104, LIT 106, LIT 120, LIT 123, LIT 130, LIT 140

Oedipal: PSY 44, PSY 54
oral: HIST 49, HIST 74, HIST 115
orgasm: TSP 16, TSP 42

patriarchy: TSP 12, TSP 17, TSP 82, TSP 117
peace: TSP 58, TSP 128
pedagogy: LIT 4, ED 27, ED 42, ED 65, ED 78, ED 81
personal: TSP 27
phallic: ART 14, PSY 8, PSY 55
phenomenology: SOC 99
philosophy: SOC 100, SOC 114
photography: ART 28, ART 59, ART 65, ART 126
pioneer: HIST 48
poetry: LIT 10, LIT 13, LIT 23, LIT 47, LIT 48, LIT 81, LIT 88, LIT 99, LIT 109, LIT 125
politics: SOC 38, SOC 41, SOC 51, SOC 108, SOC 115, SOC 120, SOC 138
pornography: TSP 48, TSP 94, TSP 102, TSP 104, TSP 107, TSP 111, TSP 122, TSP 134, ART 117
prehistory: ANTH 27
prisons: ED 71
professions: SOC 9, SOC 15, SOC 126, ART 4, HIST 12, HIST 95, ED 9
prostitution: TSP 67, HIST 7, HIST 86

quilts: ART 23, ART 84

racism: TSP 103, LIT 76, LIT 133, SOC 89, ED 50, ED 78
radical: TSP 18, TSP 27, TSP 29, TSP 30, TSP 42, TSP 53, TSP 65, TSP 71, TSP 79, TSP 118
rape: TSP 53, TSP 84, TSP 103, LIT 53, SOC 12, ART 20
realism: LIT 139, ART 46, ART 110, ART 114, ART 119
Reich: PSY 21
religion: TSP 3, LIT 29, HIST 84, HIST 117, ANTH 4, ANTH 7, ANTH 11, ANTH 16, ANTH 17, ANTH 31, ANTH 34, ANTH 38, ANTH 79, ANTH 81, ANTH 87, ANTH 88
representation: ART 11, ART 62
reproduction: TSP 52, TSP 132, PSY 6, PSY 10, HIST 42, HIST 47, ANTH 71
rights: TSP 56, SOC 16
ritual: ART 78, ANTH 24, ANTH 42, ANTH 56, ANTH 57, ANTH 60, ANTH 70, ANTH 71, ANTH 76, ANTH 78, ANTH 86, ANTH 88, ANTH 103
romance: LIT 94, LIT 124, LIT 127
rural: SOC 47, HIST 10, HIST 75, ANTH 52

science: SOC 132, PSY 46, HIST 114, ANTH 45, ED 3, ED 9, ED 49, ED 61, ED 72
sculpture: ART 12, ART 38, ART 86
segregation: SOC 64, SOC 94
semiotics: TSP 70, LIT 64, LIT 93, LIT 99, ART 103, ART 120, ANTH 93
separatism: TSP 17, ART 34, ED 5
servants: HIST 11, HIST 43
sex differences: TSP 28, PSY 8, PSY 9, PSY 13, PSY 20, PSY 31, PSY 41, PSY 43, PSY 49, PSY 55, ANTH 2, ANTH 71, ED 49, ED 60, ED 61, ED 78
sex roles: PSY 12, PSY 14, PSY 29, PSY 37, PSY 45, HIST 76, ANTH 30, ANTH 42, ANTH 73, ED 10, ED 14, ED 51, ED 57, ED 58, ED 73
sexism: TSP 8, TSP 9, TSP 11, TSP 55, LIT 25, LIT 66, SOC 13, SOC 15, SOC 18, SOC 67, PSY 33, ED 5, ED 14, ED 15, ED 16, ED 21, ED 22, ED 39
sexuality: TSP 38, TSP 73, TSP 99, TSP 122, TSP 131, LIT 133, SOC 79, SOC 87, ART 19, ART 79, ART 127, PSY 4, PSY 16, PSY 21, PSY 43, HIST 15, HIST 20, HIST 53, HIST 105, ANTH 59, ANTH 87
signification: TSP 70
sisters: LIT 138
slaves: HIST 11, HIST 35, ANTH 44
social work: SOC 57
socialism: TSP 22, TSP 33, TSP 60, TSP 79, TSP 82, TSP 89, TSP 119, TSP 132, SOC 105, SOC 133, HIST 20, HIST 53, HIST 112

Index of Subjects

spinster: LIT 83, ANTH 25, ANTH 75, ANTH 104
sport: SOC 30, SOC 37
statistics: SOC 116, SOC 138, ED 13
stereotypes: TSP 12, LIT 2, LIT 7, LIT 9, LIT 38, SOC 10, SOC 12, SOC 69, ART 14, ART 37, ART 44, ART 50, ART 91, ART 117, PSY 7, PSY 43, HIST 8, HIST 22, ED 34, ED 36
structuralism: ANTH 93
subjects: TSP 70, PSY 2
suffrage: LIT 95, ART 98, HIST 30, HIST 59, HIST 61
suicide: ANTH 52
surrealism: ART 1

taboos: ANTH 10, ANTH 53, ANTH 98
technology: SOC 134, HIST 76, ANTH 56
textiles: ART 75, ART 86, HIST 100
theatre: ART 31, ART 41, ART 68, ART 85, ART 94, ART 96, ART 97, ART 98, ART 100, ART 102, ART 113, ART 119, ART 123
therapy: PSY 18, PSY 25, PSY 29, PSY 34, PSY 38, PSY 48, PSY 53
Third World: LIT 76, ED 67, ED 76
trade unions: SOC 49, HIST 51, HIST 55, HIST 77
transsexual: SOC 85, ART 127

Utopia: TSP 6

Victorian: HIST 2, HIST 7, HIST 17, HIST 22, HIST 29, HIST 54, HIST 57, HIST 65, HIST 79, HIST 86, HIST 92, HIST 96, ANTH 29, ANTH 101
violence: TSP 94, SOC 60, PSY 39
virginity: ANTH 40, ANTH 62, ANTH 75, ANTH 90

West Indian: ED 50
widows: SOC 22
witches: HIST 18, ANTH 25, ANTH 28, ANTH 33, ANTH 57, ANTH 77, ANTH 90
women-centred: TSP 6, TSP 17, TSP 126, LIT 37, LIT 57, LIT 72, PSY 32, HIST 34, ED 80
Women's Aid: SOC 77, PSY 39
women's movement: TSP 4, TSP 13, TSP 19, TSP 20, TSP 21, TSP 22, TSP 23, TSP 39, TSP 45, TSP 47, TSP 49, TSP 54, TSP 55, TSP 56, TSP 57, TSP 62, TSP 63, TSP 68, TSP 83, TSP 86, TSP 89, TSP 113, TSP 121, LIT 116, SOC 27, SOC 97, SOC 135, ART 33, HIST 3, HIST 12, HIST 21, HIST 23, HIST 72, HIST 111, ANTH 17, ANTH 65, ANTH 103, ED 15, ED 24
working class: SOC 49, SOC 52, SOC 68, HIST 22, HIST 25, HIST 46, HIST 52, HIST 55, HIST 74, HIST 97, HIST 115, ED 37

Index of Contributors

Abbott, Sidney: TSP 31
Abel Elizabeth: LIT 82, LIT 100, ED 69
Abramson, Joan: ED 23
Acker, Sandra: ED 75, ED 76
Acuff, Betty: ART 37
Adams, Carol: ART 50, ED 30
Adams, Elsie: TSP 21
Ahlum, Carol: ED 31
Allen, Mary: LIT 21
Altbach, Edith: TSP 22, HIST 23
Amir, M.: SOC 12
Amsden, A. H.: SOC 90
Andersen, Margaret: SOC 123
Anderson, Scarvia: ED 10
Andreas, Carol: SOC 13
Anscombe, Isabelle: ART 116
Appignanesi, Lisa: LIT 5
Ardener, S: ANTH 39, ANTH 72, ANTH 98
Arms, Suzanne: SOC 45
Art Journal: ART 51
Art Magazine: ART 17
Art in Society: ART 29
Atkinson, Ti-Grace: TSP 44
Astin, Helen: ED 32
Auerbach, Nina: LIT 35, LIT 83

Babcox, Deborah: TSP 23
Babbart, Ann: ART 10
Ballan, Dorothy: SOC 14
Balmary, M: PSY 50
Bank, Mirra: ART 84
Banks, J. A.: HIST 4
Banks, Olive: HIST 89
Banner, Lois: ART 108, HIST 24
Bardwick, Judith: TSP 63, PSY 6, PSY 9, PSY 13
Barker, Diana: SOC 59, SOC 60
Barrett, M: SOC 91, SOC 105, SOC 124
Barrett, N. S.: SOC 128
Bart, Pauline: SOC 15
Basch, Françoise: LIT 9

Baxandall, Rosalyn: HIST 35
Baym, Nina: LIT 36
Beard, Mary: HIST 1
Beasley, M.: ART 60
Beaumann, Nicola: LIT 101
Beauvoir, Simone de: TSP 1
Beck, Evelyn: SOC 92
Beddoe, Deirdre: HIST 101
Bell, P. Roseann: LIT 46
Bemstock, Shari: LIT 119
Benedict, Ruth: ANTH 3
Benston, M.: HIST 6
Benton, Suzanne: ART 38
Berger, G.: ED 38
Berger, John: ART 92
Berkin, C. R.: HIST 66
Berkinow, Louise: LIT 10
Bernard, Jessie: SOC 10, SOC 28, SOC 29, SOC 46, PSY 4, ED 2
Bird, Caroline: TSP 45
Birkby, Phyllis: TSP 37
Bishop, S.: TSP 80
Blumhagen, K.: ED 42
Boneparth, Ellen: SOC 129
Borun, Minda: ANTH 21
Bose, Christine: ED 48
Boserup, Ester: SOC 61
Boslooper, Thomas: SOC 30
Boston, S.: HIST 77
Boston Women: SOC 31
Boulding, E.: HIST 36
Boumelha, Penny: LIT 84
Bowles, Gloria: ED 70
Boyd, N.: HIST 95
Branca, P.: HIST 29, HIST 56
Brée, Germaine: LIT 6
Breen, D.: PSY 23
Breugal, Irene: SOC 93
Brickman, Richard: LIT 85
Bridenthal, R.: HIST 45
Brighton Women: ED 49
Bristol Women: ED 46

Index of Contributors

Broude, N.: ART 104
Broverman, Inge: PSY 7
Brown, C.: LIT 37
Brown, Janet: ART 85
Brown, Rita: TSP 64
Brownmiller, Susan: TSP 53
Brownstein, Rachel: LIT 86
Brundsdon, Charlotte: ART 117
Brunt, Rosalind: TSP 112
Bryant, M.: HIST 78
Bulkin, Elly: LIT 70
Bullough, Vern: HIST 16
Bunch, Charlotte: TSP 46, TSP 100, TSP 101, ED 71
Burman, S.: HIST 67
Burstyn, Joan: HIST 79, ED 12
Butler-Paisley, Matilda: ART 39
Byrne, E. M.: ED 43

Cade, Toni: TSP 7
Cadogan, Mary: ART 52
Califia, Pat: TSP 102
Cambridge Women: SOC 113
Cameron, Avril: HIST 102
Cameron, Deborah: LIT 131
Canadian Research Institute: ED 77
Cantor, M.: HIST 46
Caplan, P.: ANTH 73
Carden, Maren: TSP 47
Carlson, E. R.: PSY 2
Carnegie Commission: ED 13
Carroll, Berenice: HIST 37
Carter, Angela: LIT 87
Cartledge, S.: TSP 38
Cassell, Joan: ANTH 65
Chamberlain, Mary: SOC 47
Change: ED 64
Chasseguet-Smirgel, Janine: PSY 8
Chesler, Phyllis: PSY 14, PSY 27
Chetwynd, J.: SOC 69
Chicago, Judy: ART 2, ART 40, ART 86, ART 93
Chinoy, H. K.: ART 96
Chiplin, B.: SOC 62
Chmaj, Betty: ART 7, HIST 9, ED 11
Chodorow, Nancy: PSY 44
Christ, Carol: ANTH 79
Christian, Barbara: LIT 132
Chrysalis: ART 61
Cixous, Hélène: LIT 11, LIT 22, LIT 71

Clark, Alice: HIST 103
Clausen, Jan: LIT 88
Clements, Patricia: LIT 102
Cole, Doris: ART 18
Collins, Randall: SOC 48
Comer, Lee: SOC 36
Conrad, Susan: HIST 38
Cooke, Joanne: TSP 39
Coote, Anna: TSP 113
Cornillon, Susan: LIT 3
Cott, Nancy: HIST 47, HIST 68
Coward, Rosalind: TSP 70, TSP 117, LIT 55
Cowie, Elizabeth: ART 62
Crewe, Louie: ED 44
Critcher, C.: SOC 37
Cruikshank, Margaret: ED 65
Culley, Margo: ED 81
Culver, Elsie: ANTH 11
Cunningham, Gail: LIT 38
Currell, Melville: SOC 38

Dalla Costa, Mariarosa: TSP 54
Daly, Mary: TSP 3, TSP 40, TSP 81, TSP 125
Daniels, Arlene: ED 24
Darty, T.: TSP 126
Davidoff, Leonore: HIST 17
Davidson, C. N.: LIT 56
Davies, Ross: SOC 49
Davies, Stella: HIST 5
Davin, Delia: HIST 39
Davis, Angela: TSP 24, TSP 103
Davis, Elizabeth: ANTH 22
Deckard, B. S.: TSP 55
Deem, R.: ED 45, 50
Delamont, S.: HIST 57, ED 51
Delaney, J.: ANTH 53
Delany, Sheila: LIT 103
Denmark, Florence: PSY 19
Deutsch, Helene: PSY 1
Diamond, Arlene: LIT 28
Diamond, Norma: ANTH 15
Díaz-Diocaretz, M.: LIT 133
Diner, Helen: ANTH 27
Dinnerstein, Dorothy: PSY 28
Dixon, Marlene: TSP 92
Doane, Mary Ann: ART 118
Doely, S. B.: ANTH 16
Dolan, Eleanor: ED 1

Donegan, Jane: HIST 58
Donelson, Elaine: PSY 35
Donovan, Josephine: LIT 12
Douglas, Ann: LIT 29
Douglas, Mary: ANTH 10, ANTH 40
Downing, Christine: ANTH 99
Dreifus, Claudia: SOC 83
Duberman, Lucile: SOC 50
DuBois, Ellen: HIST 30, HIST 59
Dudowitz, R. L.: ED 72
Duncan, Carol: ART 19
DuPlessis, Rachel: LIT 134
Dupont, Béatrice: ED 60
Dworkin, Andrea: TSP 48, TSP 65, TSP 104
Dyhouse, Carol: HIST 90

Ecker, G.: ART 124
Educational Leadership: ED 14
Edwards, Lee: LIT 120, ART 8
Edwards, Susan: SOC 139
Eermath, M. S.: ANTH 17
Ehrenreich, Barbara: HIST 18, HIST 60, ANTH 28
Eichenbaum, L.: PSY 53
Eichler, M.: SOC 106
Eisenstein, Hester: TSP 118, LIT 57
Eisenstein, Sarah: HIST 104
Eisenstein, Zillah: TSP 82, TSP 105
Elevson, Allana: ED 52
Ellman, Mary: LIT 2
Elshtain, J. B.: SOC 114, SOC 125
Epstein, Cynthia: SOC 9, SOC 115
Erens, P.: ART 87
Ettore, E. M.: SOC 107
Evans, Marcia: LIT 121
Evans, Mary: TSP 114
Evans, R. J.: HIST 40, HIST 69
Evans, Sara: HIST 70
Ewen, Stuart: ART 105

Faderman, Lillian: LIT 72
Falk, Nancy: ANTH 88
Farrar, Claire: ANTH 41
Fee, Elizabeth: ANTH 29
Feinberg, Jean: ART 75
Felman, Shoshana: LIT 122
Female Studies: ED 4
Feminist Art Journal: ART 63
Feminist Criticism: LIT 58

Feminist Studies: HIST 80
Ferguson, Marjorie: ART 109
Ferguson, Mary Anne: LIT 7
Ferrier, Carole: LIT 30
Fetterley, Judith: LIT 39
Figes, Eva: TSP 8, LIT 89
Film Library Quarterly: ART 3
Fine, Elsa: ART 76
Firestone, Shulamith: TSP 9
Fischer, Ann: ANTH 13
Fischer, Christiane: HIST 48
Fisher, Elizabeth: ANTH 80
Fiske, Betty: ART 9
Fitzpatrick, Blanche: ED 33
Fleenor, Julianne: LIT 104
Fletcher, S.: HIST 81
Flexnor, Eleenor: HIST 3
Fliegel, Zenia: PSY 54
Flynn, Elizabeth: LIT 105
Foreman, Ann: SOC 70
Foss, Paul: TSP 73
Foster, Shirley: LIT 123
Fowlkes, Diane: ED 78
Fowlkes, Martha: ED 53
Fox-Genovese, E.: LIT 59
Franz, von Marie-Louise: ANTH 25
Frankfurt, Ellen: SOC 24
Frazier, Nancy: ED 15
Freedman, E. B.: TSP 133
Freeman, Jo: TSP 10, TSP 11, TSP 56, TSP 57
French, Brandon: ART 77
French, M.: ART 97
Friday, Nancy: PSY 36
Friedan, Betty: TSP 2, TSP 106
Friedl, E.: ANTH 42
Frieze, Irene: PSY 45
Fritz, Leah: TSP 58, TSP 83
Frontiers: HIST 71
Furniss, W.: ED 20
Fussell, G. E.: HIST 10

Gabhart, Anna: ART 10
Gadol, Joan: HIST 41
Gale, Fay: ANTH 18
Gallop, Jane: PSY 55
Gardiner, Judith: LIT 90
Garskof, Michele: TSP 25
Garvin, Harry: LIT 40
Gavron, Hannah: SOC 6

Index of Contributors

Gay Left Collective: TSP 93
Gelpi, Barbara: LIT 13
Gentile, Mary: ART 125
Gilbert, Sandra: LIT 47, LIT 48
Gilligan, Carol: PSY 56
Gittell, M.: SOC 108
Glazer, Nona: SOC 17
Gluck, Sherna: HIST 49
Golde, Peggy: ANTH 19
Goldenberg, Naomi: ANTH 81
Gonzales, Nancie: ANTH 20
Goodale, J.: ANTH 23
Goot, Murray: SOC 51
Gordon, Linda: HIST 42
Goreau, A.: ART 94
Gorham, D.: HIST 96
Gornick, Vivian: TSP 74, SOC 18
Gould, Carol: TSP 66
Green, Rayna: ANTH 89
Greenglass, E. R.: SOC 126
Greenwald, Maurine: HIST 11
Greer, Germaine: TSP 26, TSP 127, ART 88
Grier, B.: LIT 73
Griffin, Susan: TSP 75, TSP 84, TSP 107
Gullahorn, Jeanne: PSY 51
Guttentag, Marcia: ED 34

Hacker, Helen: SOC 2
Hafkin, Nancy: ANTH 54
Hageman, Alice: ANTH 34
Hakim, C.: SOC 94
Hall, Catherine: HIST 91
Hall, N.: ANTH 90
Hamilton, Roberta: SOC 84
Hammer, Signe: PSY 24
Hammond, Dorothy: ANTH 55
Hanisch, Carol: TSP 27
Hanscombe, Gillian: LIT 91
Harding, Esther: ANTH 24
Harding, S.: SOC 130
Harford, B.: TSP 128
Harris, Ann: ED 5
Harrison, Barbara: ED 16
Harrison, Jane: ANTH 6
Harrison, Margaret: ART 64
Hart, Nicky: SOC 63
Hartmann, Mary: HIST 25
Hartmann, Heidi: SOC 64
Hartsock, Nancy: SOC 131

Haskell, Molly: ART 20
Hayden, Dolores: ART 98
Hayes, Danielle: ART 65
Hays, H. R.: ANTH 9
Heilbrun, Carolyn: TSP 41, TSP 85, LIT 92
Hellerstein, E.: HIST 92
Henley, Nancy: SOC 71
Heresies: ART 66, ANTH 74
Heron, Liz: HIST 116
Hersch, Blanche: ED 54
Herzog, Elizabeth: SOC 10
Hess, Thomas: ART 11, ART 21
Hewitt, Margaret: HIST 2
Hill, Vicki Lynn: ART 30
Hillman, James: ANTH 91
Hoch-Smith, Judith: ANTH 75
Hochschild, A.: SOC 95
Hoffman, Lois: SOC 39
Hoffman, Nancy: LIT 4
Hole, J.: HIST 12
Hollander, A.: ART 41
Holledge, Julie: ART 99
Hollis, Patricia: HIST 72
Hollister, Valerie: ART 78
Holzberg, Carol: ANTH 76
Hooks, Bell: TSP 108
Hope, Carol: TSP 86
Horner, Matina, PSY 15
Horney, Karen: PSY 3
Howe, Florence: ED 25, ED 35, ED 55
Howe, Louise: SOC 72
Huber, Joan: SOC 32
Hubert, Jane: SOC 40
Huf, Linda: LIT 106
Hughes, Mary: ED 82
Hull, Gloria: ED 66
Humm, Maggie: LIT 142, ED 73
Hussein, Freda: SOC 136

Iglitzein, L.: SOC 65
Irigaray, Luce: LIT 135, LIT 136

Jackson, Irene: ART 53
Jacobus, Mary: LIT 49
Jagger, Alison: TSP 76, TSP 119
James, Selma: LIT 137
Janeway, Elizabeth: TSP 28, TSP 49
Janz, Mildred: ART 31
Jaquette, Jane: SOC 41

Jay, Carla: TSP 32
Jehlen, Myra: LIT 74
Jelinek, Estelle: LIT 60
Jenness, Linda: TSP 33
Jensen, Margaret: LIT 124
John, Angela: HIST 82
Johnson, Barbara: LIT 61
Johnston, Claire: ART 22, ART 42
Johnston, Jill: TSP 50
Jones, Beverley: SOC 7
Jordan, Rosan: ANTH 105
Joseph, Gloria: TSP 109
Juhasz, S.: LIT 23
Jump/Cut: ART 89

Kanter, R. M.: SOC 73
Kaplan, Alexandra: PSY 29
Kaplan, Ann: ART 32, ART 79, ART 110
Kaplan, Cora: LIT 24
Kaplan, Sydney: LIT 14
Kay, Karen: ART 67
Keller, Evelyn: PSY 46
Kelly, A.: ED 61
Kelly, Joan: HIST 26, HIST 113
Kelly, Mary: ART 111
Kennard, Jean: LIT 41
Kent, Sarah: ART 126
Keohane, N.: TSP 115
Kerber, Linda: HIST 83
Kessler, Evelyn: ANTH 56
Kessler, Suzanne: SOC 85
Kessler-Harris, A.: HIST 97
Key, Mary: LIT 15
Keyssar, Helene: ART 119
King, J.: SOC 74
Klaich, Dolores: TSP 51
Klein, Viola: SOC 19
Koedt, Anne: TSP 29, TSP 42
Kolbenschlag, Madonna: ANTH 82
Kolodny, Annette: LIT 16, LIT 17
Komarovsky, Mirra: SOC 1, SOC 3
Kramarae, Chris: LIT 62
Krasilovsky, Alexis: ART 12
Kreps, Juanita: SOC 20
Kristeva, Julia: LIT 93
Kuhn, Annette: SOC 86, ART 106, ART 127

Lacks, Roslyn: ANTH 92
Ladner, Joyce: SOC 21

Lakoff, Robin: SOC 33
Lamphere, Louise: ANTH 66
Landes, Ruth: ANTH 1
Langland, E.: ED 62
Lauretis de, Teresa: ART 120
Laws, J. L.: PSY 30
Lederer, Laura: TSP 94
Leeson, Joyce: PSY 47
Leghorn, L.: SOC 116
Leonard, Eileen: SOC 127
Lerner, Gerda: HIST 13, HIST 14, HIST 50, HIST 73
Levy, Rachel: ANTH 7
Lewenhak, S.: SOC 109, HIST 51
Lewis, E.: PSY 5
Liddington, J.: HIST 61
Light, Alison: LIT 107
Lippard, Lucy: ART 1, ART 54, ART 55
Lipshitz, Susan: TSP 77
Little, Judith: LIT 108
Llewelyn, Davies: HIST 52
Lloyd, C.: SOC 96
London Feminist History Group: HIST 105
Long, Priscilla: TSP 4
Lopata, Helena: SOC 22
Lorde, Audrey: TSP 78, TSP 129
Lowe, M.: SOC 132
Lucas A.: HIST 106
Lurie, Nancy: ANTH 4

McBride, Theresa: HIST 43
Maccia, Elizabeth: ED 26
Maccoby, Eleanor: PSY 20, PSY 31
McConnell-Ginet, S.: LIT 63
MacCormack, Carol: ANTH 93
McCrindle, J.: HIST 74
McGarry, Eileen: ART 43
McGavran, Murray: TSP 120
Macintyre, Sally: SOC 75
Mackie, L.: SOC 76
Maclean, Ian: HIST 84
MacLeod, Sheila: PSY 52
McNaron, T.: LIT 138
McRobbie, Angela: SOC 117, SOC 137
Mainardi, Patricia: ART 23
Mander, Anica: PSY 25
Mandle, Joan: SOC 97
Marks, Elaine: TSP 95
Marshall, R.: HIST 107

Index of Contributors

Martin, Del: TSP 34
Martin, M.: ANTH 43
Martin, Wendy: LIT 125
Marxist-Feminist Literature
  Collective: LIT 42
Mason, M.: LIT 50
Massachusetts Review: ART 112
Matalene, Carolyn: ANTH 77
Matrix: ART 121
Mattfield, Jacquelyn: ED 3
Matthiasson, C.: ANTH 35
Mayo, M.: SOC 77
Mead, Margaret: ANTH 2
Mellen, Joan: ART 24
Mickelson, Anne: LIT 51
Miller, Casey: LIT 25
Miller, Jean Baker: PSY 18, PSY 32
Miller, Nancy: LIT 64
Millett, Kate: TSP 12, TSP 67
Millman, Marcia: SOC 52
Millum, Trevor: ART 44
Minault, Denise: ART 25
Miner, Dorothy: ART 4
Mitchell, Juliet: TSP 30, TSP 130, PSY 21, HIST 44
Mitchell, Sally: LIT 75
Moberley, Bell: SOC 4
Modleski, Tania: LIT 94
Moers, Ellen: LIT 26
Moi, Toril: LIT 139
Moore, H.: ART 68
Moragu, C.: LIT 76
Morewedge, R.: HIST 31
Morgan, Elaine: ANTH 26
Morgan, Fidelis: ART 100
Morgan, Robin: TSP 13, TSP 71, SOC 8
Mulford, Wendy: LIT 95
Mulvey, Laura: ART 45
Munro, Eleanor: ART 90
Murphy, Y.: ANTH 36
Myers, Carol: LIT 27

Nelson, C.: ANTH 30
Nemser, Cindy: ART 13, ART 14, ART 46, ART 56
Ness, E.: ED 56
Neules-Bates, Carol: ART 107
Newland, Kathleen: SOC 98
Newman, L.: HIST 114
Newton, Judith: LIT 77, HIST 108

Niethammer, Carolyn: ANTH 67
Nochlin, Linda: ART 80
Norton, Mary: HIST 85

Oakley, Ann: SOC 25, SOC 42, SOC 43, SOC 99, SOC 110, SOC 118
Ochs, Carol: ANTH 68
O'Donovan, K.: SOC 140
O'Faolain, Julia: HIST 19
Off Our Backs: ED 67
O'Flaherty, Wendy: ANTH 94
Okin, S.: SOC 100
O'Leary, Virginia: PSY 37
Olsen, Tillie: LIT 43
Orbach, Susie: PSY 48
O'Reilly, Jane: TSP 96
Orenstein, Gloria: ART 47
Orloff, Katherine: ART 33
Ostriker, Alicia: LIT 109
Owen, Ursula: LIT 110
Ozick, Cynthia: LIT 111

Packard, Sandra: ED 36
Pagels, Elaine: ANTH 83
Parker, R.: ART 101, ART 122
Paulme, Denise: ANTH 8
Pearson, Carol: LIT 78
Peck, Ellen: TSP 52
Perkins, T.: ART 91
Perry, Ruth: LIT 65, LIT 112
Petersen, Karen: ART 57
Phillips, Anne: SOC 133
Piercy, Marge: LIT 96
Pinchbeck, Ivy: HIST 93
Pomeroy, Sarah: ANTH 44
Pool, Jeannie: ART 69
Poovey, Mary: LIT 126
Porter Nancy: ED 54
Pottker, Janice: ED 39
Power, Eileen: HIST 32
Pratt, Annis: LIT 79
Purvis, J.: ED 74

Radical Teacher: ED 40
Radway, Janice: LIT 127
Rapoport, R.: SOC 66
Raphael, D.: ANTH 45
Rapp, Rayna: ANTH 84
Rawlings, Edna: PSY 38
Raymond, Janice: TSP 87

Redstockings: TSP 68
Reed, Evelyn: TSP 14, TSP 15, ANTH 46
Reeves, Nancy: ED 6
Reinhardt, N. S.: ART 113
Reinharz, Shulamit: SOC 101
Reiter, Rayna: ANTH 47
Rendell, Jane: HIST 117
Reuss, Richard: ANTH 48
Rich, Adrienne: TSP 69, TSP 88, TSP 97, ED 47
Rich, Ruby: ART 95
Richardson, Betty: ED 21
Rigney, Barbara: LIT 44
Riley, Denise: HIST 109
Roberts, E.: HIST 115
Roberts, Helen: SOC 119
Roberts, J. I.: PSY 33
Roberts, Joan: SOC 67
Roberts, J. R.: LIT 80
Robinson, Lillian: LIT 45
Robinson, Lora: ED 17
Roby, Pamela: SOC 53
Rogers, Katherine: LIT 1, LIT 97
Rogers, R. L.: SOC 111
Rohrlich-Leavitt, Ruby: ANTH 49, ANTH 50
Romero, Joan: ANTH 31
Rosaldo, M.: ANTH 37, ANTH 95
Rosen, Marjorie: ART 26
Rosenberg, Jan: ART 114
Rosenberg, Marie: SOC 54
Rosenberg, Rosalind: TSP 116
Rosenfelt, Deborah: ED 18
Ross, Heather: SOC 55
Rosser, C.: SOC 5
Rossi, Alice: SOC 11, SOC 34, SOC 78, ED 19
Roszak, Betty: TSP 5
Rothschild, J.: SOC 134
Rover, C.: HIST 7
Rowbotham, Sheila: TSP 35, TSP 43, TSP 89, TSP 121, HIST 20, HIST 53
Rowe, Karen: ANTH 85
Roy, Maria: PSY 39
Rubin, Gayle: TSP 59
Rubin, Lillian: SOC 68, SOC 102
Rubinstein, Charlotte: ART 115
Ruddick, Sara: ART 70
Ruether, Rosemary: TSP 60, ANTH 38

Rule, Jane: LIT 18
Rush, Anne: ANTH 57
Russ, Joanna: TSP 134, LIT 113
Ruth, Sheila: ED 58
Ruthven, K.: LIT 128
Ryan, Mary: HIST 33

Sabrosky, Judith: TSP 90
Saffioti, H.: HIST 62
Safilios-Rothschild, Constantina: SOC 26, SOC 79
Sage, Lorna: LIT 140
Sanday, Peggy: ANTH 100
Sandler, Bernice: ED 7
Sarah, E.: HIST 110
Sargent, Lydia: TSP 110
Schapiro, Miriam: ART 34
Schlegal, Alice: ANTH 69
Schneider, David: ANTH 5
Schramm, Sarah; HIST 75, ED 27
Schwartz, Therese: ART 27
Scott, Anne: HIST 8, ED 8
Scully, Diane: SOC 35
Segal, Marcia: SOC 103
Shapiro, J.: ANTH 58
Sharpe, Sue: ED 37
Sherfey, Mary: TSP 16, PSY 16
Sherman, J.: PSY 10, PSY 40, PSY 49
Showalter, Elaine: LIT 8, LIT 31, LIT 52, LIT 141
Shulman, Alix: TSP 98
Shuttle, Penelope: ANTH 78
Siltanen, Janet: SOC 138
Singer, June: ANTH 59
Skiles, Jacqueline: ART 5
Smart, Carol: SOC 80, SOC 87
Smith, Barbara: LIT 32, LIT 114
Smith, Hilda: HIST 98
Smith, Sharon: ART 48
Smith-Rosenberg, Carroll: HIST 15, HIST 34
Snitow, Ann: TSP 122
Snyder, Eloise: SOC 104
Sochen, June: HIST 27
Social Science Quarterly: SOC 44
Sokoloff, Natalie: SOC 112
Solanas, Valerie: TSP 17
Spacks, Patricia: LIT 19, LIT 33
Spender, Dale: TSP 123, TSP 135, LIT

Index of Contributors

66, HIST 99, HIST 111, ED 59, ED 63, ED 68
Spivak, Gayatri: LIT 115
Spretnack, Charlene: ANTH 101, ANTH 103
Springer, Marlene: LIT 34
Squier, Susan: LIT 129
Stacey, Judith: ED 22
Stacey, M.: SOC 120
Stack, C.: ANTH 51
Staley, Thomas: LIT 98
Stamboulian, G.: TSP 91
Stanley, L.: SOC 135
Stanworth, M.: ED 79
Starr, Elizabeth: ANTH 96
Staxbler, Sookie: TSP 18
Steinem, Gloria: TSP 124
Sternburg, Janet: LIT 67
Stetson, Erlene: LIT 81
Stevens, Evelyn: ANTH 32
Stewart, Grace: LIT 53
Stimpson, Catherine: TSP 99, SOC 121
Stites, R.: HIST 63
Stone, Merlin: ANTH 60, ANTH 86
Stromberg, A.: SOC 88
Strouse, Jean: PSY 22
Stuard, Susan: HIST 94
Stubbs, Patricia: LIT 54
Suhr, Elmer: ANTH 14
Swan, Susan: ART 71
Synder-Ott, Joelynn: ART 72

Take One: ART 15
Tate, Claudia: LIT 116
Tauvis, Carol: PSY 41
Taylor, Barbara: HIST 112
Theodore, A.: ED 9
Thompson, Jane: ED 80
Thompson, Mary Lou: TSP 19
Thompson, R.: HIST 28
Thonnessen, W.: HIST 21
Thorne, Barrie: SOC 56, SOC 122
Thorsten, Geraldine: ANTH 97
Tilly, Louise: HIST 64
Todd, Janet: LIT 68, LIT 69
Todd, Susan: ART 123
Torre, Susanna: ART 73
Trescott, M.: HIST 76
Trible, Phyllis: ANTH 61
Troll, Israel: PSY 42

Tuchman, Gaye: ART 81
Tucker, Anne: ART 28
Tufts, Eleanor: ART 35

Ulanov, Ann: PSY 11
Unger, Rhoda: PSY 26

Valparaiso University Law Review: SOC 23
Van Vuran, Nancy: ANTH 33
Vance, Carole: TSP 131
Velvet Light Trap, The: ART 16
Vetterling-Braggin, M.: TSP 72
Vicinus, Martha: HIST 22, HIST 54
Visual Dialog: ART 49
Vogel, Lisa: TSP 132, ART 36

Walker, Alice: LIT 117
Walker, Cheryl: LIT 99
Walkowitz, Judith: HIST 86
Walters, Margaret: ART 82
Walton, R. G.: SOC 57
Walum, Laurel: SOC 81
Wandor, M.: TSP 36, LIT 118, ART 102
Ware, Cellestine: TSP 20
Warner, Marina: ART 128, ANTH 62, ANTH 102
Washbourn, Penelope: ANTH 70, ANTH 87
Wasserman, Elga: ED 28
Watson, James: SOC 82
Weideger, Paula: ANTH 63
Weigle, Marta: ANTH 104
Weinbaum, Batya: TSP 79
Weinberg, Martin: PSY 17
Weiner, Annette: ANTH 64
Weiner, Gaby: ED 83
Weisstein, N.: PSY 12
Wertheimer, Barbara: HIST 55
West, Uta: TSP 61
Westergaard, John: SOC 58
Westervelt, Esther: ED 29
Whitelegg, E.: HIST 100
Whitworth, Sarah: ART 58
Widdowson, Frances: HIST 87
Wiesenfeld, Cheryl: ART 59
Wilding, Faith: ART 74
Williams, Elizabeth: PSY 34
Williams, Juanita: PSY 43
Williams, Merryn: LIT 130

Williamson, Judith: ART 83
Willis, Ellen: TSP 111
Wilson, Amrit: SOC 89
Wilson, Elizabeth: ART 129, HIST 88
Wittig, Monique: TSP 6
Wohl, A.: HIST 65
Wolf, Margery: ANTH 52
Wolff, Janet: ART 103
Wolpe, Anne-Marie: ED 41

Women and Art: ART 6
Women and Literature: LIT 20
Wortis, Helen: SOC 27

Yates, Gayle: TSP 62
Young, Frank: ANTH 12

Zelman, Elizabeth: ANTH 71